W9-ASR-137

THE ROOTS OF NATIONAL SOCIALISM

THE ROOTS OF NATIONAL SOCIALISM

1783–1933

by

ROHAN D'O. BUTLER

NEW YORK

Howard Fertig

1968

HOWARD FERTIG, INC. EDITION 1968
Published by arrangement with E. P. Dutton & Co., Inc.

Library of Congress Catalog Card Number: 67-24579

PRINTED IN THE UNITED STATES OF AMERICA
BY NOBLE OFFSET PRINTERS, INC.

To

WILLIS

PREFACE

This examination of the roots of national socialism was planned before the outbreak of the present war in the west. I think that I can truthfully say that the circumstance of this war has not induced me to modify to any considerable extent either my treatment of the subject or my views concerning it; in so far as there have been alterations they have been chiefly occasioned by the immediate pressure of war upon time, labour and materials, which has made it necessary to give the book a rather slighter form than it might otherwise have assumed. It has, in particular, been found necessary to omit nearly all the footnotes giving exact references to passages quoted. This course has been reluctantly adopted in view of war-time restrictions upon paper and printing. But at a time when a number of the near-necessities of life are rationed one can accept in good part restrictions upon such a luxury as a book. If, however, the reference to any quoted passage is particularly desired, it can be obtained on application to the author through the publishers.

This book is not a comprehensive study based upon exhaustive research. It is a critical survey. Those who are already familiar with the field will readily appreciate my obligation to the work of previous historians who have covered different parts of it, and more especially to that of Friedrich Meinecke, Edmond Vermeil and Reinhold Aris. I am also deeply obliged and grateful for certain quotations which I have derived from the works of other authors and editors, including Miss P. R. Anderson, Mr. R. R. Ergang, Professor Alexander Gray, Professor F. J. C. Hearnshaw, Doctor O. Levy, Miss E. O. Lorimer, Professor H. Oncken, Professor Arthur Rosenberg and Mr. H. Wickham Steed.

Of my more personal debts the first is to Mr. E. L. Woodward, not only for reading the manuscript and for many valuable criticisms and suggestions, but also for his constant encouragement and support. I have received additional help from other friends, and my especial thanks are due to Mr. R. Tymms for his advice and interest. There is also my debt to Mr. B. H. Sumner; its magnitude precludes specification. But the responsibility for the statements and conclusions contained in this book is mine alone.

I am further most grateful to the Warden and Fellows of All Souls College, but for whose liberality this book could scarcely have been written; and I am under a corresponding obligation to certain other persons who need not here be named.

R. D'O. B.

Box 100,
W.D.O.,
London, W. 1.

CONTENTS

THE ROOTS OF NATIONAL SOCIALISM

Chapter I

BACKGROUND

The Germans are a great people, and they have played a great part in the making of Europe and the affairs of the world. They play it still. Former German achievements in music, literature and science are justly valued as important contributions to the common heritage of the peoples of the west. The political enterprizes and military master-strokes which, for the past two hundred years, have signalized the German rise to power, are widely renowned: but often more renowned than relished by those who are themselves not German. Indeed many foreigners are apt to be almost nonplussed when, as in the Great War and in the great war after the Great War, the German nation marches into action. For it is not always easy for other peoples to understand how individual Germans, respected as decent, warmhearted men and women, lovers of family and the home, orderly, upright and industrious, can suddenly, to all appearance, forget themselves completely and eagerly merge their being in a national whole distinguished for its aggressive ferocity and its ruthless disregard of the accepted principles of conduct in civilized society. Tentative explanations of this phenomenon have been advanced; it is sometimes held that the Germans have a peculiar psychological kink which periodically produces otherwise inexplicable lapses from normality; sometimes that the Germans, pleasant enough individually, somehow contaminate each other as soon as they draw together for social and political purposes.

Such sketchy generalizations are not so much explanations as indications of the fact that many people, though tolerably well acquainted with Germans as individuals on the one hand

and with the deeds of the German nation on the other, fail to discover any very satisfactory connection between the two. But the basic tie between the individual and the society in which he lives is what he thinks about the ordering of society. The niceties of political theory may often seem remote from life, but ultimately it remains true that men behave in human society in accordance with their conception of that society and of their function in it. In the case of Germany this middle link, the distinctive outlook on society, has won much less recognition than the superficial characteristics of the German individual and the historical actions of the German people. This fact is the more remarkable since the dominant German outlook springs from a very bold and imaginative corpus of thought, and one which, almost throughout the course of its growth during the last century and a half, has been intimately interconnected with the politico-social development of the nation. The interconnection is, indeed, implicit in the name commonly given to this German code of thought: the historical school.

In order to appreciate the full significance of this historical school with its novel stress upon the subjective and the particular it is especially important to take into account the conditions and circumstances of its inception. It is necessary to sketch in the background, both political and intellectual.

When at the beginning of the sixteenth century Martin Luther led the revolt against the catholic church, his adversaries justly charged him with unloosing a pent torrent of disorder whose volume and impetus no man could check or gauge. Luther himself soon perceived as much and threw up earthworks of state to stem the rising tide. In 1525, when the oppressed German peasantry rose in revolt, he came forward for the princes and, while admitting that the peasant cause was 'not at all contrary to natural law and equity', sought to cow them with the admonition: 'Suffer! Suffer! The Cross! The Cross! That is the law taught of Christ. There is no other.' The rebel monk of Wittenberg now proclaimed that 'revolt is never just, however just may be the motive'. Defection from the single church under the authority of the pope was stabilized for the time at the state and its princely ruler.

And the time was about two hundred and fifty years. It was the hey-day of the princes. They ruled almost untrammelled either from above or from below; for the medieval ideal of supernational christendom was gone, and the stature of every man as an individual was not yet accorded recognition. The sixteenth-century sovereign has been described as a kind of new Messiah.

But religious issues continued to vex relations between princes and notably between German princes. The climax came with the Thirty Years War. This last great war of religion issued in 1648 in the first of those great political settlements which have determined the face of modern Europe. The reformation had originated in German territory, and it was on German territory that the religious struggle in Europe was fought to a standstill. In 1648 the German states lay desolate and exhausted, the battleground of Europe, fought over and pillaged off and on for thirty years by German, Austrian, British, French, Walloon, Czech, Hungarian, Spanish, Swedish, and Danish forces. But one state was less exhausted than the rest: Brandenburg-Prussia.

The house of Hohenzollern had done well from the early reformation. In the same year as the revolting peasants were being admonished by Luther and crushed by the princes the knights of the Teutonic Order, converted to Lutheranism, dissolved the order and constituted their East Prussian territory into a duchy hereditary in the house of their grand master, Albert of Hohenzollern. This event was more than a stage in the fortunes of a princely house. It was the beginning of a great geographical shift of stress. The geography of ill-bounded Germany hinges roughly upon the river Elbe. South and west of it lie the historic lands, the mountains and forests, Bavaria and the Rhineland, the places which focused the life of medieval Germany, the imperial cities, bishoprics and commercial centres, Regensburg, Mainz, Aachen, Nuremberg, Bamberg, Cologne and Augsburg. North and east of the Elbe lie the new lands and shallow soil, the beginning of the great lowland plain which stretches away to the Ural mountains, the country which had been wrested from the heathen bit by bit and colonized with toil. From the reformation onwards these new lands under Hohenzollern tutelage were to play an ever larger part in the destiny of the German nation.

And now in the last stages of the reformation Brandenburg-Prussia did better than most other German states. In 1643 Frederick-William, later known as the Great Elector, early withdrew from the war and in five years managed so to restore the estate of his dominions as to be in a position to press his claims with authority in the negotiations at Münster and Osnabrück. The most bloody of all German wars set Brandenburg-Prussia upon the road to dominion. This road she pursued with inflexible purpose.

The treaty of Oliva and the battle of Fehrbellin were the first stages in this progress. The Great Elector held his own against the Swedes, double-crossing them first and then defeating them: at the same time he set about the ordering and welding of his scattered dominions, extending the central power of his personal authority, subduing provincial diets, and in particular reducing to submissiveness East Prussia and Cleves, which looked respectively to Poland and to Holland for support of their autonomous leanings. The Great Elector was succeeded by the elector Frederick, who profited from the War of the Spanish Succession to the extent of the annexation of upper Guelderland and, more important, international recognition of the newly constituted kingdom of Prussia. In the year of the Treaty of Utrecht, which sanctioned these increases of territory and dignity, Frederick-William I ascended the Prussian throne. For twenty-seven years this remarkable man devoted himself to the task of stamping upon his parvenu dominion, still backward, boorish, and poor, those indelible characteristics that were to make Prussia famous among nations. More than any other one man he evolved Prussianism as a political factor. Later Prussians have rightly named him their greatest king in internal affairs.

Frederick-William I perceived that a sound economy was the essential precondition of national development. He infused new life into Prussian agriculture and commerce, and reformed the local administration. In 1723 the machinery of Prussian government was transformed almost overnight by the institution of the *Generaldirectorium* which, under the personal supervision of the king, was to control all branches of the administration. From this rigidly centralized machine developed the great Prussian bureaucracy. Correspondingly a new legal code was promulgated. A uniform law was to govern a land uniform in its submission. But the progress of Frederick-William's reign is best measured by the index of Prussia's military strength. The numerical strength of the army rose from about 38,000 in 1713 to 89,000 in 1740. It was a very expensive army. Approximately five-sevenths of the yearly state revenue were spent upon it at the end of the reign. It was a very up-to-date army. The marching-step, bayonet, and iron ram-rod were introduced; the precision of Prussian drill aroused the admiration of Europe. And the novelty went deeper. The officers were taught to regard themselves not as a band of financial speculators and military careerists, but as members of an honourable *élite*; thus the foundations of the Prussian military caste were laid. In 1733, for the first time in any great European country, the principle of universal military conscription was laid down. Many exceptions were as yet permitted. But the principle held. The triple obligation of every Prussian was military service (*Wehrpflicht*), taxation (*Steuerpflicht*), and education (*Schulpflicht*). This latter was of an elementary kind, for learning was not likely to flourish in a country in which the royal princess Wilhelmina was forced to hide her few books under beds and tables, and thought that her father would have whipped her if he had ever found her reading or writing. Christian Wolff, the leading German philosopher of the time, was expelled from Prussia at forty-eight hours' notice. The young art-critic Winckelmann fled to Dresden, whence he cursed his native land. 'I shudder', he said, 'at the thought of this country; it is oppressed by the greatest despotism that has ever been conceived of. It is better to be a circumcised Turk than a Prussian. In a land like Sparta (a very ideal description of the rule of the corporal's stick) the arts cannot flourish and must degenerate.'

Frederick-William I was a cruel man by nature, and he was formidable in his tyranny. He bullied his own family not less than the nation. One German historian has remarked that in this reign 'every personal enjoyment is ruthlessly sacrificed to state ends'. And so Frederick-William, gradually and without remorse, pursued his purpose of regimenting his people and their every occupation in the interests of the omnipotent, authoritarian state which he was determined to establish, in his own words, like a 'rock of bronze'. To those who groaned under its weight the king replied: 'In affairs of state the good of the whole always takes precedence over that of the individual.' The needy patient Prussians acquiesced. Despotism was nothing new to most of them. It was the normal basis of local everyday life under the feudal lords, the Junkers. And Frederick-William's despotism was in general efficient. In 1736, for instance, when neighbouring states were agriculturally distressed, the provident Prussian government distributed to the peasantry seed-corn which it had amassed. That, and actions like that, were much to be thankful for.

The 'King of the Beggars' well knew what he was about. He found Prussia small and poor. He left her strong. He thought she had much to achieve. He enabled her to achieve it. Frederick-William used to say: 'I know very well that in Vienna and Dresden they call me a money-grubber and a pedant, but it will stand my posterity in good stead.' And again: 'The kings want to create land and people with the pen: I say with the sword, or you will get nothing.'

The work of this plodding purposeful king was put to good use by his more brilliant son, as is well known. But the logic informing the sum of the achievement of Frederick the Great is not always fully appreciated. In the War of the Austrian Succession Frederick swooped on Silesia and seized it with no shadow of moral justification. In the Seven Years War he defended his hold upon it; Prussia was tried to the limit, but by her blood and sweat she held it. Materially, she consolidated her possession of Silesia. By engineering the first partition of Poland Frederick not only extended his dominion; much more, he committed his two great neighbours, Austria and Russia, to an act of international immorality beside which even the seizure of Silesia paled. Morally also, Prussia consolidated her possession of Silesia.

In 1786 Prussia entered upon what have been called the least-known and most maligned years of her history under the direction of Frederick the Great's nephew, Frederick-William II, who has been described as a boozy mystic. This king learnt his political methods from his great predecessor, who told him, if we are to believe the *Matinées du Roi de Prusse*: 'By the word politics I mean that one must always try to dupe other people,' and enjoined him: 'Above all follow zealously this maxim: that to despoil your neighbours is to deprive them of the means of injuring you.' On the whole Frederick-William II learnt these lessons well; but he lacked the judgement and determination necessary for their most effective application. With regard to Poland he managed, if anything, to outdo Frederick II in perfidy. In 1790 Prussia concluded an alliance with Poland. In 1793, by arrangement with the Russians, the Prussians were marching as conquerors into Greater Poland and occupying Danzig, with whom undeclared war had long existed, the Prussians harrying her customs officials and virtually maintaining an economic blockade. In 1794 Prussian forces stormed into Cracow and besieged Warsaw. In 1795 the third partition was completed and Poland ceased for the time to exist as an independent nation.

Prussia now sought to consolidate her new position by deserting her allies and withdrawing from the war against France which she had very largely originated. It is needless to detail here the chain of particular circumstances which made it impossible for Prussia promptly to effect this consolidation. The deeper cause lay in the fact that wild work and great things were afoot, greater things than the eighteenth century had ever witnessed. To appreciate them it is necessary to see what Europe was thinking about the ordering of society during those years in which Prussia was carving her way to greatness.

When after the reformation the state largely took over from the church it was natural that political theory should by slow degrees become more secular in outlook, concentrating upon the practical and ideal relation of the individual to the state. Thus the great school of natural law developed. This school of thought tried to define absolutely the status, rights, and obligations of the individual in a society that was itself absolute as being the embodiment of the rule of natural law. Natural law was held to be law that is natural as nature itself, law the observance of which is the mark of rational man, law that is man's own sense of justice, the supreme law which enjoins obedience to the laws. Natural law had in Roman times been identified with international law (*jus gentium*), and its place in the corpus of medieval thought was succinctly indicated by Saint Thomas Aquinas, who held that natural law was the sharing of the rational creature in the eternal law of God. It was idealistic in that it looked back to a hazy better time, to that golden age in the state of nature when sociable man lived under the regimen of the most natural of all laws which could not therefore be otherwise than good. It was idealistic in that it strove to ground its teaching in those absolute values such as good and right and truth which civilized man cannot define absolutely, let alone attain, but without which life for him would lose its meaning. It respected the sanctity of absolute values, that cardinal principle of western civilization.

In practice, however, the theory of natural law often tended to become an elaborate justification of state-reason in politics. Bodin, the learned and genial French theorist of the sixteenth century, stood at the head of the main line of political thinkers who were concerned to justify according to natural law the absolute territorial state as it then existed. The defence of absolutism by this code reached its peak in the age of Bossuet, who held that the people cannot be conceived of apart from the ruler who is 'the state itself', and of his sovereign Louis XIV who proclaimed: *L'état c'est moi.* But democratic tendencies had been early discernible in such theorists as Hotmann, Mariana, and Althusius. These tendencies steadily developed during the eighteenth century, particularly in France. The age of reason began to perceive that it was irrational to deny that the sanctity of the individual was the counterpart to the sanctity of absolute values, that his freedom followed from the reformation, that the princely state of absolute authority was but a temporary expedient with no anchor in enduring justice. Or if it did not perceive these things, it perceived what amounted to as much. And so the events of 1517 found their logical complement in those of 1789.

The deeds of the Terror bore witness to the intensity of the change. But fundamentally France in her revolution of 1789 crowned her former ample contributions to the betterment of European society. In the revolution France equated the individual, the state, and the supernational order in fresh terms. She set forth those rights of man which were to safeguard the dignity and estate of the free individual. She conceived *la patrie* in which every individual should find equal and untrammelled scope for his activities within the rule of the impartial popular law that was their guarantor. She proclaimed fraternity with all peoples of good faith, like-minded with herself. Those were the ideals: liberty, equality, fraternity.

France was not insulated from the body-general of the continent, and the currents which supplied the power for her great activity were running also in those lands which were still members of the Holy Roman Empire, no longer holy, or Roman, or an empire.

In Germany such currents were indeed much less highly charged. In a territory dominated by some three hundred despots, benevolent, malevolent, or indifferent as the case might be, political theorists of the so-called Cameral school found it difficult to imagine or imprudent to suggest that the acme of satisfactory governance could be other than a benevolent despotism, decently justified according to the recognized canons of natural law. For the most prominent political writer of the time, Schlözer, benevolent despotism was indeed not enough; he hankered after representative constitutional government. But Schlözer was a Hanoverian under English rule and could afford such ideas, though even they did not take him very far since he reverenced monarchy as a divine institution and thought that an enlightened prince was the best guarantee of progress. Nevertheless, developments in France necessarily had their effect in Germany as elsewhere. Rousseau in particular did much towards opening up new lines of thought for German thinkers. In the main these lines led ultimately in a direction very different from that taken in France. Probably the most important single factor which made for this deflection was the fact that Germany did not then exist, though Prussia did. Whereas in 1789 France was essentially France. The revolution meant, in practical terms, the reorganization of her social system, the ordering of the *patrie* in an attempt to realize the ideals outlined above. And how greatly this middle term, the nation, bulked in practice became evident even before the Napoleonic era.

The response which the revolution evoked from Germans naturally varied according to temperament, class, and state. On the whole the response of prominent German thinkers was at first decidedly favourable, sometimes even rapturous; but as the revolution got into its stride very many were bitterly disappointed and became correspondingly hostile. This circumstance may in some measure be taken as an indication of the gap which existed between France and Germany as far as practical realities were concerned. In their admiration of the revolution Germans often tended to concentrate upon the ideal rather than the political aspect. They, not less than Frenchmen, were enraptured to a degree now difficult to imagine by this new vision of the noble individual living in oecumenical brotherhood with his fellows. *Weltbürgertum*, world-citizenship, was a word on many lips. But the Germans lacked the middle, national, term. It was perhaps partly this lack, and partly a peculiarly German bent, which accounted for the fact that German thinkers, unlike the French, were in the main not primarily concerned with defining and safeguarding the position of the individual in society and of formulating proposals for the regulation of practical international politics according to something other than purely nationalistic standards. They plunged in deeper forthwith. The great German romantics sought to increase the stature of the individual by exploring unplumbed depths within him. And correspondingly some envisaged a supernational, as distinct from an international, order: that is, an order not among nations but above them, not a mere compromise between nations but nationality transcending itself.

But other Germans wished for political interpretation and practical realization of their ideals. They brooded upon the missing middle term.

Earlier Von Steuben and his German followers had sent home great tidings from America: how thirteen small states had banded together, and had broken the shackles of an effete empire, and had in free federation created a new nation. At the same time many Germans were taught by the Holy Roman Empire and its great Germanic past to look, not indeed up to that now withered incubus, but out over other German lands, beyond the confines of the principalities of their birth, beyond the archbishopric of Mainz, or the duchy of Mecklenburg-Strelitz or the landgraviate of Hesse-Darmstadt, or their peers in miniature sovereignty. And what the lookers mostly saw was Prussia. And Prussia was as we have seen her.

Within the empire there were princes who imitated Prussia's despotism, if not her efficiency, as the inhabitants of states like Hesse-Cassel and Württemberg knew to their cost. But the educated subjects of enlightened rulers such as Friedrich August III of Saxony and Karl Friedrich of Baden were far from regarding Prussia as a paragon. They tended to despise or hate this unlovely parvenu crouched upon the shallow sandy soil of the north, ready to spring, violent and crude, the state whose children were taught that Benkelsz, the discoverer of a process for salting herring, was more valuable to the fatherland than Voltaire. But when it came to practical politics the German states in the latter half of the eighteenth century mostly looked to Prussia.

The Prussian victories in the Seven Years War, and especially the defeat and humiliation of the French at Rossbach, were more than a stage in the Prussian progress; they were an inspiration to the German lands at large. For long years the German principalities had been used as pawns in the designs and combinations of the great foreign powers; time and again German territory had been the chosen battleground whereon foreigners fought out their quarrels. And now at last a German power rose by its own exertions, and went out against the great foreigners, and chastened them, and held her own against them all, Russia, Austria, and France. Throughout his reign Frederick the Great, superficially an untypical German, continued to develop his position as a patriotic leader. He fought the War of the Bavarian Succession in order to prevent Austria from achieving her long-cherished design of absorbing Bavaria. He succeeded. By the treaty of Teschen, concluded in 1779, Austria renounced her Bavarian design and the position of Prussia was safeguarded while Frederick at the same time considerably enhanced his reputation as the defender of the rights and liberties of the empire. The smaller states looked to Prussia. This tendency was confirmed six years later when the emperor Joseph II renewed his project for annexing Bavaria under cover of one of those complicated exchanges of territory of which eighteenth-century princes made a speciality. In this scheme the other great continental powers, Russia and France, were to play their part. Karl August, Duke of Zweibrücken, heir to Karl Theodor the debile Bavarian elector, appealed to Frederick the Great. Frederick at once sent protests to St. Petersburg, Versailles, and Vienna, and accused the emperor of seeking to infringe the imperial constitution. In March 1785 he set Prussia at the head of the *Fürstenbund*, the League of Princes, with the avowed object of maintaining the constitution of the empire and protecting individual princes against aggression. This league was joined by the princes of Saxony, Brunswick-Luneburg, and Anhalt, the dukes of Saxe-Weimar and Gotha, Zweibrücken, and Mecklenburg, the margrave of Baden, the landgrave of Hesse-Cassel, the archbishop-electors of Mainz and Trier and the bishop of Osnabrück. This time Joseph II was defeated without a war. Such was Frederick's crowning achievement. He died next year. His successor attempted to maintain this policy, especially after 1795, when Prussia sought to lead the smaller states in a policy of northern neutrality, laying down a demarcation line and instituting a joint observation-corps, each state contributing the quota fixed at the congress of Hildesheim. That Frederick-William II was largely unsuccessful in this policy is perhaps the greatest measure of his failure. But the tradition was there, and deeper currents were running that way.

Prussia, the authoritarian hero of a century-old epic of peculiarly cynical statecraft, was thus the focus of something greater at a time when German thinkers were beginning to envisage a powerful national state.

Coupled with the absence of a single German state there has been mention of a peculiarly German bent, thus skirting the edge of the deep. It is not possible here to explore these depths, but only to remark in passing that in Germany as early as the seventeen-seventies the cult of *Sturm und Drang* betokened the first serious revolt against the intellectual order which France had given to the continent, an order based upon delicate precision, rational restraint, and cultivated taste. This order was, indeed, threatened also from within. But the French following of Mesmer and Cagliostro and their likecould not compare with the extraordinary vogue of mysticism, magical superstition, and pseudo-scientific spiritualism in Germany. To a certain extent this was, indeed, only the latest manifestation of a standing German tradition.

Towards the end of the sixteenth century religious thought in Germany had already begun to feel the influence of mystics like Giordano Bruno, Sebastian Franck, and Jacob Böhme. The great undertaking of these mystics was the reversal of the previous relation between Christianity and the universe; instead of seeking to absorb the universe into a rigid creed of Christianity, they attempted to evaluate Christianity in terms of a wider universe of historical life and cosmic experience. From such sources ultimately issued the later German and romantic tendency towards a species of lay piety in the face of the mystery of the world (*Weltfrömmigkeit*). Midway in the course of this development stood the pietist movement which, under the guidance of Spener, gained ground rapidly in Germany towards the end of the seventeenth century. Pietism aimed at a revival of the indivisible Church of the spirit, preaching rebirth, dwelling upon the mystic significance of the community (*Gemeinschaft*), and developing the concept of 'individuality and diversity' which held that the relation between the individual and his fellows was comparable to that between the organs of a living body—an organic theory which was to exert powerful influence upon the great romantics.

The appeal of pietism was largely lower-class. It stressed German culture as opposed to the classical and French civilization of the upper classes. It set up will and enthusiasm over against intellect, revelation against reason; it ended by attacking the universalism and intellectualism of the enlightenment. This movement was at its height during the first half of the eighteenth century, and was particularly stimulated by Count Zinzendorf, Spener's godson, who founded the first

Moravian community in 1722. Later in the century other mystical sects made headway, and throughout Germany secret orders like that of the Rosicrucians flourished exceedingly, reaching their zenith under Frederick-William II of Prussia and his ministers of obscurantist mysticism, Wöllner and Bischoffswerder. Still more significant was the fact that the main body which expressly sought to combat superstition and promote the cause of the enlightenment was itself a secret mystical body of the first order, organized in a series of classes and ranks with titles such as Plant-School, Magus, Scottish Knight, and Minervalis. That this sect of the Illuminati should have posed as the promoter of the enlightenment is a notable commentary upon the then climate of opinion in Germany.

Such cults were in their mystical aspect the extreme outcome of a popular German tradition in religious thought; in their pseudo-scientific aspect they were a debasement of the main intellectual outlook of the eighteenth century, which derived its typical modes of thought from the physical sciences and from mathematics. The ways of nature were being laid bare with precision; formulae of absolute validity were being discovered. Political thinkers, glad with a new sense of the perfectibility of man, sought to adapt these exact techniques in order to determine the right ordering of society. It was a question of discovering the right formulae, of solving the right equations. But gradually some deeply pondering Germans began to look to a new and different mode of thought. For them history began to take on fresh meaning at about the same time as the concept of the nation was acquiring novel significance. This conjunction was far-reaching in its effect.

Chapter II

ROMANTICISM

1783–1815

While Prussia was climbing to fame in the latter half of the eighteenth century new thoughts were sweeping in from her eastern domains.

In 1762 an East Prussian youth of seventeen, poor, introspective, and given to solitary communion with nature, came to the local university-town of Königsberg. There Johann Gottfried Herder learnt much from Immanuel Kant. But he learnt more and more readily from Johann Georg Hamann, an ardent patriot and francophobe and an intensely subjective thinker, who readily championed the emotions against reason. This needy hypochondriac, delving back into the German mysticism of Jacob Böhme and others, pronounced obscure and oracular dicta which gained for him the name of the Magus of the North. His disjointed effusions commonly bore subtitles such as *Hierophantic Letters* or *A Rhapsody in Cabbalistic Prose*.

Herder's choice between his masters was significant. Later in life he once confessed to his wife, 'I have too little reason and too much idiosyncrasy'[1]: that from one who may justly claim to stand at the head of the new school of German political thought.

Herder, an unamiable character but a highly original and somewhat neglected thinker, exercised a quite remarkable influence over his contemporaries. A friend writing to him in

[1] *Errinerungen aus dem Leben Johann Gottfried von Herders.* Caroline Herder (Tübingen, 1820), vol. ii, p. 37. Quoted, R. R. Ergang, *Herder and the Foundations of German Nationalism* (New York, 1931), p. 74. I am further greatly indebted to Mr. Ergang's study for quotations given in the following pages.

1785 hailed his works as 'inspired of God. I also heard this opinion voiced unanimously on my long journey from Pyrmont to Hanover, Bremen, Oldenburg, Hamburg and back by way of Lüneberg, Celle and Brunswick'. And later German theorists in the most various fields of thought felt his influence; for his ideas were of astonishingly wide range, if often tantalizing in their incompleteness.

Herder gave Germans a new pride in their common past. He sought to modify the high regard in which Greek art was then held by the Germans who followed Winckelmann and Lessing in appreciation. He extolled Dürer and everything Gothic, remarking once that he wished that he had been born in the Middle Ages, and asking whether 'the times of the Swabian emperors' did not 'deserve to be set forth in their true light in accordance with the German mode of thought?' He equated the German with the Gothic.

As in the sphere of art so in that of language Herder proclaimed a national message. He crowned the line of German authors who, since 1617 when Martin Opitz wrote, in Latin, his *Aristarchus, sive de contemptu linguae Teutonicae*, had urged Germans to take pride in their own despised language. Herder's collections of folk-poetry created a great vogue in Germany for that type of hitherto neglected literature. In one of his mediocre verses he urged his countrymen to 'spew out the ugly slime of the Seine. Speak German, O you German'. But he went much further. In 1772 he published his work *Uber den Ursprung der Sprache* (*Concerning the Origin of Speech*) which laid the foundations of that study of comparative philology which was to bear directly upon the development of the new political outlook.

It is fitting that the ideas of the thinker who so largely originated the school of historical thought should have culminated, insofar as they ever did culminate, in his great work, the *Ideen zur Philosophie der Geschichte der Menschheit* (*Ideas upon the Philosophy of the History of Mankind*). Herder began work on this book in the year 1783. It is an important date in the history of German thought.

Herder's philosophy was of a strongly subjective turn. It stressed the influence of physical and historical environment upon human development. Herder proclaimed, in particular, that in history 'one must go into the age, into the region, into the whole history and feel one's way into everything'. The historian must be a 'regenerated contemporary' of the past. Herder further maintained that 'if any science is an instrument of the most genuine patriotic spirit, it is history'. Historical subjectivity and patriotism issued in a new concept of the nation.

Herder replaced the traditional conception of the politico-juridical state by that of the folk-nation, which was represented as an organic historical growth. Each nation was an organic personal whole. Herder laid particular stress upon this biological aspect. He held that 'a nationality is a plant of nature', and talked further of the 'national animal' and of the 'physiology of the whole national group'. This organism was completed by the 'national spirit', the 'soul of the folk'.

To this national organism Herder attached exceptional significance. Patriotism for him was almost the touchstone of individual worth. 'He that has lost his patriotic spirit has lost himself and the whole world about himself.' He taught that 'in a certain sense every human perfection is national'. Nor was he afraid to push his concept of the organic folk to its extreme, maintaining that 'there is only one class in the state, the *Volk* (not the rabble), and the king belongs to this class as well as the peasant'. The then necessity of explaining that the word folk[1] was used not in the sense of the rabble but in that of the popular corporate body of the nation is an incidental tribute to the novelty of the conception: both novel and mature with Herder, for already we dimly see the folk emerging as the basis of a hierarchic but classless national body.

If the nation was very important it was also very separate. Each nation according to Herder was distinguished by its climate, education, foreign intercourse, tradition, and heredity. Providence is extolled as having 'wonderfully separated

[1]Here as elsewhere *Volk* is translated by *folk* rather than by *people*. The folk is not merely an association of citizens, but tends rather to mean the tribal community considered as a nation; the word *folk* goes further than the word *people* in its connotation of racial homogeneity. *Folk* is an imprecisely suggestive word; it surpasses *people* in the very German quality of *Innigkeit*, a blend of inwardness and fervour.

nationalities not only by woods and mountains, seas and deserts, rivers and climates, but more particularly by languages, inclinations and characters'. Herder appreciated the consequent limitations of the human outlook and approved them. He praised the tribal outlook, holding that 'the savage who loves himself, his wife and child with quiet joy and glows with limited activity for his tribe as for his own life is in my opinion a more real being than that cultivated shadow who is enraptured with the shadow of the whole species'. The nation need not look beyond itself since 'each nationality contains its centre of happiness within itself, as a bullet the centre of gravity'. Nor should it look beyond itself, for 'every nation bears in itself the standard of its perfection, totally independent of all comparison with that of others'. Here then is the total separation, with this to complete it: 'Do not nationalities differ in everything, in poetry, in appearance, in tastes, in usages, customs and languages? Must not religion which partakes of these also differ among the nationalities?' This question was further pointed when the person who was made to ask it went on to lament that Luther did not establish a national church. In another place Herder expressed a doubt whether Germany did not buy Christianity at too high a price, that of true nationality. Here as elsewhere Herder's theorizing upon the nation can hardly be disassociated from his German patriotism, which sometimes bordered upon national pantheism. He once wrote, for instance:

> 'Since according to the ideas of the [Red Indian] Americans every river, every tree, every meadow has a spirit, should not the German rivers and mountains also have one? Let someone, therefore, defend the national spirit . . . and show by examples that Germany has since the earliest times had a fixed national spirit in all classes, still has it at the present time, and according to its organisation will have it everlastingly. The writer of such a history deserves more than one civic crown; a wreath of oak, beech, spruce and linden boughs.'

German national spirit demanded German territorial unity: 'He is deserving of glory and gratitude who seeks to promote the unity of the territories of Germany through writings, manufactures, and institutions.' Herder also sounded a deeper and more ringing call:

'But now! Again I cry, my German brethren! But now! The remains of all genuine folk-thought is rolling into the abyss of oblivion with a last accelerated impetus. The light of the so-called enlightenment [*Aufklärung*] is eating round about itself like a cancer. For the last half century we have been ashamed of everything that concerns the fatherland.'

Here is a formal defiance of the age of reason and enlightenment. One specimen of Herder's folk-thought will perhaps suffice. In the *Ideas upon the Philosophy of the History of Mankind* he wrote: 'Compare England with Germany: the English are Germans, and even in the latest times the Germans have led the way for the English in the greatest things.'

Thus did Herder the historical theorist turn away from the light of the eighteenth century at about the same time as Justus Möser, the pragmatic historian of Osnabrück, began to draw upon history in support of his opposition to the enlightenment, maintaining that for a happier ordering of society one should look to the feudal past and to the careful preservation of those historical institutions which had proved their worth in withstanding the test of time. But whereas Möser's outlook was mainly bounded by the confines of the little state of his birth, Herder, who hated absolutism and Prussian militarism, was imbued with the spirit of the whole German folk. And his sweeping thought ranged wider yet. Herder sought to reconcile his teaching of the folk-nation with the eighteenth-century climate of opinion. This attempt was largely a reflection of his underlying desire to harmonize sentiment with reason, an undertaking present to German thought at least since the time of Leibniz and his theory of knowledge, according to which there exists between the extremes of unconscious matter and perfectly conscious God a hierarchy of monads, graded according to clarity of perception. All knowledge is implicit in the soul; the most elementary stage is sensuous and intuitive perception, which is thought in the raw; by a process of development within the human soul this perception becomes self-conscious, rational, thought. Great importance accordingly attaches to the method of this development, the crowning achievement of which is the harmonization of primitive and derivative truth, of experience and intelligence, feeling and reason. Herder was only among the first of a long line of Germans who were preoccupied with the possibility of this splendid achievement. It is the key to much in German theory. But it is not here possible to follow up this line of thought or the many paths of speculation opened out by Herder himself. It must be enough to notice certain points of immediate significance.

Herder was too penetrating a thinker not to perceive the extremes to which his theory of the folk-nation tended. And he issued specific warning against them. While regarding the Jews as Asiatic aliens in Europe, he nevertheless refused to commit himself to a rigid racial theory, remarking that 'notwithstanding the varieties of the human form there is but one and the same species of man throughout the whole earth'. He warned his countrymen of the snares that lay ahead, holding that 'national glory is a deceiving seducer. When it reaches a certain height, it clasps the head with an iron band. The enclosed sees nothing in the mist but his own picture; he is susceptible to no foreign impressions.' And yet, more pointedly:

> 'It is the apparent plan of nature that as one human being, so also one generation, and also one nationality learn, learn incessantly, from and with the others until all have comprehended the difficult lesson: 'No nationality has been solely designated by God as the chosen people of the earth; above all we must seek the truth and cultivate the garden of the common good.' Hence no nationality of Europe may separate itself sharply, and foolishly say, 'With us *alone*, with us dwells *all* wisdom.'

Time was to show that many Germans were able to respond to Herder's immediate enthusiasms and convictions, but fewer to his more far-sighted saving stipulations.

One of those, however, who did not permit himself to be carried away was Immanuel Kant, who criticized the *Ideas upon the Philosophy of the History of Mankind* and provoked Herder to a retort in the form of a *Metacritique upon the Critique of Pure Reason.* Herder quarrelled with Kant and indeed he eventually succeeded in striking up dreary quarrels with nearly all his friends and admirers even including Hamann. But his difference with Kant is a measure of the latter's aloofness from the heady enthusiasms which inspired Herder. The author of the Project for Eternal Peace was properly speaking no party to the origination of the historical school; but it is nevertheless notable that according to Kant the categorical imperative of conscience left no room for mere happiness; he preached duty for duty's sake, holding that the criterion of good laws is their consistency with reason, not their aptitude for promoting happiness; at the same time he taught that 'the ruler has only rights against the subject, no duties'. Combinations and modifications of these doctrines were to play an important part in that line of thought which derived from Kant's early pupil, Herder, who attracted a number of his later ones. Even in Kant's immediate following there were young men who, as will be seen, developed opinions very different from his own.

But Kant was not alone. The two greatest German minds of the age were the two great exceptions, aloof and elevated. Beside Kant stood Goethe. They ranged from the individual to the universe untrammelled by any mediate allegiance. Goethe owed much, indeed, to Herder, deriving his appreciation of the Gothic from him and once confessing that the *Ideen zur Philosophie der Geschichte der Menschheit* was to him the 'most congenial of gospels'. But both as an administrator in the service of Duke Karl August of Saxe-Weimar and as an artist in the service of his genius he held aloof from politics. Goethe's works were indeed largely reverenced by his countrymen as being of peculiarly German import; how far this was the case may perhaps subsequently appear. But Goethe, the distant conservative, the admirer of Napoleon, never allowed himself to be fettered by such admiration. Perhaps the most specific and serene statement of his supernational position is to be found in his conversation with Eckermann on Sunday, 14th March, 1830, when as an old man he rather sadly dwelt upon the reproaches levelled against him and in particular upon that of being 'quite without love for my fatherland and my dear Germans'. He said simply that political poetry was limited poetry and that he had never been able to write war-songs or share the hatred of nation against nation.

Schiller should also be reckoned of this company, although some of his writings can be twisted to support the national school of thought. He was a passionate advocate of untrammelled freedom, although with him as with Kant and Luther before him there is noticeable, particularly in *Don Carlos*, a significant divorce of the cult of abstract ethical freedom from practical political safeguards and the maintenance of social dignity. Whither this led and how far it is a peculiarly German trait may later become apparent. Schiller himself, like Wieland and other classicists, was a cosmopolitan spirit; at the same time, however, he proclaimed the majesty of the German, holding that 'every folk has its day in history, but the day of the Germans is the harvest of all time'. But this exceptional German quality was according to him 'a moral greatness; it dwells in the culture and in the character of the nation, which is independent of his political fates'. This was written to soothe the self-esteem of Germans in the face of political humiliation, probably soon after the peace of Lunéville in 1801. It illustrates something of the attitude which a number of the early romantics adopted towards political issues; on the whole they were not uninterested in them, but they tended to approach by way of the idealistic and the aesthetic. In this connexion it is worth instancing the way in which the concept of the nation was treated by a prominent member of Schiller's circle, his young protégé, the hellenist Johann Christoph Friedrich Hölderlin; the form, not less than the content, is of significance. In Hölderlin's poetical novel *Hyperion*, in which the spirit of storm and stress was infused into the then prevalent cult of ancient Greece, a major incident turns upon consideration of the significance of the nation-state. The titular hero remarks to his friend Alabanda,

> 'A folk in which spirit and greatness no longer begets any spirit and greatness has nothing in common any longer with others that are still men; it has no more rights, and it is an empty farce, a superstition, if one still insists upon honouring such corpses, which have no will of their own, as if the heart of a Roman still beat within them. Away with them! It should not stand where it does, the rotten barren tree; it steals light and air from the young life that is ripening towards a new world.'
>
> Alabanda flew to me, embraced me, and his kisses penetrated to my soul. 'Brother-in-arms!' he cried, 'dear brother-in-arms. . .'.
>
> 'That is my melody, once and for all,' he continued in a voice that stirred my heart like a battlecry; 'there is no need of anything further! . . . Oh! light me a torch that I may burn the weed from

the heath, let someone prepare me a mine that I may blow the inert clods out the earth! . . .'

Alabanda was silent a while.

'I have my joy in the future,' he finally began again, and ardently clasped me by both hands. 'Thanks be to God, I shall accept no common end! In the mouth of the churl to be happy means to be sleepy. To be happy! When you speak to me of being happy I feel as if I had mush and tepid water upon my tongue. So foolish and so wicked is everything for the sake of which you renounce your laurel-crown, your immortality.'

The two then proceed to eulogize the sons of the sun who 'live upon victory', until Hyperion cries,

'O heaven and earth! . . . This is joy. . . . Yes! Yes! by thy splendid soul, man, thou wilt save the fatherland with me.'

'That will I', he [Alabanda] cried, 'or go under.'

From this day on we became ever more sacred and beloved one to another.

Hyperion and Alabanda subsequently went on 'a splendid trip to Chios'. Further rhapsodizing ensued, culminating in Hyperion's exclamation, 'we are having our betrothal-day together.' But he then added,

'But let us return to our former talk!

Thou yet concedest too much power to the state. It should not demand what it cannot compel. But the product of love and of the spirit does not allow itself to be compelled. Let it [the state] leave that untouched, or else may its law be taken and thrust into the pillory. By heaven, he who would make the state into a school of morals does not know how he sins! The fact that man has wished to erect the state as his heaven has always turned the state into hell.

The state is the coarse husk round the kernel of life, and nothing further. It is the wall around the garden of human fruits and flowers.

But of what use is the wall round the garden, where the ground lies barren? In that case only rain from heaven can assist.

O rain from heaven! O inspiration! Thou wilt bring us once more the springtide of the peoples. The state cannot impose its law upon thee. But if it does not disturb thee thou wilt come, thou wilt come with thy almighty bliss, thou wilt wrap us in golden clouds and bear us aloft above mortality. . . . Dost thou ask me when this will be? At the time when the beloved of the age, the youngest most lovely daughter of the age, the new church, shall issue from out of these polluted outworn forms, when the awakened apprehension of the divine shall return to man his divinity, and to his breast fair youth, when—I cannot proclaim it, for I can scarce surmise it, but it comes certainly, certainly. . . .'

Alabanda was silent and looked at me astonished for a while. . . .

'Come,' I cried, and seized him by his raiment, 'come, who continues longer in the prison which surrounds us with night?'

'Whither, my fine enthusiast!' answered Alabanda dryly, and a shadow of mockery seemed to play across his face.'

That was the beginning of the end of their friendship, and Hyperion went away, alone, and found Diotima.

Hyperion and Alabanda were of one mind, then, in denying to peoples whom they styled decadent the right to live, and in extolling the sacrifice of individual happiness to national glory. But Alabanda, at least by implication, identified the folk-nation with a repressive state; whereas to his friend the state was a concept without moral content in itself, and only by heavenly inspiration were the peoples to attain their true fulfilment.

But when Hyperion parted from Alabanda after their dispute it was not for ever. And as the course of their lives went forward so, in some sense, did that of the development now under survey.

Not a few of Hölderlin's contemporaries sought to soar with Hyperion, but like him, could not wholly break with Alabanda. One such was Friedrich Leopold von Hardenberg, the Saxon-Prussian nobleman who devoted much of his time to the mining of salt, better known as Novalis, that very pure and short-lived spirit of the early romanticism.

Novalis provides an outstanding example of the romantic contempt for system. But among the products of his wayward brilliance it is possible to discern, fragmentarily, the kernel of much that later Germans built up with system enough. For Novalis, as for other romantics, the French revolution was no absolute revelation, but rather the antithesis only to the preceding political mode; it was the creative work of synthesizing these two that was of major concern. Novalis' outlook may fairly be thus evaluated in that he gave some attention to that triple terminology which won renown with Hegel. According to Novalis 'thesis and antithesis are the terminal points of a line. The line is the synthesis'.

He perceived that in this synthesis the state was no final

term, remarking for instance that 'the states must become aware that the attainment of all their aims is only possible by means of joint measures. Systems of alliance, rearing towards the universal monarchy'. For the attainment of this end Novalis turned increasingly to religion, hoping thereby to restore the much-regretted unity of medieval Christendom, the 'general Christian union'. But he was also greatly taken with the state, holding, for example, that the citizen should pay taxes to the state as a man gives presents to his mistress. 'With us', he wrote, 'the state is too little *proclaimed*. There should be state-announcers, preachers of patriotism'. Herder's conceptions of the novel significance of history and of the state as a biological organism were shared by Novalis. According to him 'the state has always been a makroanthropos'. The state was not only political, but cultural. 'All culture arises from the relations of a human being to the state.' Novalis saw that the state was a toilsome thing, and he indicated no rosy path. He held that 'the state spares man no trouble, but much rather does it increase his hardship to infinity; though not, indeed, without increasing his strength to infinity'. And with Novalis strength stood for much. He maintained that 'all men are by nature only relatively equal, which in fact is the old inequality, the stronger has also the stronger right. Likewise men are not by nature free, but only more or less bound'. The stronger has also the stronger right: the phrase went echoing down the corridors of German thought.

If the state was an ideal to Novalis, so was Germanity. For him 'the instinctive universal policy and tendency of the Romans also resides in the German people. The best thing that the French have won in the course of their revolution, is a portion of Germanity [*Deutschheit*]'. This 'Germanity is true popularity and therefore an ideal'. And finally Novalis can be observed pursuing this line of thought home to its ultimate term, and equating Germanity with cosmopolitanism. In 1797 he wrote to the elder Schlegel that 'Germanity is cosmopolitanism mixed with the most powerful individuality'. Such thoughts were big with the future.

The year of Novalis' birth, 1772, also saw that of the younger brother of the recipient of the letter just quoted. The Hanoverian romantic Karl Wilhelm Friedrich von

Schlegel outlived Novalis by some twenty-eight years, but he may yet be fitly noticed here. This eclectic philosopher, a rather extravagant figure, was typical of his time in being absorbed in the problems of the individual. In *Lucinde*, his unfinished romance of 1799, he sought to translate into practical ethics the romantic demand for full individual freedom. But the principle of individuality applied to the sphere of state-politics tends to become the principle of nationalism. Schlegel was not less typical of his age in his stress upon the nation or in his enthusiasm for ancient Greece. The merging of the two is evident in his dictum that 'the Greek culture was in general thoroughly original and national; it was a whole complete in itself which, through internal development, reached a very high peak and, in full circle, also sank back again into itself. . . . Their poetry was, not only in the first beginning, but also in its whole progress, constantly national'. It is accordingly not surprising to find Schlegel declaring that 'each state is an individual existing independently for itself [*ein selbständig für sich bestehendes Individuum*]; it is unconditionally its own master; it has its peculiar character and governs itself according to peculiar laws, customs, and usages'. Earlier, in 1791, Schlegel had said that he wished 'to derive everything from the immense peculiarity of our nation'. And he led where others were to follow in stressing the relation between national peculiarity and historical continuity. Schlegel held that 'the state comprises a coexisting and successive continuity of men, the totality of those whose relation to one another is determined by the same physical influence; for instance all inhabitants of a country or descendants of one tribe'. this tribal aspect of the nation was of particular significance since according to Schlegel 'the older, purer and less mixed the stock is, so also are its customs, and the more that this is so as regards customs and true persistence in an attachment to them, so much the more will it [the stock] be a nation'.

But Schlegel like others went beyond the nation. In the early period, while still under the influence of democratic theories of natural law, he held that 'the idea of a *world-republic* has practical validity and characteristic importance'. But, again like others, he outgrew this phase, laying increasing stress upon conservative aristocratic nationalism and, especially after his conversion to catholicism in 1808, turning like Novalis to religion for the supernational order. The rationalistic concept of a league of nations was accordingly displaced by the romantic ideal of an oecumenical empire, not indeed an expansion of the Napoleonic empire which was held to be egoistic and 'mechanical', but a holy empire under a pope-emperor. This romantic idealism pointed towards realistic imperialism, as is apparent from a passage in which Schlegel talked of

'the empire, as specifically differentiated from the kingdom, as a kingdom over the kings. In this connection the nation which, through the empire, exercises a fixed overlordship over the neighbouring peoples is presumed to be a strong one, if not the strongest. . . . The idea of the empire is much more powerfully adapted than is that of a union of nations to the introduction of a moral relation between nations. This is already demonstrated by the comparison of the Middle Ages with more recent times. Furthermore this system is much better suited to the natural relation in which the nations stand to each other in respect of the great difference of their cultures.

Schlegel propagated these ideas in the popular lectures which he delivered at Cologne from 1804 to 1806. This fashionable theorist had a friend who experienced a change of outlook somewhat similar to his own, and who was to deliver a series of lectures of even greater renown.

Johann Gottlieb Fichte stands next after Herder as the second great figure in the line of German national thought. In Upper Lusatia this son of a poor Saxon linen-weaver was born in the same year that Herder first came to Königsberg. The diligently pious youth, later to be accused of atheism, used to listen with such attention to the sermons of the local pastor that he could afterwards repeat them by heart. This accomplishment attracted the attention of a neighbouring patron who set him in the way of learning. He endured the gruelling régime of the great monastic school at Pforta, which left its flinty impress on many of Germany's greatest men.

Fichte early came under the influence of Kant and in 1792, stimulated and assisted by him, published the *Versuch einer Kritik aller Offenbarung* (*Sketch of a Critique of all Revelation*) which was commonly attributed to Kant himself. Fichte had begun, significantly enough, as an opponent of the enlightenment and defender of the edicts of the obscurantist Prussian minister Wöllner. But in the early seventeen-nineties Fichte, influenced by Kant and the French revolution, devoted his attention in the field of social theory to such concepts as the liberty of the individual, natural law, and a cosmopolitan order, which were reflected in *Die Grundlage des Naturrechts nach Principien der Wissenschaftslehre*, published in 1796.

It is not here possible to trace in detail how Fichte, from being a disciple of Kant, gradually evolved a romantic philosophy of his own, and became the metaphysical precursor of Hegel. But since Fichte, like so many of his German contemporaries, worked out his social and political theories in close relation to his metaphysical tenets, it is pertinent to note the main issue which parted him from Kant. Fichte was like Kant convinced that knowing was not independent of the knowing mind; but whereas Kant retained a distinction between knowing and the unknowable thing-in-itself, between perception and the reality of the thing perceived, Fichte transcended all such limitations. He established transcendental philosophy, proclaiming the identity of the knowing mind and the process of knowing and the known reality. He thus perfected the subjective system of knowledge according to which all is flat before the ego. The subjective unity is complete. Within this unity discord and opposition may indeed arise, but that is only the ego surpassing itself, goading itself to finer exertion. The ego creates the world, which is non-ego. The ego realizes itself by producing the world of objects. Non-ego is enveloped by ego. Logical idealism crows in exultation. The ego is creation, being, fulfilment, totality.

In the face of such colossal egotism it is hardly surprising that Fichte was charged with atheism. In this connexion in 1799 he made an unnecessary exhibition of himself at the university of Jena and was forced to seek refuge in Berlin. Fichte described the first work which he produced on Prussian soil as a link in the chain of the system which he was gradually forging. This book appears to have attracted but slight notice, though it influenced other thinkers, and notably

Friedrich Schlegel. Nevertheless its importance is very considerable. Not only does it strikingly illustrate the transition from Fichte's early radicalism to his maturer political outlook, but it is also almost, if not actually, the first socialist treatise in German. In the light of contemporary economic development in Prussia and France and of his metaphysical concept of totality Fichte worked out his ideal economic ordering of national society. In the autumn of 1800 appeared *Der geschlossene Handelsstaat* (*The Closed Commercial State*).

In this treatise, published less than twenty-five years after *The Wealth of Nations*, Fichte deliberately denied almost everything that Adam Smith had taught. He started from the thesis, familiar by now, that 'it is the state alone that unites an indeterminate multitude of human beings into an *enclosed whole*, into a *totality* [*Allheit*]'.

'In modern Europe', according to Fichte, 'there have been no states at all over a long period of time. At present attempts are still being made to construct them. . . . The deeper-lying duty of the state has been overlooked; this is to install each [citizen] in the possession suitable to him. It is only possible to achieve this last, however, if commercial anarchy is removed in the same way as the political is being gradually removed, and if the state encloses itself as a commercial state in the same way as it has been enclosed with regard to its legislative and judiciary functions.'

The general romantic tendency to hark back to the Middle Ages is already here apparent on the economic side; stress is laid upon guaranteeing to every individual his due measure of social security; it is the duty of the state to see to it that each man lives, in medieval phraseology, *convenienter*, as befits him.

In accordance with the above the state is to institute a rigidly planned corporate economy wherein all uncontrolled individual enterprize is made impossible. For instance,

'each person who . . . proposes to devote himself exclusively to an occupation must moreover, in the course of law, give notice to the government, which as representative of all and in their name confers upon him the exclusive right, and in the place of all affords the necessary renunciation [of the common right to engage in that particular occupation]. Now if somebody gives notice in respect of a branch of occupation after the highest number of workers which is legally allowed in it is already full, then the right shall not be granted him, but much rather shall there be suggested to him other branches in which his strength is needed.'

All production and trade will be under state supervision. 'No tradesman', for example, 'will be appointed who does not render account of whence he proposes to procure his goods.' And similarly in agriculture. Fichte was somewhat worried that the state could not control good and bad harvests. He tried to meet this difficulty by a device whereby 'whoever has cultivated more than his allotted quota announces it to the state, which does not compensate him for the surplus on the spot by an equivalent, whereby an increased circulation and all the disadvantages thereby entailed would follow; but it only *credits* this surplus to him; but at all events, with a view to his security, it issues him with a certificate for it'.

Fichte pointed out as one of the main advantages of his scheme the fact that 'in a state organized according to the principles here advanced no goods can be brought to a commercial house for sale for which an early vent cannot be counted on, since the permitted production and manufacture has already been calculated according to possible requirements in the foundation of the state. The commercial house can even compel this sale'. The aim of such a state is declared to be 'the wellbeing of the *nation*; not of a few individuals whose very high level of comfort is often the most striking indication, and true cause, of the greatest distress of the nation; this wellbeing should accordingly be extended pretty generally in the same measure'.

The economic basis of the state is, as far as possible, complete autarky. Fichte clearly perceived that the necessary complement to internal economic control was accordingly the most rigid supervision over foreign trade. He proposed to effect this by the following means:

'All direct traffic by the citizen with any foreigner should be absolutely done away with: this is the demand. Absolutely done away with is only that which has been made impossible. Direct traffic by the citizen with any foreigner must be made impossible.

'All possibility of world trade rests upon the possession of a medium of exchange that is valid throughout the world, and upon the serviceability of the same for us. . . . Consequently the solution of our problem would be as follows: *All world-currency, i.e. all gold and silver, which is in the hands of the citizens, should be taken out of circulation, and exchanged against a new land-currency, i.e. one which would only be valid inside the country.'*

All internal payments would be made exclusively in this land-currency. Fichte discussed the possibility of a purely paper currency but, with the recent warning of the French republican *assignats* evidently in mind, dismissed it as unlikely to command general confidence. He proposed that the government should mint its internal currency from some quite new unspecified substance the value of which could be fixed at will by the government without fear of popular suspicion; he only stipulated, first that 'the new money should . . . commend itself to the imagination: it should therefore be handsome to look at', and secondly that 'the preparation of this money must cost the government as little as possible of the former world-currency, since it needs this last for other purposes outside the country. . . . The new money must have as little true inner worth as possible'. But this is only one side of the operation, for 'at the same time as the currency transaction inside the country a manifesto from the government appears everywhere abroad' proclaiming that it is taking over all direct international trade from its citizens and warning 'foreigners, as from the day of the appearance of this manifesto, to enter directly into commercial dealings with no inhabitant of the state that is to be enclosed, without the express permission and intervention of the government'. Henceforth 'the amount of trade that is still to be carried on provisionally with abroad will be fixed; i.e. it will be settled what kind of goods should be imported or exported, what quota of the same for each year, and how long such imports and exports shall continue at all; also how much thereof for each district, and for each trading concern. This trade is from now on conducted not by the private person, but by the state.'

The reference to the 'provisional' maintenance of foreign trade leads naturally to the thesis that

'with every year imports must lessen. From year to year the public needs less of those [foreign] goods which can be produced in the country either in the form of the genuine article, or of substitutes; for it should accustom itself to do without these same [foreign goods] entirely, being actively held to it so to accustom itself by the ever rising prices of the same. The import and use of goods, of which the estimation rests only upon [public] opinion, can even be forbidden on the spot. . . . In measure as the internal production and manufacture, conducted according to plan and calculation and no longer left to blind chance, steadily increases, so are foreign goods replaced by those produced in the country.'

Elsewhere Fichte considered the prohibition of fashionable luxury goods in greater detail, mentioning for instance sable furs, silks, and, particularly, embroidery-work 'by which clothes are made neither warmer nor more lasting'—a truth which his father, the poor weaver, may early have impressed upon him.

In order to complete the commercial isolation of the state Fichte correspondingly envisaged an almost total elimination of exports. But he at once proceeded to supply the argument against this, remarking that

'in order to base this national independence of foreign countries not upon needy circumstances, but upon the highest possible prosperity, the government possesses the most efficacious means in the world-currency which it has gathered in; with this money it can buy and borrow from abroad as many of the forces and auxiliary means as it can ever need. . . . Machines are bought abroad and copied in the country. The promise of cash overcomes every prohibition [made by other states].

After it has been worked out which branches of occupation can be introduced into the country the government should promote production with particular regard to the raw materials for those branches of occupation, tending towards the building up of substitutes if the genuine products cannot be reared in this climate. Almost every climate has its own substitutes for every foreign product, the only point being that the first cultivation does not repay the pains.'

In a long note Fichte then emphasized that this difficulty could be overcome by enterprizing long-term planning and state subsidy. He took as a concrete instance the case of a northern country which set out to produce a substitute for cotton.

Fichte specifically allowed one exception to his scheme for a self-contained economy, stating that 'only in one case can the retention of some foreign trade be considered; in the following: the cultivation of a given product. . . . in a given climate, . . . although not altogether impossible, may be very disadvantageous, but highly advantageous in another . . .', and inversely with another given product. 'A trade agreement could be established between such states, which are designed by nature itself for a permanent barter-trade'. Fichte instanced a possible state barter agreement between a northern and a southern state to cover wheat and wine.

Fichte realized that 'in order', in particular, 'to be able to maintain these laws with regard to export a strict supervision would certainly be necessary in the harbours and frontier-towns; this would allow nothing to pass out of the country for whose export the permission of the Commercial Board was not produced'. Nor did he hesitate to admit that 'it is true that in order to maintain equipoise in the public traffic and the undisturbed relation of all to all it [the government of the closed commercial state] has to conduct a mass of transactions, calculations and inspections which present governments do not have to'. But Fichte nevertheless maintained that 'the facility of state administration, as of all work, depends upon setting to work with order, perspective of the whole, and according to a firm plan'. He perceived that others would probably not agree entirely, and that 'at any rate to start with, there would be grounds for apprehending a considerable emigration of persons to whom the new order, which alone is the true order, would appear to be tiresome, oppressive and pedantic'. But he went on to detail grimly the power of the absolute autarkic state to prevent such persons from taking anything but a very small fraction of their property out of the country. As regards foreign travel in general he admitted that special currency arrangements would have to be made for travellers abroad, but he added a significant qualification: 'Only the scholar and the higher artist need to travel outside a closed commercial state: idle curiosity and dissipation should no longer be allowed to purvey their boredom through all countries'. For the ordinary man, then, the closed commercial state was to be prison as well as home.

Fichte rightly saw that his system, in order to be fully successful, must be operated as an indivisible whole. He said that

'it is clear from what has been said that the system advanced here, if it should come to be carried out in practice, must be accepted or rejected in all its parts, and that no government, indeed, should take up the described currency operation as a comfortable means of enriching itself, while on the other hand neglecting as troublesome affairs the enclosure of the commercial state, the regulation of public traffic, the fixing of prices, and the guaranteeing of the condition of all; it should also restrain itself from creating [internal] money according to caprice and putting it into circulation on the first occasion on which it may need money. Through such a procedure there would arise insecurity of property and a monstrous disorder whereby the people would soon be driven to despair and to revolt against the thoroughly dishonest government.'

Almost the main argument which Fichte advanced in favour of the creation of closed commercial states was that, according to him, it would promote international peace. By abandoning an economy of maximization and reverting to the medieval concept of an economy of sufficiency the chief cause of war would be removed. Fichte, however, did not neglect what later German theorists might have called the geopolitical imperative. According to him a state which is in the process of enclosing itself should enter into its 'natural frontiers' since 'certain portions of the surface of the earth, together with their inhabitants, are patently designed by nature to form political wholes', and because the enclosing state 'in order to . . . satisfy the demands of its citizens needs an extensive territory which contains within itself a complete and enclosed system of necessary production'. In the fourth section of the sixth chapter of the third book of the treatise Fichte gave a most illuminating glimpse of the reverse side of the picture which he otherwise kept dark. He therein proclaimed that

'thanks to its wealth in cash the government of which we are speaking has the capacity to arm itself to such an extent, and to this end to buy and bargain for so many foreign auxiliary means and forces, that no opposition could be made to it; accordingly it would attain its object [of securing "natural frontiers"] without bloodshed and almost without a stroke of the sword, and its operation would be more of a march of occupation than a war.

Directly after the occupation the same currency operation as was carried out in the mother country would be undertaken in the added provinces; and thereafter the improvements in agriculture and manufacture which exist in the mother country. By the first means the new citizens would be most forcefully bound to the mother-country in that the means of trading with others would be torn from them. . . .

It ought to suit the object in view if a part of the inhabitants of the new provinces were attracted by friendly means into the mother country, others being sent in their place from the mother country into the new provinces; and thus the old and the new citizens would blend. . . .

According as the occupation is completed, there would appear a manifesto from the government to all states, in which it would render account of the grounds for this occupation, according to the principles advanced here, and, according to these principles themselves, which as far as the government is concerned are henceforth no further applicable, would give security, and solemnly bind itself and give assurance that: it would henceforth have no further part in any foreign political concern, would enter into no alliance, would undertake no mediation, and simply would not cross its present frontiers under any pretext':

fair words with which to palliate foreign reaction to aggression. German romantics were, as has been shown already, claiming that only national standards were applicable to national affairs. It might, of course, be rather inconvenient for other nations if the government of the enclosing state were from time to time to revise its opinion as to what constituted the necessary extent of a portion of the earth designed by nature to form a political whole and of a territory containing within itself a complete and enclosed system of necessary production. And indeed perhaps such adjustments on the part of the enclosing state were almost to be expected in view of the novel and intensified form of nationalism which it would nurture within its confines. For according to Fichte

'it is clear that very soon a higher level of national honour and a distinctly more decided national character would arise among a nation so enclosed, whose members only live among each other and extremely little with foreigners, who by those measures maintain their peculiar way of living, arrangements and customs, who love with attachment their fatherland and everything pertaining to the fatherland. It becomes a different, entirely new nation.'

In *Der geschlossene Handelsstaat*, then, Fichte argued in favour of total national autarky, a planned economy, quota systems, concealed inflation, a blocked currency, state barter agreements, artificial production of substitute materials, intensive armament, living-space, forcible unresisted occupation of territory, complete economic co-ordination of such territory, transfer of populations, and cultivated nationalism. The words are different: *Lebensraum* and *Gleichschaltung* do not appear; it is as yet not *ersatz* but *stellvertretend*, not *Einmarschierung* but *Occupationszug*. But the ideas are the same. This embryonic German socialism is national-socialism.

Fichte fully appreciated the revolutionary nature of his proposals. In his dedication to the cautious Prussian bureaucrat Struensee he said that 'the author resigns himself to the fact that this project too will very likely remain a mere school exercise without success in the real world'. Struensee said he thought so. And so it did; but not for ever.

Fichte closed his economic treatise of 1800 by perfunctory and rather unconvincing tribute to the idea of a society of closed commercial states enjoying intellectual and scientific co-operation on an international basis. But the whole tenour of the argument is such that it is not surprising to find that by the summer of 1806 Fichte was proclaiming his belief 'that really no cosmopolitanism can exist at all, but that in reality cosmopolitanism must necessarily become patriotism'.

Between these two dates Fichte established himself as a popular lecturer in Berlin. His great series of lectures culminated in those delivered in the winter of 1807–8. Here again the development of German thought is indissolubly linked to the course of political events. While the German romantics were exploring new ways of thought the French armies had been conquering new territories. In 1806 came the clash with Prussia. Napoleon and his Marshal Davout destroyed the Prussian army at Jena. The French swept over the country from west to east, right up to Tilsit on the river Niemen. There in the summer of 1807 was concluded the treaty by which Prussia was dismembered territorially, bled financially, forbidden to maintain an effective army, and subjected to French military occupation.

Before the war of 1806–7 Prussia had comprised approximately 5,700 square miles and 9¾ million inhabitants: after it she was left with about 2,800 square miles and some 4½ million inhabitants. More than half had gone It has been reckoned that during the two years in which the French were in occupation the Prussian reparations and contributions amounted approximately to one milliard and 129 million francs. The exact figure may, indeed, be questioned, but not the general scale of depredation which it indicates.

In the winter of 1807, when the fortunes of Prussia were thus at their nadir, Fichte, who had lately studied Machiavelli with approval, delivered in Berlin his celebrated *Reden an die deutsche Nation* (*Addresses to the German Nation*) which he gave to Germans for a new sign of the greatness of the nation, of their nation.

Fichte entitled his fourth address *The Chief Difference between the Germans and the Other Peoples of Teutonic Descent.* For him

> 'the difference . . . consists in this, that the German speaks a language which has been alive ever since it first issued from the force of nature, whereas the other Teutonic races speak a language which has movement on the surface but is dead at the root. To this circumstance alone, to life on the one hand and death on the other we assign the difference. . . . Between life and death there is no comparison; the former has infinitely more value than the latter. All direct comparisons between German and Neo-Latin languages are therefore null and void.'

Fichte consequently deplored the introduction of foreign words into the German language; he took three particular examples, and his choice is significant. They were the words *Humanität*, *Liberalität*, and *Popularität*, words which had been very much at home in the *Grundlage des Naturrechts*. But they were now declared to be 'verbal images, which even in their pure form among the Romans arose at a low stage of ethical culture or designated something positively base'. The 'base associations' of these words should be obviated by the substitution of a corresponding, but truly Germanic, trio, respectively *Menschfreundlichkeit*, *Edelmut*, and *Leutseligkeit*.

This originality and superiority of language was the index of all-pervading originality and superiority. Fichte extolled 'the Germans as an original folk [*Urvolk*] and as the folk that has the right to call itself simply *the* folk, in contrast to other branches that have been torn away from it; for indeed the word German [*deutsch*] in its real significance denotes what we have just said'. As a practical corollary to this Fichte proclaimed that 'all who either are themselves alive and creative and productive of new things, or who, should this not have fallen to their lot, at any rate definitely abandon what is null . . . all these are original men; they are, when considered as a folk, an original folk, the folk simply, Germans'. It is hence apparent that the concept of the folk-nation must bulk for Germans beyond normal measure. Fichte maintained that according to his thesis it was 'obvious at once that only the German . . . really has a folk and is entitled to count on one, and that he alone is capable of real and rational love for his nation'. And the spirit of the nation is all-compelling.

'What spirit', Fichte asks, 'has an undisputed right to summon and to order everyone concerned, whether he himself be willing or not, and to compel anyone who resists, to risk everything including his life? Not the spirit of the peaceful citizen's love for the constitution and the laws, but the devouring flame of higher patriotism, which embraces the nation as the vesture of the eternal [*Hülle des Ewigen*], for which the noble-minded man joyfully sacrifices himself, and the ignoble man, who only exists for the sake of the other, must likewise sacrifice himself.'

Fichte, who made a special study of education, asserted that the 'spirit which is to be produced [by it] includes the higher love of fatherland, the conception of its earthly life as eternal end and of the fatherland as the support of this eternity'. It naturally followed that 'folk and fatherland in this sense, as a support and guarantee of eternity here on earth and as that which can be eternal here below, far transcend the state in the ordinary sense of the word, viz., the social order as comprehended by mere intellectual conception'.

Here, then, is the ultimate term of German romantic political theory which imbues the German folk-nation with a mystical unity and virtue beyond 'mere intellectual conception'. Fichte gloried in this extreme and plumbed its depths. He said that 'the inner essence of foreign ways, or of non-originality, is the belief in something that is final, fixed, and settled beyond the possibility of change, the belief in a border-line on the hither side of which free life may indeed disport itself, but which it is never able to break through by its own power, and which it can never of itself render fluid, making it part of itself'. In another passage Fichte made rather clearer what was involved in this unoriginal respect by foreigners for the border-line of free life by remarking that 'in the demand that one must take everything as it is meant, but must not go further and call in question the right to have opinions and to express them—in that demand the foreign spirit [*Ausländerei*] always betrays itself, however deeply it may be concealed'.

Such was the theoretical counterpoise by which Fichte sought to restore the German equilibrium, so gravely threatened by the practical humiliation of Tilsit. The romantic school of German political thought had since its inception been very largely a subjective self-vindication, an attempt on the part of Germans to think and feel themselves out of the prevalent sense of inferiority in the face of the maturity and precision of French thought and culture. And on the political side the fact that the new German cult of nationalism was to a considerable degree imitative, looking to the already flourishing national life of France and England, tended to make it only the more emphatic in proclaiming its high originality. When this sense of cultural inferiority was reinforced by that of military defeat, the trend of German thought was, as if by reflex action, immediately made sharper and pushed to the extreme.

But it was not in theory alone that Prussia reacted to the French domination. The great Prussian national revival of 1807–13 is as familiar as it is important. Those years saw, indeed, one of the most remarkable concentrations of national effort that history has to show. In the first place Prussia sought to set her own house in order. The reforms of Stein and Hardenberg embraced the social structure, central administration, local government, trade, and finance. Stein was influenced by British ideas of self-government, and it was Hardenberg who, however unwillingly, first summoned a general assembly of the notables of Prussia; during his administration the first 'provisional national representative body' met; but the liberal tradition of co-operation in national assembly was quite lacking, and the government found these assemblies unhelpful bodies. The reforms, particularly those of Hardenberg, were carried out in the Prussian tradition of bureaucratic centralization and sometimes, as in the case of the Gendarmerie Edict of 1812, actively promoted it. Prussian political society was brought up to date somewhat; serfdom was formally abolished and the Jews were emancipated. But the fundamentals persisted: autocracy and bureaucracy at the centre and, locally, the rule of the Junker and the obedience of the peasant.

Meanwhile Wilhelm von Humboldt was ordering Prussian education anew. This new order was symbolized in the university of Berlin which was created in 1810. Humboldt rejected Fichte's proposals whereby the university was to be used primarily as a political instrument for promoting patriotism on the lines laid down in his addresses. But Fichte was its first elected rector. Among those who received chairs in the new university was the Prussian pastor Friedrich Daniel Ernst Schleiermacher. Schleiermacher was an eclectic philosopher like his close friend Friedrich Schlegel. This connexion with one of the most vehement of the romantics indicates the position which Schleiermacher occupied as the main link between protestantism and the romantic movement in Germany. And, more than that, this theologian might almost claim to stand next after Luther in working out the German equation between protestantism and politics. Just as Luther had stood firmly by princely authority in politics, so did Schleiermacher support the monarchical and aristocratic ordering of society. And as Luther had heightened the prestige of the princely state, so did Schleiermacher, who despised mere personal happiness, exalt its modern counterpart, the nation, which he viewed in terms of the current organic theory, laying stress upon language and racial unity. Nationality was God manifesting himself upon earth. According to Schleiermacher

> 'every nationality is destined through its peculiar organization and its place in the world to represent a certain side of the divine image. . . . For it is God who directly assigns to each nationality its definite task on earth and inspires it with a definite spirit in order to glorify itself through each one in a peculiar manner.'

The German nationalists could press on confident of the support of the Church of Luther.

While such provision was being made for the minds of the Prussian youth, their physical education was seen to by Jahn, an unpleasing boor who combined an extraordinary medley of uncouth notions about the German folk with a novel appreciation of the value of gymnastic exercises. On the one hand he published in 1809 his *Deutsches Volkstum*, one of the earliest assertions of the racial superiority of the Germans; on the other he did much out on the Hasenhaide to toughen the youth of Berlin; but even Treitschke, among the most Prussian of later historians, thought it a pity that 'the sons of a gifted people honoured a noisy barbarian as their teacher'.

At the same time as Jahn was promoting physical training Scharnhorst was directing the reconstruction of the army. True to her tradition, it was in the military sphere that Prussia exerted herself to the greatest purpose and achieved her most remarkable feat of organized determination. By the convention of Paris, which Prussia was compelled to sign in September 1808, the strength of the Prussian army was limited to 42,000 men. This insignificant force was, however, completely reorganized and modernized by the tousled Hanoverian peasant and his lieutenants, Gneisenau, Grolmann, Boyen, and Clausewitz, Scharnhorst's young and very special pupil. But the reforms went much farther. Scharnhorst and his followers were determined that the army of the nation should be the nation in arms. To achieve this they organized an enormous national conspiracy to thwart the aims and provisions of the convention of Paris. Tirelessly Scharnhorst pushed forward with the programme of rearmament, plotting to evade the vigilance of French spies with which the country was honeycombed even when it was not actually held down by French garrisons. Scharnhorst planned to train a series of complementary paramilitary bodies, the *Bürgergarde*, *Landsturm*, and *Landwehr*. But Napoleon would have none of this, and Scharnhorst was temporarily driven to institute a system whereby men were, as unobtrusively as possible, passed through the army at high speed. In this way some 150,000 men were gradually trained. This took time. Some could not last it out. In 1810 all Prussia mourned the death of the beautiful young queen Luise, whose spirited and patriotic conduct had so won the devotion of her subjects. She died broken-hearted at the humiliation of her country. In the dark days after Jena she had proudly proclaimed: 'We are going under with honours, respected of nations.' The Prussian leaders were determined that their country should rise again with honours, compelling respect by force of arms.

It is well known how Prussia did rise again, how Napoleon sought to prevent this by forcing nearly half of the Prussian standing army to follow him into Russia, and how he failed; how Prussia put some 200,000 men into the field against him, and fought her war of liberation, culminating in the Battle of the Nations, the invasion of France, and the final stroke at Waterloo.

Thus Prussia once more placed herself at the head of German resistance to France. The reaction in Germany was great. By 1813 Fichte was urging King Frederick-William III of Prussia to become the *Zwingherr zur Deutschheit*, the master compelling to Germanity.

In 1805 Ludwig Achim von Arnim thought that 'without folk-activity there is no folk-song, and there is seldom folk-activity without it'. Certainly the experience of the following years seemed to confirm this dictum. During the years in which Prussia was vindicating her national existence the singers of the folk came into their own. These poets did not for the most part embody any very novel concepts in their work, but they afford striking illustration of the fervour which the new awareness of nationality was beginning to generate and of the popularization of the romantic idea of the German folk. And, above all, they bear witness to the degree in which the German folk-activity (*Volksthätigkeit*) of which Arnim spoke was thus early identified with war, an identification which was subsequently never wholly allowed to lapse.

Prominent among such poets was Arnim himself. This Prussian aristocrat collaborated with the catholic Clemens Brentano in producing *Des Knabens Wunderhorn*, a collection of folk-poetry of such popularity that it may almost be reckoned the literary harbinger of the new folk-era. As an example of Arnim's patriotic style an extract from *Der Landesvater*, written in 1806, may perhaps be quoted:

Unteroffizier. *Lied der Lieder*
Hall' es wieder,
Gross und deutsch sei unser Muth,
Seht hier den geweihten Degen,
Thut wie brave Preussen pflegen
Und durchbohrt Franzosenbrut.

Soldaten. *Sehet den geweihten Degen,*
Fruchtbar ist ein Sommerregen,
Weihend ist der Feinde Blut.[1]

But Arnim with his bellicose non-commissioned officer never rose to the heights attained by Bernd Heinrich Wilhelm von Kleist. Kleist was a man of extremes. In an early poem called *Der höhere Frieden* (*Higher Peace*) he wrote:

Wenn sich auf des Krieges Donnerwagen
Menschen waffnen, auf der Zwietracht Ruf,
Menschen, die im Busen Herzen tragen,
Herzen, die der Gott der Liebe schuf:

Denk' ich, können sie doch mir nichts rauben,
Nicht den Frieden, der sich selbst bewährt,
Nicht die Unschuld, nicht an Gott den Glauben,
Der dem Hasse, wie dem Schrecken wehrt;

Nicht des Ahorns dunklem Schatten wehren,
Dass er mich im Weizenfeld erquickt,
Und das Lied der Nachtigall nicht stören,
Die den stillen Busen mir entzückt.[2]

Making all allowance for change of circumstance, it is yet almost disconcerting to find Kleist in 1809 writing *Germania an ihre Kinder* (*Germany to Her Children*), of all German battle-songs perhaps the most terrible in its sheer delight in carnage. The *leitmotif* is given in the first chorus:

Stehst du auf, Germania?
Ist der Tag der Rache da?[3]

Germania addresses her children as:

Unbesiegtes Marsenblut,
Enkel der Kohortenstürmer,
Römerüberwinderbrut!

[1] *N.C.O.* Let the song of songs resound; may our spirit be great and German; see here the consecrated dagger; do as honest Prussians should and cleave through the brood of Frenchmen.

Soldiers. Behold the consecrated dagger; fruitful is the summer rain, and the blood of foes gives consecration.

[2] When, upon the thunder-chariot of war, men arm at the call of discord—men who have hearts in their bosoms, hearts created by the God of love: then I think that they yet cannot rob me of anything, not of peace which certifies itself, not of innocence, not of belief in God, which forfends hate as it does fear; they cannot prevent the deep shade of the maple from refreshing me in the wheatfield; they cannot disturb the song of the nightingale which delights my quiet bosom.

[3] Dost thou arise, Germania? Is the day of vengeance there?

Chor. *Zu den Waffen, zu den Waffen!*
Was die Hände blindlings raffen!
Mit dem Spiesse, mit dem Stab
Strömt ins Tal der Schlacht hinab![1]

These German heroes are to sweep over the French like a boundless sea. They are exhorted thus:

Alle Triften, alle Stätten
Farbt mit ihren Knochen weiss;
Welchem Rab' und Fuchs verschmähten,
Gebet ihn den Fischen preis;
Dämmt den Rhein mit ihren Leichen, . . .
Chor. *Eine Lustjagd, wie wenn Schützen*
Auf die Spur dem Wolfe sitzen!
Schlagt ihn tot! das Weltgericht
Fragt euch nach den Gründen nicht![2]

These two poems by Kleist illustrate how one German could comprehend those extremes of idyllic benevolence and steeled ferocity which have sometimes nonplussed observers of the German character in general. Such extremes posit high tension. In the particular case of Kleist perhaps it was some such tension that ultimately accounted for the picnic with his sweetheart beside the Wannsee, and the pistols in the picnic-basket, and the double killing.

Whatever their intrinsic interest it would perhaps have been hardly fitting to include poems by Arnim and Kleist in the present survey had they merely been isolated poets. But, far from that, they were both political figures of no small significance. It was largely they who harnessed romanticism to reaction in practical politics. They were both active supporters of the Prussian Junkers, led by Von der Marwitz, who were in reactionary opposition to the Hardenberg reforms. Kleist edited their anti-liberal organ, the *Berliner Abendblätter*, which maintained for instance that 'things

[1]Unconquered Martian blood, scions of the cohort-stormers, brood that overcame the Romans!

Chorus. To arms! To arms! Hands snatch them blindly up! with pike and stave, pour down into the valley of battle!

[2]Colour all the pastures, all the steads, white with their bones; those which the raven and the fox disdain, deliver them over to the fish; dam up the Rhine with their corpses. . . .

Chorus. A joy-hunt, as when marksmen are on the track of the wolf! Strike him dead! At the last judgment you will not be asked for reasons!

would have been better in Europe if Voltaire had been forgotten in the Bastille and Rousseau had been put into a lunatic asylum'. Arnim distinguished himself, among other things, by founding the Christian Germanic Society from which 'Jews, Frenchmen and Philistines' were specifically excluded. The exclusion of Jews reflected one of the main tenets of the party. Prejudice against the Jews had thriven in Germany for centuries, but the Junker conservatives were the first to erect anti-Semitism into a political principle. They accused the reforming Hardenberg of turning Prussia into a Jewish state. This anti-Semitism of Von der Marwitz and his followers was based not upon racial grounds but, tellingly enough, upon the theory that the Jews constituted a state within a state and thus disrupted the unity of the nation. As background to this theory lay the fact that many of the newly emancipated Prussian Jews were speculating in landed property and acquiring a hold over nobles who had been ruined by the war.

If Arnim and Kleist were political poets their Saxon contemporary Karl Theodor Körner went yet farther. He was the warrior-bard. Like Kleist he died young, but in the cause which he celebrated. Perhaps he touched the highest key in his *Schwertlied* (*Sword Song*) in which the sword says:

Wohl klirr' ich in der Scheide;
Ich sehne mich zum Streite
Recht wild und schlachtenfroh.
Drum, Reiter, Klirr' ich so.
Hurrah!

Lass mich nicht lange warten!
O schöner Liebesgarten,
Voll Röslein blutigrot,
Und aufgeblühtem Tod.
Hurrah![1]

The rider is thus adjured:

Denn drückt den leibeheissen
Bräutlichen Mund von Eisen

[1] I do indeed clank in the scabbard; I long for the strife, right wild and battle-joyous. For this reason, rider, do I clank so. Hurrah! Do not keep me long a-tarrying! O fair garden of love, full of little blood-red roses and blossomed death. Hurrah!

An eure Lippen fest
Fluch! wer die Braut verlässt!
Hurrah!

Nun lasst das Liebchen singen
Dass helle Funken springen!
Der Hochzeitmorgen graut.—
Hurrah, du Eisenbraut!
Hurrah![1]

This is the very passion of the fight. A few hours after writing these verses, on the 26th August, 1813, Körner went out and attacked a French convoy near the village of Lützow not far from Gadesbusch. And he was killed there. His comrades took him up and buried him near the village of Wöbbelin in the neighbourhood of Ludwigslust, under an oak, to the strains of his own 'Prayer during Battle'. Körner was twenty-one years old.

But of all the patriotic poets none rivalled Ernst Moritz Arndt, who has been called the most German of all the Germans. He was among the first to give practical content to the new idea of greater Germany. In his poem *Des Deutschen Vaterland*, written in the same year as the *Schwertlied*, Arndt asked what it is that the German should call his fatherland; he ran through a fairly comprehensive list including Prussia, Swabia, the Rhineland, Bavaria, Pommerania, Westphalia, the Tyrol, Switzerland, and Austria. But to each suggestion the reply was:

O nein! nein! nein!
Sein Vaterland muss grösser sein.[2]

Finally came the answer:

Was ist des Deutschen Vaterland?
So nenne mir das grosse Land!
So weit die deutsche Zunge klingt
Und Gott in Himmel Lieder singt,
Das soll es sein.
Das wackrer Deutscher, nenne dein!

Das ist des Deutschen Vaterland,
Wo Zorn vertilgt den welschen Tand,

[1]Press fast to your lips, then, the love-hot bridal mouth of steel. A curse upon whomsoever deserts the bride. Hurrah! Now let the beloved sing so that the bright sparks fly up! The marriage-morning dawns. Hurrah, thou bride of steel! Hurrah!

[2]O no! no! no! His fatherland must be greater.

Wo jeder Franzmann heisset Feind,
Wo jeder Deutsche heisset Freund—
Das soll es sein
Das ganze Deutschland soll er sein![1]

But Arndt did not confine himself to poetry. He was a polemical writer of the first order. In 1807, in the rather curiously entitled *Friedensrede eines Deutsche* (*Peace-address of a German*), he was proclaiming to his beaten people, 'We are Germans. . . . We are the navel of the European earth, the middle point between north and south. You know that the Greeks set their Delphi in the midst. . . . Where are our oracles and prophecies? . . . The fighters and the avengers will come; let this be the newest oracle.'

During the peace congress at the close of the Napoleonic wars Arndt consistently preached the formation of a unitary Greater Germany in the spirit of *Des Deutschen Vaterland.* It is instructive to find Arndt defining more precisely what he meant by the phrase 'as far as the German tongue sounds'. In the *Zeit der Geist*, his most considerable work, he wrote:

'The compass of our language is not merely confined to Germany and its dialects. We are joint heirs to the Netherlands, Denmark, Sweden, and Norway, just as we concede to them joint inheritance as far as we are concerned; indeed we are also joint heirs to England and Scotland. . . . South Britain has been more romanized since the eleventh century, but north Britain and three-quarters of Scotland have always remained almost entirely Germanic, and only much later accepted the Roman-English language as the written language. In the fine romances and ballads of northern England and southern Scotland there breathes throughout a pure Germanic spirit in sense, tone, colour, and language; of this about a third is to be credited to us, and two-thirds to the Scandinavians. For . . . all the best Scottish historical experts are agreed that the ancient Picts, also, were Scandinavian Teutons.'

[1]What is the fatherland of the German? Name to me the great country! As far as the German tongue sounds, and as God sings songs in heaven, that's what it ought to be. Call that thine, valiant German! . . . That is the fatherland of the German—where anger roots out foreign nonsense, where every Frenchman is called enemy, where every German is called friend—that is what it ought to be. It ought to be the whole of Germany!

Arndt proceeded to expatiate at some length upon fruitful Nordic unity, with passing reference to Alsace and to Switzerland. He concluded:

'Must this be a dream? No, I hope not. . . . If we survive politically, if our fatherland still has the virtue and the good-fortune to create a political body and form for itself, then will the German eagle fly higher and higher with new spirit and exertion, and the sound of its wings will attract the white nordic falcon, which hangs its wings in lonely sorrow upon its rocks and cliffs now that the gods and heroes are gone to the grave and history is silent. . . . And can we, who live upon the Rhine, the Elbe and Danube, do without our northern brothers? We have done without them for long, but in which age? In the Middle Ages they were always fresh and with us, indeed they lived and bloomed right in our midst; and in the sagas and heroic songs they embraced our most intimate life.'

Arndt was a native of the island of Rügen, and his northern upbringing probably accounts for such Nordic fervour. It should not be supposed, however, that he was thereby blinded to the claims of other territories to inclusion in the glorious Germanic body-general. For instance he wrote a tract entitled *Der Rhein Teutschlands Strom, aber nicht Teutschlands Grenze* (*The Rhine Germany's River, but not Germany's Frontier*). The argument is implicit in the title.

Arndt's views deserve the more consideration in that he was Stein's secretary and pet propagandist. He wrote a whole series of patriotic writings, and achieved a reputation hardly less than that of Fichte. But in tracing the trend of political thought from Fichte to Arndt attention has been more or less concentrated upon north-eastern Germany. In order to correct the balance we may turn to Joseph Görres, a middle-class native of the prosperous Rhineland, and a fit representative of Germans in the south-west who were very far from identifying themselves automatically with Prussia and its modes of thought.

Görres, born at Coblenz, exemplified the influence which revolutionary France exerted upon many Germans, particularly in the Rhineland. In the seventeen-nineties he edited a republican paper, published a work entitled *General Peace, an Ideal*, hotly opposed clericalism amd was, in general, in the van of the 'enlightened' and 'cosmopolitan' radical movement, even demanding the union of the Rhineland with France. But in 1800 Görres went on political mission to Paris and came back disabused of most of his Gallic enthusiasm. Above all, he found the French lacking in depth. On his return he recompensed himself for this disappointment by plunging into the romantic circle, coming under the influence of the mystical medievalist Brentano and, in particular, of Schelling.

Görres, like Schelling, devoted particular attention to art and the sciences but, like him, wove them into the pattern of his political thought in accordance with the romantic conception of all-embracing unity. A passage in Görres's *Aphorisms upon Art* indicates his transition from the republican to the historical school of thought: 'The fatherland, the republic is the mother of all daughters, of all sons, the daughter of all parents, the beloved of all lovers; it is only there that original beauty is enthroned in high majesty.' He strayed yet farther from republicanism in remarking that 'in the midst of nations rulers rise up; law materializes itself in them'. But he qualified this in another set of aphorisms, laying down that 'the single individual has only partial life; only the whole immortal species attains to the totality of the ideal'. The species, the folk, and the nation were very present to Görres although like other romantics he dreamed of supernational empire. He followed dutifully in the path first blazed by Herder, regarding the state as a living organism, and grounding his theory in historical growth. In the historical process Görres saw the reconciliation of free-will and necessity, the 'free subjection to the eternal world-law'. This semi-religious concept of history was implicit in Görres's main historical work, *The Growth of History*, which was planned as the first part of a larger whole entitled *Religion in History*. In *The Growth of History* Görres particularly stressed the concept of the folk-myth which comprises the essence of the whole biological development of the folk; he said of it that 'all history is nothing but the growth of this plant of heaven; it goes creeping through all species; it has struck its roots in the matter of the primeval world. The ties of race and blood are the basis of the unity of the folk: 'Like cannot sunder itself from like, and blood of like mixture cannot belie itself, no matter into how many side-streams it may have branched off.' 'Each stock is an enclosed whole rounded off in itself; a common bond of blood-relationship clasps all members; just as all speak one language externally, so must they internally also have one disposition, and hold together to a man: that is the first rule and law.'

The Napoleonic age was not conducive to cloistered scholarship. Under the stress of events Görres, like many of his contemporaries, became a political publicist. He edited the *Rhenish Mercury*, which was for two years the prime organ of public opinion in Germany. The influence of Görres as a publicist was remarkable and rivalled that of Friedrich Gentz. But whereas Gentz was the well-paid and somewhat unoriginal apologist of benevolent despotism, the balance of power and other notions of the old order, quite out of sympathy with rising nationalism, Görres, deducing practical measures from his general theories, was a much more significant figure for the future. In the first place, as was logical, he demanded the creation of a united Greater Germany. He was, indeed, more modest than Arndt in this respect, asking only for the incorporation of Denmark, Holland, Belgium, Switzerland, and Alsace-Lorraine. Among his typical remarks may be included:

'Denmark, in her present hopeless position, should remember that she was once a fief of Germany.'

'She [Switzerland] should join herself to Germany because it is there that are to be found the stem and root from which she proceeded, and because this neutrality, in which she has dragged herself along for centuries, has now come to an end once and for all as far as the future is concerned.'

'The Burgundian inheritance . . . will be restored; Lorraine with the bishoprics and Alsace with all appendages will return.' 'We must already regard Alsace as a German province, bought back by good German blood.'

It was Görres who first described the French as the hereditary foe (*Erbfeind*).

Görres was far from being an original thinker; throughout almost his whole lifetime he managed to crest the wave of popular German thought. His very unoriginality renders him the more significant. There can be small doubt that the greater part of German opinion was with Arndt and Görres in their support of German efforts at the Congress of Vienna to lay the foundations of a Greater Germany. These efforts were mainly made by Prussia and Württemberg. Both strove, in particular, to secure the annexation of Alsace.

But with Görres and the south in general it was by no means a matter of course to look to Prussia for leadership. Görres strongly disliked Prussia and her political traditions. He called the Prussia of the years before Jena 'the seat of a hard rigid military spirit which threatens to swallow up every peaceful property—the focus of a devouring, burning political egoism'. And about 1810 he was writing to the Prussian Arnim about 'your fatal country'. The hegemony of Austria in Germany seemed more natural and desirable than that of Prussia to the southern outlook of catholic Görres, who was becoming increasingly subject to religious influences. And it was not only in the south that a non-Prussian hegemony seemed to be the necessary condition of German unity. Stein, for instance, looked to Austria at one time while Gneisenau toyed with the idea of a Germany united under an English prince, a conceit which would certainly not have commended itself to Görres, who wrote of English policy that 'since Germany appears to be another India divided between many rajahs and having beside these its Sikhs and Mahrattas, it [English policy] takes council how it may divide and rule it also as another India'. England for Görres was a 'money-power', a nation of 'maritime leopards'.

But gradually Görres swung in his opinion as to the right way of achieving German unity. He hailed the Prussian regeneration of 1813 with such enthusiasm in the *Rhenish Mercury* that his enemies accused him of being in Prussian pay. Prussia was now to be junior partner to Austria in securing German unity, the Prussian king being field-marshal-general of the empire. Prussia's stock continued to rise with Görres, and her vigorous action during the hundred days confirmed him in his conviction that it was to Prussia rather than to Austria that Germans should now look for leadership. In 1814–15 Görres strongly supported Prussia's efforts to secure agreement to her annexation of all Saxony. It is a rather unpleasing spectacle to watch him seeking to justify by the most remarkable sophistries, largely drawn from racial theory, those crude Prussian power-politics which he had earlier so roundly condemned. He maintained, for instance, that Saxons should welcome annexation to Prussia since they would thus be at last reunited with their long-lost brethren, the Lower Saxons of Westphalia and the lower Elbe. He was correspondingly active in urging his fellow Rhinelanders to rejoice at their incorporation in the Prussian state. True to form, the Prussians, upon their occupation of the Rhineland, repaid these services by suppressing the *Rhenish Mercury* and depriving Görres of his local office of director of public education. Görres's general disappointment at the Viennese settlement and the loose nature of the new German Confederation was thus heightened by personal indignation at his treatment. In 1819 he published his best-known work, *Germany and the Revolution*; its liberal flavour was distasteful to the Prussian authorities of the period of the restoration, and Görres was forced to flee from arrest. His life petered out in religiosity.

The life and views of Görres may be taken as the type of many others. All Germans who were not Prussians certainly did not do and think as he. But Görres is nevertheless an example which sheds much light. Thus early one is presented with the spectacle of the rather easy-going unstable German, inclined towards liberalism but clinging to tradition in many things, a romantic spirit fired with the ideal of the greater German unity; and we see how display of power-politics by other Germans, more single-minded and tougher than he, attracted him like steel to a magnet, and how the impact came with something of a shock.

In order to round off the picture it is necessary to give some brief account of the man who exercised great influence upon Görres, the Württemberger who made a name for himself in Bavaria, in all Germany, Friedrich Wilhelm Joseph Schelling.

Schelling stands with Fichte as the main bridge between Kant and Hegel. He belonged to that group of romantics who held, as their organ the *Athenäum* once expressed it, that 'Kant has introduced the concept of the negative into world-wisdom. Would not it be a more useful attempt to introduce also the concept of the positive into philosophy'. Schelling sought to effect this largely by equating the realization of absolute reason with historical development; as he put it:

'Since everything that is realized is only the development of absolute reason, we must also find everywhere in history, and particularly in the history of the human spirit, traces of that absolute reason which, from the empirical and purely practical standpoint, appears to us to be providence, which has as it were ordered everything in advance in the way in which we find it in reality.'

Freewill and necessity were reconciled in the historical process since freewill was not constrained by any *a priori* theory, the very negation of history, but realized itself in the absolute indwelling reason of historical determinism. Harmony between history and religion was assured by the fact 'that in Christianity the universe is in general regarded as *history*, as a moral empire, and that this general outlook constitutes the basic character of the same [i.e. of Christianity]'.

But for Schelling the process in which freewill and necessity were reconciled was not merely historical but, even more markedly, organic. It was he who most firmly established the organic theory as a component of the school of historical thought. Schelling elaborated the so-called philosophy of nature which sought to reconcile the dualism between nature, the realm of necessity, and morality, the realm of freedom, in interpreting the world as an organic whole. The organism is the highest form of the spirit in nature; it is at the same time both natural and intellectual in so far as it belongs both to the realm of nature and to that of morality.

Schelling's main approach to philosophy was aesthetic, not social; it is fitting that he, the most romantic of all the philosophers, should be primarily concerned with the beautiful rather than with the good. Nevertheless he did also draw social and political inferences from his philosophy. He summed up his position succinctly with the remark: 'The same intellectual substance which represents itself in nature as a biological organism creates in the sphere of human mind and history an adequate form in the organism of the state.'[1] This is the formal statement of the organic theory of the state. For Schelling, too, society centred in the state. Three of his main works stand for three main periods in his estimation of its significance.

[1]Quoted: R. Aris, *History of Political Thought in Germany*, *1789-1815*, p. 289. Cf. generally for this paragraph and the last.

In the *System of Transcendental Idealism*, published in 1800, Schelling still regarded the state as an instrument for the maintenance of individual liberties, a function which could best be performed by the separation of the three branches of sovereignty. But the influence of Fichte and Hegel steadily gained ground with him, and in the *Method of Academic Study* which appeared three years later Schelling adopted a middle position. As regards the relation of Church and state Schelling was already maintaining that 'the state, in its opposition over against the Church, is again itself the natural side of the whole, wherein both are one. In its absoluteness it must supplant what is opposed to it in appearance simply for the reason that it [the state] includes it [the Church]: just as the Greek state knew no Church, unless one reckons the mysteries as one, but they were themselves only a branch of the public life'. In the following year the state came at last fully into its own in the *System of Total Philosophy*. This work culminated in the assertion, in the 325th section,

'*that wherein science, religion and art become one, in living fashion, interpenetrating and becoming objective in their unity, is the state*. . . . It is to be noticed that here . . . there is no thought of a state that is merely formal, that is constituted with a view to an external end, perhaps only in order to ensure mutual assurance of rights (as is the case with the previously constituted states). These are merely states based upon compulsion and need. . . . The Church is not outside such an [organic] state; it is inside it. It would only be outside it in a state comprising merely *worldly ends and institutions*; but such a one is no longer a state.'

Here, then, is the state transcendent.

With Schelling, as with Görres during this period, science, art, and religion were the three primary concerns. Schelling proceeded to elaborate the way in which they all achieve perfect realization in the state:

'With regard to the way in which those [three] are comprehended in the state—they are not so comprehended only insofar as each of the three, science, religion and art, must be a particular concern of the state, but they are comprehended in its very being; they are gone over into the state, and live objectively in it itself—science by means of legislation; . . . religion through public morality and the heroism of a nation; art through the creative spirit which hovers over the whole and animates it artistically, not mechanically—through the living rhythmic movement of public life, the beauty of its apparition.'

The state is the embodiment of science, of art, of religion itself. The book closed with the triumphant equation: 'Reason: world-structure = philosophy: the state . . . Philosophy which is no longer learning but comes to life is what Plato calls πολιτεύειν—life with and in a moral totality.' This metaphysical totality of the folk-nation was very dear to Schelling. In a later work he remarked that 'metaphysics is that which creates states organically and allows a mass of human beings to become of one heart and mind, i.e. a folk. In a word . . . all metaphysics . . . rest upon the sense of totality [*auf dem Sinn für Totalität*]'. Schelling did not shrink from pushing totality to its extreme. He denied outright the reality of the individual. For him 'individuals are only phantoms like the spectrum. They are not modifications of the absolute substance, but merely imaginary apparitions'. This is the final term. The state is religion, is total; the individual is snuffed out, a phantom. Fichte's ego has passed over into the state.

But if Schelling denied the individual he exalted the German. He along with the others reserved a special place for Germans. 'Should not the lot of the Germans', he asked, 'be the general lot of mankind in that he alone runs through all the various stages which other peoples represent as separated, so that he finally displays the highest and richest unity of which human nature is capable?' The corollary followed: '. . . In respect of this relation of the German nation to the rest we must, in order to win [for ourselves] the true being of its spirit, the original direction of its sense, separate out everything which was engendered by the whoring of our fathers and grandfathers after foreign peoples. . . .'

In 1806 Schelling broke with Fichte, and next year with Hegel. He went in ever deeper. Romantic thought came wheeling round full circle.

We have seen how in the person of Herder the German school of historical thought first emerged from a murky background, from the obscurities of Hamann, who derived from Böhme and other mystics. And now Schelling, reverencing Hamann, plunged back into the welter of mysticism. He came under the influence of Franz Benedict von Baader, the mystical metallurgist, the great expositor of Jacob Böhme. Schelling went down dark ways, exploring magic, somnambulism, and the night-side of the soul; but not down into oblivion, as will appear.

The compass of the new trend in Germany is now apparent. In the sphere of practical politics Prussia emerged in 1815 much stronger over against Austria than heretofore; the Holy Roman Empire had given way to the German Confederation and the imperial overlordship of the Habsburgs dwindled to Austrian presidency of the diet of the confederation; the hundreds of principalities that had made up the empire were superseded by less than two-score confederate states. That this new constitution, based upon a permanent alliance of sovereign princes, should have so disappointed Arndt, Görres, and many who thought with them is an indication of the new spirit of national consciousness which the Napoleonic venture had roused in Germany as elsewhere. But in no other country on the continent were such developments matched with a novel mode of political thought comparable to that which derived from the romantic impulse that inspired the most brilliant age of German thought.

The German thinkers, linking historical development to biological growth, were imbued with the conviction that they had established contact with vivid, pulsating reality untouched by the scientific constructions of earlier ages, that they had given intellectual perception a new depth, that they had found the key to life itself, the realm in which being is becoming. And just as life was the organic whole, so was historical growth the totality, containing its own standards within itself, supplying its own terms of reference, embracing both practical and ideal. History was the supreme synthesis: in it freewill and necessity were one. As historical growth was the highest term of organic growth, so was the nation the highest organism—a total entity for transcending in depth and compass the state as commonly conceived. This superstate was the organic realization of the folk in its every aspect.

Thus objective and subjective merged. It might further be deduced that the Germans, who had been the first people to perceive this philosophical significance of the folk, were, as a people, different from all others and superior to them. They were the greatest, the original, folk. And since Germany did not exist as a single nation, was not the unity demanded by totality, the concept of the German nation was an ideal not only in theory, but also as an unrealized goal towards which all practical effort should be concentrated. Since Germany had no clearly defined or satisfactory natural geographical frontiers the totality of the German nation was transcendent not only in theory but also in that its limits were not adequately defined by existing state-delimitations, but only by the extent of the area occupied by peoples of Germanic stock and kin. Since Germany was not of one mind in religion, but was most notoriously divided between catholicism and protestantism, a new Germanic faith was not only theoretically an ideal, but also in some sense a necessary practical achievement if the unity of the total folk was to be rendered complete. Thus in each case did existing practical conditions promote enthusiastic acceptance of the theoretical ideal. This circumstance largely accounts for the hold which the romantic theory of the folk-nation in its various forms was to exercise upon many Germans for generations to come. As yet its devotees were limited in number. And their influence was likewise limited, since popular politics in any form were a novelty in Germany where the ordering of political society had for centuries been according to the statecraft of its rulers. But by 1815 the new forces were already gathering momentum.

Chapter III

REACTION
1815–1848

The revolutionary and Napoleonic wars left the Europe of 1815 with new fears and new enthusiasms. There was fear of Russia and, perhaps more immediate, fear of that which Russia had been so largely instrumental in crushing—the fear with which the old, the rich, the aristocrats, the reactionaries, the power-holders tended to regard those new forces which they loosely stigmatized as Jacobinism. Correspondingly the young, the poor, the new, the subject were in many cases stirred with novel enthusiasm for those ideas which came under the convenient headings of liberalism and nationalism. The interplay of these forces constituted the groundwork of the political history of Europe for decades to come.

The Holy Alliance of 1815 invested political reaction with the cloak of religion, indicating the direction in which things were moving. Russia was the major force behind the alliance. She was ruled by the Czar Alexander I, whose liberal vagaries did not prevent him from standing by reaction. In the years after 1815 Austria looked largely to Russia, and Prussia to Austria. The German powers led the reaction in Europe. By the decree of May 1816 the Prussian government limited the measure of freedom so recently accorded to its peasants. Among its chief anxieties were the liberal tendencies in the German universities, as exemplified in particular by youth-movements such as the *Burschenschaften*. These bodies mostly advocated a nebulous programme compounded of liberalism, Christianity, and German unification. It is a curious commentary upon the beginnings of German liberalism that the *Burschenschaften* derived largely from the enterprise of the baleful gymnast Jahn. At the Wartburg celebration and ceremonial bonfire the movement overreached itself. It finally did for itself in 1819, when Kotzebue, a second-rate playwright in Russian pay, was murdered by Karl Sand who was associated with the *Unbedingten*, an extreme group of the *Burschenschaften*. The authorities seized the opportunity, and in that year representatives of Prussia, Austria, Hanover, Saxony, Mecklenburg, Bavaria, Baden, Nassau and Württemberg came together in conference at Carlsbad; there measures were concerted which provided for strict censorship, the prohibition of unauthorized societies, a purge of the German universities, and the institution of the *Zentral untersuchungskommission* (Central Committee of Investigation) at Mainz in order to hold things down for the future. In the same year Metternich met Frederick-William III at Teplitz and obtained from him an undertaking that no measures of popular representation would be introduced in Prussia. At the end of the year Wilhelm von Humboldt, who had liberal tendencies, was dismissed from the Prussian government. The years up to 1830 have been described as the classic age of the Prussian bureaucracy. The Prussian minister of police, Prince Wittgenstein, was a secret tool of Metternich.

Accordingly in the eighteen-twenties a hush hung over the political life of Germany. Almost the only stir was caused by the government of Württemberg and its sympathizers in the south. They put about the *Manuscript from Southern Germany* which was published in London and did some fairly effective propaganda on behalf of the 'triadic idea' by which a third block should be set up over against the two great German powers, Prussia and Austria. It would be an Allemanic *bloc*, that is a grouping of south German states under the leadership of Württemberg and Bavaria, thus in some sort resurrecting the Napoleonic Confederation of the Rhine. These states were represented, not without a measure of truth, as being the centres of German enlightenment and liberalism in contrast to reactionary Austria and Prussia. Those two powers broke off diplomatic relations with Württemberg and brought King William and his minister Wangenheim sharply to heel. Liberties were suppressed in Württemberg as elsewhere, and King William had to make humble apology to Prussia and

Austria for his insubordination. Henceforth it was clear that whatever might be the future course of German political development there could be hardly a question of the smaller states adopting a concerted and independent policy with regard to major issues. Prussia and Austria held the field and no third party would be allowed to intervene with effect.

The interconnexion between the development of German politics and of the theory of the historical school is such that it is but natural to find the new German theory adapting itself rapidly to changed conditions and flourishing, indeed, with renewed vigour in the climate of opinion which prevailed from the Congress of Vienna to the July Revolution. But the transition of the school from its first to its second period necessarily involved adjustments of stress. Arndt fared hardly better than Görres in this process. The man who in 1803 had by his writing largely induced King Gustavus Adolphus IV to abolish serfdom in Rügen found in 1819 that his criticism of the reactionary policy of the German powers and his demand for reform were sufficient to prompt the government of Frederick-William III to arrest him and put him on trial. This criticism of Arndt's was contained in the fourth part of his largest work, *Geist der Zeit* (*Spirit of the Time*). The reaction which it provoked is a fit commentary upon the title. For the next twenty years Arndt lived in retirement.

It is perhaps indicative of the general trend of the political thought of the new German school that two of its most distinguished representatives should have accomplished the transition from the high-romantic period to that of the restoration with a minimum of friction. Both achieved fame in the earlier period, but the significance of their work is such that it may best be considered here.

Adam Heinrich Müller stands out not only as one of the foremost of the romantic political theorists and as a link between the first and second phases of that theory, but also as an illustration of the connexion between north and south, Prussia and Austria. And he further demonstrates the main English influence upon German political thought at that time. Müller, like many of his romantic and historically minded contemporaries, greatly reverenced Burke.

In 1779 Müller was born in Berlin. Soft-natured, an untypical Prussian, this melancholic sickly youth used to evaluate his ailings in terms of astrology. In 1805 he followed in the way of many romantics and was received into the Catholic Church. Müller was a close friend of Kleist and like him he supported the reactionary Prussian Junkers under Von der Marwitz against the Hardenberg reforms; this made it impossible for him to secure employment in the Prussian civil service at that time, but Austria took him in, and he worked many years as an official of that state. In reward for this service he was ennobled in 1826 at the instance of Metternich, who represented to the emperor that

'in the last twenty years he has employed his talent as an author on behalf of good and right, of the monarchical principle and of religion in such measure that, even though a decisive success has not thereby been achieved with the great mass of the people, it can yet be asserted with confidence that by this means many waverers have been strengthened, many strays led back into the way, and also many won for the good cause who, but for the penetrating word of truth, would have adhered to the tirelessly active party of the innovators.'

The state was the corner-stone of the teaching which won this handsome encomium from Metternich. According to Müller the state is 'not merely a plaything or instrument in the hand of a person . . . but it is *itself a person*, a free whole, existing and growing in itself by means of endless interaction of contending and self-reconciling ideas'.[1] Consequently 'private life is nothing other than national life observed from below, and public life is ultimately nothing other than the same national life viewed from above'. Müller identified 'real nationality' with 'true freedom and independence', holding that neither can be achieved

'so long as state and citizen serve two masters . . . so long as hearts are internally rent by a double desire, the *one*, to live as a citizen in the state . . . the *other*, to extract himself from the whole civil order, to cut himself off from that same state along with his domestic and whole private life and with his most sacred feelings, indeed even with religion.'

Private life and religion, then, must be swallowed up by the great Leviathan if 'real nationality' is to be achieved. This is

[1] *Vermischte Schriften*, vol. i, p. 221. For quotations from Müller's works, cf. F. Meinecke, *Weltbürgertum und Nationalstaat*, chap. vii, *passim*.

a corollary of Müller's proposition that the state is 'the necessity of all necessities of the heart, the spirit and the body': of the body as well as of the other two, for the state is itself, in a very real sense, a huge living body. Müller maintained that

'all these states, which we have represented as being great human beings, human in bodily structure, disposition and mode of thinking, in movement and life, should be independent and free like the individual in the single state . . . they should grow and live and make themselves mutually valid and tangible in their peculiar national forms and manners.'

Müller, who thought that Germany's economic existence demanded political unity, was particularly concerned with questions of political economy and was at pains to construct an economic system to correspond to his conception of the supreme organic super-individual, the state. It is typical of his approach to economics that in his chief economic work, the *Versuche einer neuen Theorie des Geldes* (*Essays in a New Theory of Money*), he remarked that 'nothing is worthy of admiration that can be expressed in numbers'. Müller's economic works, even more than his others, engender sympathy with the publicist Gentz, one of Müller's oldest and closest friends, who once said of his writings that 'everything swims before me as if wrapt in a cloud of fine words, through which no figure stands out in firm outline. At best I am depressed, not instructed'. Accordingly a mere summary of Müller's economic teaching shall suffice.[1]

Müller held that, corresponding to the total unity of the state, all property should ultimately be common, private property being regarded merely as the right of usufruct. Müller's ardent veneration of the feudal system was largely based upon the belief that it was the expression of this principle. All wealth, production, and consumption must be primarily regarded in the light of their reaction upon, and interconnexion with, the state; and this interconnexion is in all three cases fundamental. The relation between wealth and the state rests upon the fact that while mere price reflects what is momentary, true value is the significance which a thing has in

[1]For a concise account in English of Müller's economic doctrine, cf. Alexander Grey, *The Development of Economic Doctrine*, chap. viii. The present summary is greatly indebted to this account.

the state. As regards production and consumption, it is from the perpetual conflict between these two that there emerges the higher product, which is national credit, national power, belief in the state, the state itself. In the state the other two conflicting terms of the triad are reconciled. The state alone can give them true meaning. And it follows that national wealth is not merely a static question of addition and subtraction. For national wealth depends not only upon production and possession, but also upon consumption and use.

For Müller the economic trio, land, labour, and capital, became nature, man, and the past. Capital is the legacy of the past to the present. And this capital is spiritual not less than material. Müller, who fully realized what he was about and deliberately challenged the orthodox economists who followed Adam Smith, made one of the main charges against him the fact that he had neglected this element of spiritual capital. And since capital was identified with the past it was necessarily identified with the state since, according to the romantic formula, the state which is the national growth is a dual alliance, uniting not only one man with another, but also past with present. The organic state is the practical expression of historical continuity. The folk is 'the exalted community of a long succession of species—those who have departed, who are now living, and who are still to come—who are all associated for life and death in one great intimate union.'

Division of labour is likewise rooted in the state, since it can only achieve its full purpose if all work for all in the true commonwealth which is the state. And only true national capital can prevent possible abuses of the division of labour.

Müller's economics reached their climax in his theory of money, according to which money, the cash nexus, is the economic expression of man's need for union with others, just as law is its juridical expression; and this union is achieved in the state. Money is relationship. The citizen, in that he is necessary to others, is money; law is money; the state is money. Consequently, chiming with Fichte, the state must have its own individual currency. Gold and silver are world-money, fostering notions of world-trade and the like. It is paper money that binds a man to his fatherland. Müller indeed refused to go the whole way with Fichte. He specifically rejected the closed commercial state. But this did not prevent him from reproaching Adam Smith for paying too little attention 'to the enclosed personality of states in their rounded-off character'.

Here, then, is the state dominating all economics as it does politics, embracing all, embodying wealth, value, production, consumption, capital, labour, and money. It is a very complete construction. 'Totality' was a favourite word with Müller.

In his economic theory, as elsewhere, Müller pointed the way which much of later German thought was to follow. And as in economics so in war. Müller was one of the earliest German thinkers specifically to draw the conclusion that since the nation is a natural growth, greatly to be revered, so is war, the ultimate means by which the nation asserts its rights. Just as the nation is something deep, elemental, so is war. According to Müller

> 'it was not the opinions of cabinets which determined war; it was never the wilfulness of rulers, as the effeminate decadent mob liked to think was the case: it was always deep-lying reasons reposing in the necessary construction of the whole relationship between states. An inner urge towards living growth, wholly unknown to the present generation, deriving from the impact of earlier generations, was the true motive-force of the wars which certain states have in the last centuries undertaken for the sake of aggrandisement.'

Elsewhere Müller further equated war and the state in that it is war 'which gives states their outlines, solidity, individuality and personality'. That is high praise from him.

Müller would not have been the romantic that he was if he had not caught glimpses of what lay out beyond the state. He held that 'there must exist a law that is even higher than the self-maintenance of the individual state, a league for mutual guarantee among the individual states; and this law, with its necessity, must penetrate every single state right into its most secret place; it must penetrate every single citizen'. But here again, as with Novalis, Friedrich Schlegel, and other romantics, the very concept of a supernational order is informed by nationalism in that the German folk is of such high genius and wisdom that Germanity becomes a supernational ideal. Müller foresaw that

'the great federation of European peoples, which will come some day as sure as we live, will also bear German hues, for everything great, fundamental, and eternal in all European institutions is certainly German. . . . The seed of German life has indeed, in these recent folk-tumults, only been extended ever further and further over the ground of our continent; it will proceed in its rampant growth, and from quite unpretentious beginnings will gradually advance to mighty effects; let its growth be left to eternal nature.'

Thus did German romanticism rise to its climax in political and economic thought. And Müller carried it over from one age to the next. But the figure who stood with him in the transition was a greater than he, looming up above his romantic contemporaries.

In 1814 Fichte died. His chair in the university of Berlin was filled by Georg Wilhelm Friedrich Hegel. The event is symbolic of the change, and the continuity, and the gathering volume.

Hegel, the compatriot and early friend of Schelling, took over the triadic formula from Fichte. This is no place to map out his whole philosophy, but only to throw a glancing light upon those facets of it which are of immediate concern; they were also the facets which, then and since, dazzled men most.

Hegel based his whole structure upon the identification of reason with reality. For him 'reason . . . is . . . substance as it is endless power'; and 'the only concept which philosophy brings with it is . . . the simple concept of reason, the concept that reason rules the world, that the history of the world accordingly presents a rational process'. World-history is reason on the move; it is the realizing of the world-spirit. 'Therefore in the first place it must be manifest from the contemplation of world-history itself, that it has been a rational process, that it has constituted the rational, necessary, progress of the world-spirit, of the spirit whose nature is indeed always one and the same, but which unfolds this, its one nature, in world-existence.' The motive force of this historical dynamism resides in the dialectical process, in the constantly renewed interaction of thesis, antithesis, and synthesis, of struggle, tension, and reconciliation, and the consequent re-emergence of struggle and tension at a higher level. In this way reason moves forward in human history as distinct from nature, which is non-progressive and therefore quite distinct from, and lower than, history in its processes. While world-history thus exhibits historical dynamism as the progression of reason, this fundamental reason does not in practice exclude human passion. On the contrary

'we must say particularly that *nothing great in the world* is accomplished without passion. There are two elements which enter into our subject: one is the idea, and the other is the human passions; the one is the warp and the other the woof of the great carpet which is spread out before us as world-history. The concrete midst and union of the two is the moral freedom of the state.'

The state is the nodal point between the latent process of the spirit, which is rational necessity, and man's full co-operation in this process, which is freedom. Freedom is recognition of, and adaptation to, the absolute historical process through the medium of the state. In Hegel's words 'the idea of the state in modern times has this peculiarity, that it is the embodiment of freedom, not according to subjective liking, but to the conception of the will, the will, that is, in its universality and divinity'. In fact, 'everything depends upon the union of universality and particularity in the state'. Accordingly 'we have . . . to do in world-history with individuals that are peoples, with wholes that are states'.

With the state occupying this unique position in the world-historical rational order of things it necessarily followed that its reality was superlative. Hegel spoke of the state's 'abstract reality or substantivity', stating that 'to the complete state essentially belong consciousness and thought; hence the state knows what it wills, and knows it as something thought'. According to him 'the idea of the state has . . . direct reality and is the individual state as a self-referring organism'. The fact that the state recognizes no terms of reference outside itself is the logical consequence of its being the practical manifestation of the world-spirit which is defined as being 'precisely that which has its centre in itself; it does not have unity outside itself, but it has [already] found it; it is in itself and to itself. . . . The spirit is the *being-by-itself* [*das Bei-sich-*

selbst-sein]. It is precisely this that is freedom'. And so 'the rational state is in itself infinite'.

Since 'the state is the spirit which stands in the world' it is the realization of morality. 'The state is the reality of the moral idea—the moral spirit as the manifest, self-evident, substantial will, which thinks for itself and knows and fulfils that which it knows in so far as it knows it.' 'The state is the sole condition of the attainment of the particular end and good': only the condition, indeed, since Hegel held that the function of the state was not to suppress the 'subjective freedom' of the individual, but rather to achieve its absolute realization in the higher being of the state itself. But the state remained the sole condition of that realization, and it was of such high value in itself that it tended to swallow up the particular end and good; understandably, for the Hegelian 'state is the march of God in the world'. In fact, 'the state is divine will as a present spirit expanding into the real form and organization of a world.—Those who wish to stand by the form of religion in opposition to the state conduct themselves like those who think they are correct in perception if they merely remain always concerned with the essence and do not advance from this abstraction to real existence.' On the practical plane it followed that 'in so far as the religious commonalty of individuals erects itself into a congregation, a corporation, it stands in general under the superior police-superintendence of the state'.

With Hegel, as with his predecessors, the state was grounded in the folk. For him 'the folk as state is the spirit in its substantial rationality and direct reality, hence the absolute power upon earth'. But this absolute power of the folk did not imply any absolute concession to democratic notions of public opinion and the like. According to Hegel 'public opinion deserves to be equally respected and despised, the latter in accordance with its concrete consciousness and expression, the former in accordance with its essential basis'. The state, then, must have folk-thought as its essential basis, but should not countenance popular institutions for the specific expression of public opinion. In so far as Hegel concerned himself with the forms of constitutions he favoured the rule of a constitutional monarch and government by means of a 'universal' class of administrators. These super-bureaucrats were to be the effective organ of government rather than the council of estates, whose functions were hardly more than advisory. This was indeed necessarily the case, since there could be no division of powers as a safeguard against tyranny owing to the fact that 'the idea that the functions of government should be independent contains the fundamental error that they should check one another. But this independence is apt to usurp the unity of the state, and unity is above all things to be desired'. These words go far towards explaining much that is typical in the political practice of Germany. In general, moreover, detailed elaboration of constitutional forms was ultimately beside the point for Hegel, who held that it is strictly essential that 'the constitution [of the state], though it is begotten in time, should not be contemplated as made; for it is much rather to be thought of as above and beyond what is made, as self-begotten and self-centred, as divine and perpetual'.

Just as the whole Hegelian historical process rests upon recurring struggle and tension, so is the existence of the Hegelian state bound up with war. Hegelianism is a sombre doctrine of strife. It maintained that 'world-history is not the soil of happiness. The periods of happiness are blank pages in it'. It proclaimed 'the ethical element of war', holding that war saves peoples from stagnant corruption just as the wind saves the sea. Hegel taught that 'the military class is the class of universality; to it are assigned the defence of the state and the duty of bringing into existence the ideality implicit in itself. In other words it must sacrifice itself'. The universal man must sacrifice himself on behalf of the state.

In the 272nd paragraph of the *Philosophie des Rechtes* Hegel summed up his political teaching with the words: 'We must hence honour the state as the divine upon earth [*wie ein Irdisch-Göttliches*]'. And the state, being divine, was a law unto itself. The conduct of the self-referring state was quite incapable of judgement according to standard concepts of morality. In a final passage Hegel wrote:

'At one time there was much discussion of the opposition of morals and politics, and the demand was made that the second should conform to the first. At this place it is in general only proper to remark on this score that the good of a state has a justification quite other than the good of the individual; and that the ethical substance, the state, has its being, i.e. its right, directly, not in an abstract existence, but in a concrete one; and that the only possible principle of its conduct and behaviour is this concrete existence, and not one of the many general concepts that are held to be moral commands. The view that politics in this assumed opposition is presumptive always in the wrong rests, furthermore, much rather upon the shallowness of the conceptions of morality, of the nature of the state and of its relations to the moral point of view.'

Thus did Hegel tell man to worship the state and not to judge its actions by any recognized standard of morality.

Hegel invested historical thought with a new authority that was both theoretical and practical: theoretical in that he organized romantic notions and aspirations into a coherent and deeply grounded philosophical system wherein the state was transfigured and history achieved the ultimate elevation of philosophy itself so that, according to the Hegelian maxim, the philosophy of history is the history of philosophy: practical in that this man, who had written to a friend the day before the battle of Jena anticipating with satisfaction the overthrow of Prussian militarism and bureaucracy, came during the eighteen-twenties in Prussia to be regarded as the great master expounding a doctrine which almost ranked as the official faith of the German intelligentsia. Hegel was decorated by the king of Prussia; converts and disciples came flocking in to Berlin from all parts of Germany and beyond. There they listened with reverence to the lacklustre lecturer, old before his time, sitting bowed over his notes, apparently ill at ease, bringing out every sentence with an effort, coughing, only sometimes rising to a natural eloquence in the most abstruse passages. The heady enthusiasm engendered by this pedagogue assumed extraordinary proportions. Hegel, like Herder before him, influenced contemporary German learning by and large; indeed he almost transformed it. Hegelianism conquered key positions in ethics, aesthetics, philology, historiography, in the gamut of the humanities.

The Germans had good reason to welcome Hegelianism. For besides proclaiming the historically absolute state it further taught the supremacy of Germanity. Hegelian history was schematized into four main periods: oriental, Greek, Roman, and German. The construction was the more complete in that the Hegelian historical process culminated in the present rather than in the future. For Hegel 'the Germanic spirit is the spirit of the new world, whose object is the realization of absolute truth as endless self-determination, of freedom which has its absolute form itself for content. The vocation of the Germanic peoples is to furnish bearers of the Christian principle'. This may seem a rather surprising statement until it is realized that 'Frederick [the Great] . . . comprehended the protestant principle from the temporal side and, while discountenancing the religious controversies, . . . he possessed the consciousness of universality, which constitutes the uttermost depth of the spirit and the self-conscious power of thought'. Correspondingly on the more immediate plane 'Frederick II can be called the ruler with whom there enters into reality the new epoch in which true *state-interest* receives its universality and its highest right. Special attention must be devoted to Frederick II in that he has grasped intellectually the general purpose of the state, and that he was the first among the rulers who adhered to the general in the state, and did not allow the particular further validity if it was opposed to the purpose of the state'.

Hegel's stress upon the state coincided with Prussian traditions but, more than that, the identification of the real with the rational, with world-historical right, naturally lent its support to the thesis that whatever is is right. The reactionaries, however, were not suffered to add this valuable acquisition to their armoury unchallenged. In Germany, as elsewhere, things after 1815 were not as they had been before 1789, and still less so after 1830.

It is perhaps a further proof of the vitality of Hegelianism that the challenge to its orthodox creed was made within the framework of the creed itself. The radical Young Hegelians reversed the basic formula, maintaining that only the rational was real, and that the existing order was very far from being rational. This is no place to plunge into the intricacies of the ensuing controversy, into the theories of Gans, the brothers Bauer and their like, but only to notice how German thought, having rejected the rationalism of the eighteenth century, now painfully won through to a rational critique of its own by way of romanticism and the Hegelian philosophy of the spirit; and in particular how two of the earliest and most important manifestations of radical Hegelianism occurred in the fields of theology and economics, corresponding to two main, and often conflicting, European trends of the time—the religious revival in which romanticism and reaction were so often reconciled, and the industrial revolution. In 1835 David Strauss published a Hegelian life of Christ, which provoked not only a storm of opposition from the orthodox, but also an attack from the even extremer Hegelian Bruno Bauer, who wholly denied the historical existence of Christ. And it is better known how in the economic field the Jew Karl Marx based his theories of historical materialism and communism upon Hegelian teaching. In Marxism Hegelianism re-emerged with economic environment substituted for the spirit and, up to a certain point, the class for the state. Henceforth Marxist radicalism is a force to be reckoned with in political thought and practice in Germany as elsewhere. But as yet its following was relatively small.

The very violence of the polemic of the Young Hegelians tended to indicate that left-wing opposition to the political order was inclined, as so often in Germany, to be intellectual rather than practical. The government of Prussia and the other German states continued much as before. But the fortunes of the Hegelians did not. It is understandable that from being looked upon by the authorities as patriotic thinkers who might even be encouraged, they came to be regarded as dangerous extremists who called for repression. Action was taken accordingly. In 1840 some hoped that the death of Frederick-William III of Prussia and the accession of Frederick-William IV might signal a more liberal order. It did not. The new king had, indeed, more imagination than the old. Under him absolutist government was accordingly conducted with greater imagination. Among other things Frederick-William IV had, as crown prince, admired the quality of the wisdom which the aged Schelling was imparting to his fellow crown prince of Bavaria. In 1841 Schelling was called to Berlin to testify against the teaching of his old rival Hegel, a function which he performed with some alacrity and less success.

The Young Hegelian movement showed clearly that the historico-nationalist line of thought was not the only one in Germany, but the very nature of its revolt, deriving as it did from that line itself, indicated also that the historical school was well on its way to becoming the established and traditional outlook by which deviations were measured up. Pointing in the same direction is the fact that the theories of the sublime folk and the supreme nation were in this period percolating through very many different branches of German thought independently of strict Hegelianism, though in sympathy with the main features of its political teaching. The historical school as a whole was now moving forward with too wide a sweep for its influence and fortunes to be identified absolutely with those of Hegelianism or any other single exposition of nationalistic historicism.

The philosophy and general outlook of a political society is in the main embodied and given practical application in its code of law. The new doctrine of the total folk-nation demanded a new system of jurisprudence to correspond. The man primarily responsible for laying the foundations of such a system was among the most measured, certainly among the most learned, exponents of historical thought. This man was Friedrich Karl von Savigny, the friend of the Grimms and the other romantics, the brother-in-law of Clemens Brentano. He was for long years professor at the university of Berlin and for six, in the eighteen-forties, Prussian minister for legislation.

Among Savigny's earlier and most famous works stands the *Vom Beruf unserer Zeit für Gesetzgebung* (*Of the Vocation of Our Time for Legislation*), which was written in answer to Thibaut, a civil lawyer at Heidelberg, the focus of the romantic movement in Germany. Thibaut claimed that now was the time for a unified recodification of German law in the sense of the German folk. Against this Savigny, a cooler head, defended the Roman and provincial elements in existing German law, but at the same time maintained the necessity of 'an organically progressive jurisprudence, which may be common to the whole nation'; organically progressive because for Savigny the nation was a dynamic organism, and there was an organic connexion of law with the being and character of the people'. It followed that 'we first inquire of history, how law has actually developed itself amongst nations of the nobler races'. As far as Germany was concerned—and since it was a question of the nobler races Germany was very much concerned—this inquiry established that 'as there is no Prussian or Bavarian, but a German, language or literature, just so is it with the remote sources of our laws and the historical investigation of them'.

According to Savigny 'the being of law now becomes more complicated in that it has a double life, in one instance as part of the whole folk-life, and then as a special science in the hands of the jurists'. It was upon this special science that jurists since the Renaissance had tended to concentrate, and Savigny, who spoke of such things as 'the general conviction of the folk-spirit', tended to stress the novel concept of law as part of the whole folk-life. He summed up the legal position of the historical school as follows: 'The substance of law is derived from the whole past of the nation, but not arbitrarily so that it might accidentally be of one kind or another, but as having proceeded from the innermost being of the nation itself and from its history.'

Many jurists followed in the way which Savigny indicated; and it is not a long step from Savigny's position to the assertion that each nation, unique in its being and becoming, is a law unto itself; particularly when one appreciates the implications of the fact that in German the word *Recht* embraces right and law in one, a sinister overlap.

As in law, so in other fields.

It has been noted how geographical and other factors tended to cause Germans to lay particular stress upon language. It was not purely coïncidental that leaders of historical thought like Herder, Fichte, and Arndt were well versed in philology. As an example of the effect which such study of philology was apt to produce upon Germans at that time few cases are more instructive than that of Friedrich Wilhelm Christian Karl Ferdinand von Humboldt, who has been noticed before in other connexions.

In his early years Humboldt stood out sharply from among most of his German contemporaries in that he sought to determine the necessary practical safeguards of individual liberty in political society by rigidly restricting the powers and functions of the state. But it is significant that the book in which he worked out such a system, the *Ideen zu einem Versuch die Grenzen der Wirksamkeit des Staats zu bestimmen*, written in 1792, was not published in full until 1851, some fifteen years after his death. Meanwhile Humboldt devoted himself increasingly to philology, and where it led him is evident from his last considerable work, the *Über die Verschiedenheit des menschlichen Sprachbaues und ihren Einfluss auf die geistige Entwickelung des Menschengeschlechts* (*Concerning the Diversity of the Human Structure of Language and its Influence upon the Spiritual Development of the Human Race*).

This treatise opened with the assertion that 'the division of the human race into peoples and tribes and the diversity of their languages and dialects are directly interdependent'. This relation rests upon the fact that 'every language derives a definite peculiarity from that of the nation and conversely exerts a uniformly determining influence upon it. National character is maintained, reinforced, and even to a certain degree produced by community of dwelling-place and activity; but it properly rests upon the similarity of natural predisposition which is usually accounted for by common descent'. The basis of the nation is the stock, and its insignia is the language. But all languages, hence all nations, are not of equal value. Humboldt gave a more restrained version of Fichte's distinction between living languages and dead ones, which are for practical purposes to be equated as good and bad languages. Humboldt maintained that 'in the countless multiplicity of existent and extinct languages we can now establish a distinction, which is of decisive importance for the development of the human race: namely a distinction between languages which have developed powerfully and with consequence from a pure principle, in legitimate freedom, and those which cannot glory in these advantages'. He proceeded to expatiate upon this distinction, rich in possibilities.

Humboldt's new perception of the significance of the nation connoted a new equation of the individual with the nation in the light of the fact that 'there is revealed . . ., if indeed only darkly and dimly, a view into the time in which for us the individuals lose themselves in the mass of the folk'.

In accordance with this view 'the individual human being is always associated with a whole, with that of his nation, of the stock to which this belongs, and of the whole species'. Each national whole is an entirely distinct and self-sufficient totality. 'The individualities which are to be found inside the same nation are . . . embraced by the *national uniformity* which in its turn separates every single disposition from its like in another folk'. Humboldt correspondingly maintained that 'in the concepts, as much as the language, of each folk, however uncultivated it may be, there lies . . . a *totality* corresponding to the compass of the unrestricted human capacity for cultivation, from which may be created without foreign assistance every single thing comprehended by humanity'. Here, then, is the individual identified with humanity at large exclusively in so far as he is a member of the total folk. Philology and philosophy, Humboldt and Hegel, advanced together.

Philologists were not behindhand in applying such theoretical discoveries as these to the sphere of practical politics, as may be instanced by Jacob Grimm who, together with his brother, stood perhaps most directly in line with Herder as a philological and literary explorer and expounder of old German folk-lore and folk-ways. And the popularity of the many books which the Grimms produced was comparable to that of Herder's.

Jacob Grimm in dedicating to Gervinus his major work, the *Geschichte der deutschen Sprache* (*History of the German Language*), remarked that it was 'political through and through'. What he meant by this was explained later in the introduction in which he wrote that

> 'the destinies of the whole of the Middle Ages were particularly guided by it [the German people]; but what a height of power would have been assigned to it had the Franks, Burgundians, Langobards and Visigoths, like the Anglo-Saxons, asserted their hereditary language. With their surrender they were lost to us and largely to themselves; Lorraine, Alsace, Switzerland, Belgium and Holland are our empire; we say that they are not yet irrevocably alienated.'

Grimm was writing at a time when the Schleswig-Holstein question was already looming up, and he said in reference to it:

'And just as from out of the recent enmity between Sweden and Denmark there has awakened the sleeping impulse of their close union, so also will our present quarrel with the Scandinavians resolve itself into that brotherly league between us and them which the community of language loudly demands. For if the great [German] union is established internally how could it be that the contentious peninsula should not be wholly joined to the mainland in accordance with the demands of history, nature and position? How should the Jutes refrain from returning to their old union with the Angles and the Saxons, the Danes to their union with the Goths? As soon as Germany has transformed herself it will be impossible for Denmark to exist as formerly.'

The certain measure of archaic quaintness which flavours these observations should not deceive one into supposing that ordinary Germans, even very hard-headed Germans, looked upon them merely as fanciful conceits. Bismarck, for instance, made it his early business to prove Grimm's last observation correct. Thus did Görres and Arndt and Grimm and many lesser figures stand as indices to the rising curve of Pan-Germanism.

It was but fitting that history itself should rank high among the branches of learning which came under the influence of the historical school. And among the German historians of the time two great figures bulked above the rest: Barthold Georg Niebuhr and Leopold von Ranke.

Niebuhr did for Roman history in Germany what Savigny did for Roman law. This very learned man, whose scholarship was as fine as his memory was prodigious, laid the foundations of the modern approach to ancient history. In his political outlook, however, Niebuhr was rather the reverse of modern, being a staunch opponent of the French revolution and all that it subsequently entailed. He held that 'with us in Germany aristocracy can never become so disgusting as superficial liberalism'. But the conservative Niebuhr agreed with more liberal thinkers like Arndt and Grimm in wishing to see a greater united Germany. At the congress of Vienna he forecast that the days of the small German states were numbered, and he thought, for instance, that 'it is quite by chance that the Swiss were no longer present at the [German] imperial diet, and it is to be ascribed to a piece of bungling at the peace of Westphalia'. Niebuhr was equally like-minded with his fellow Germans of the time as regards the divinity of the state itself, and he said as much in the lectures which he delivered at the university of Bonn in the late eighteen-twenties. According to him 'it is a correct, deep idea of the ancients that the constitution of most states should have been bestowed by means of an oracle. Therein lies the obscure feeling that the state is a revelation of God, and it is a much higher view than that of the eighteenth century'. In other words, 'the state is an institution ordered of God, which belongs to the essence of the human being. . . . But this institution cannot completely exhibit itself upon this earth; what we see of the state in reality is only a shadow of the divine idea of the state'.

What Niebuhr did for the study of ancient history Ranke did for that of modern history. Ranke was born in 1795 in Thuringia in the heart of Germany. Like Niebuhr he was a delicate boy, but in contrast to Niebuhr's unhappy childhood, permeated by the marsh-fevers of Meldorf, Ranke's early years passed pleasantly enough in the little town of Wiehe, set placidly in its valley and deriving its only excitement from a garrison of hussars. Ranke was small of growth, but his head was disproportionately noble and his brain won him speedy recognition. In the middle eighteen-twenties he began his association with the university of Berlin, which lasted for half a century. This historian, the greatest that Germany has produced, refused to allow his scrupulous historical methodology to be tampered with by Hegelianism or any other form of theoretical folk-historicism. But although he did not permit his views on politics and national questions unduly to influence his history, he held very decided views and he gave them publicity at the time, and particularly from 1832 to 1836, when in co-operation with Perthes and others he edited the *Historisch-Politische Zeitschrift*. This journal was of a moderately conservative complexion, and in general it defended the Prussian government against the liberal press. Ranke contributed a number of articles which give a fair idea of his political outlook.

In an article entitled 'France and Germany', published in 1832, Ranke proclaimed: 'the idea of humanity—God gave it expression in the different peoples'. In accordance with this stress upon national peculiarity 'our teaching is that each folk has its own policy. But what does it mean, this national independence with which all minds are permeated? Can it only mean that no foreign superintendent should sit in our towns and no foreign troops march through our country? Does it not much rather imply that without depending upon others we should work up our spiritual characteristics to the degree of completion of which they are capable in themselves?—that we should independently cultivate the nature which we have received from God, our original property, our being, in the way demanded by it.'

What this meant exactly for Germans was brought home in a passionate finale:

'But did we allow ourselves to be talked over by them [the French] at the time when they wanted to hand over to us that philosophy of the eighteenth century (which was also partly brought over from England) and its dependent view of religion and nature? It is precisely in opposition to them that we, as they themselves now admit, have penetrated so much deeper and have approached nearer to the truth. Nobody will deny that in all branches of knowledge their view has been defeated and supplanted. Their poetry and art? Happily we have not followed further in their tracks since we have had a literature [of our own]. All the spiritual exertions of our good age, all the scientific acquisitions of our great men, everything which gives Germans a name has succeeded in opposition to France. And we are to imitate and take over the state which the French have produced from observation, moreover, of foreign forms but which rests entirely upon the selfsame connection of ideas, upon that mechanistic view of things, which is so natural to them—a state which for that very reason threatens every moment to disintegrate of itself! . . . Far be it from us! Everything that we live and are, everything that we have acquired in the centuries of our past, revolts against it.'

That is as good a summary of the trend which things had taken, and were taking, in Germany as it is a powerful appeal against any German toying with the ideas of the July revolution.

Ranke was, however, no idealistic intellectual who believed that it was sufficient for Germany to draw upon her cultural enterprise in order to assure herself of her rightful place among nations. In an article entitled 'Über die Trennung und die Einheit von Deutschland' ('Concerning the Separation and the Unity of Germany') he emphasized two facts in particular: first, that 'over and over again the talk is of the unity of Germany', and secondly that 'the esteem in which this country [Prussia] is held in Europe depends upon its military power. . . . This military power demands its needs, undiminished, without interruption; it demands unity and stern subordination. How easily could even an apparently trifling interference with this endanger the stability of things and therewith the general German element in the common life of Europe!' The conjunction of the two has its significance. But Ranke went deeper than that.

Ranke's most original treatment of the problems of political theory is found in a treatise entitled *Politisches Gespräch* (*Political Conversation*). This work was published in 1836 when Ranke was forty-one years old, in the prime of life and mental vigour. In a sense it may be regarded as summing up the progress which German political thought of the historical school had made during its first half-century; it shows very well whither the line of thought was tending; for Ranke had a judicious mind; he saw the tendency and equated it against that which it deliberately denied.

The political conversation is a dialogue between Carl, a state-counsellor, and Friedrich, a Benedictine monk. Carl maintained that 'the state is no doctrine' and asked Friedrich, who was warming to debate, 'what do you mean by the positive spiritual content of the state?' Friedrich led off thus:

> 'I maintain that genuine politics must have a historical basis, that they must rest upon observation of powerful states which have of themselves thriven in renowned development.
>
> '*Carl.* Is it impossible to proceed from the general to the particular?
>
> '*Friedrich.* One certainly cannot reach the particular from the general without a spring, without a new beginning. The spiritual reality which suddenly stands before your eyes in unsuspected originality cannot be deduced from any higher principle. You can certainly rise with careful boldness from the particular to the general; there is no way leading from general theory to the observation of the particular.'

Here is a clear formulation of the basic position of the historical school, with its stress upon the inductive method grounded upon historical fact and rejection of deduction from general principles.

The implications of this theory in the political field were

made clear when Carl said, 'You will not deny that the different states have something in common', to which Friedrich replied:

'but it seems to me that we must distinguish the formal from the real. The formal is the general; the real is the particular, the living. Certain constitutional forms, . . . the due establishment of relations between classes, may be necessary to all states. But they are not the original life through which it is, much rather, that all forms first obtain their content. Something exists by virtue of which each state is not a division of the general, but life, an individual, in itself.'

Friedrich closely allied this something with transcendent nationalism, maintaining that

'our fatherland is not that place in which, in short, things merely go well for us. Our fatherland is much more with us, in us. Germany lives in us; we exhibit it, whether we will or not, in every country to which we betake ourselves, beneath every zone. We are founded upon it from the start and we cannot emancipate ourselves. This secret something which fills the least even as it does the most superior—this spiritual air that we breathe in and out—surpasses all constitutions, and vivifies and fulfils their every form.

'*Carl.* It seems that with you nationality and the state coincide.

'*Friedrich.* And yet this is less the case than one might suppose. Nations have a tendency to be states; but I could not say that I knew of one that was really a state. Perhaps France most nearly attains this goal; but she does not include nearly every Frenchman, neither . . . Canadians . . . nor even her nearest neighbours in Savoy and Switzerland. England is still further from it. Her colonies have in the main detached themselves from her, and have developed in a way opposite to that of the motherland. One need not even speak of Germany. Even if one was prepared to regard the German confederation as a kind of state . . . all Germans would still not be included in it by a long way.'

The crux of the conversation was reached soon after when Carl quietly remarked, 'It seems that in your policy foreign relations will play a big part.' Friedrich answered:

'The world is, as stated, included [in the calculation]. In order to be something one must raise oneself by means of one's own strength; we must develop free independence and we must fight to obtain the right which is not conceded to us.

'*Carl.* Then would not everything come down to naked force?

'*Friedrich.* Not as much as the word 'fight' seems to indicate. The foundation is present; a community has been definitely established; but if it is to erect itself into universal significance moral energy is necessary above all. By this means alone is it possible to overcome the rivals, the enemies in the contest.

'*Carl.* You regard the bloody handiwork of war as a contest of moral energies. Take care that you do not become too sublime!

'*Friedrich.* You know quite well that our forefathers, who were certainly not sublime, saw it that way. It was thus that those Tenctrians, those Amsivarians contested with the Romans for the land which stood empty. But, as a matter of fact, you will not be able to give me the names of many important wars from which it may not be inferred that true moral energy determined the victory.

'*Carl.* And now you also want to deduce the forms of the internal organisation [of the state] from the fight and the victory.

'*Friedrich.* Not entirely, not in the first place, but [I do] indeed [wish thence to deduce] its modifications. The measure of its independence gives a state its position in the world; at the same time it imposes upon it the necessity of ordering all internal relations with a view to asserting itself. This is its highest law.

'*Carl.* You seem to favour a military tyranny.' Friedrich protested at this and asserted that, 'the great communities gradually evolve through the secret efficacy of mutually supporting ideas. Happy event if one person has the genius to lead them! He will never possess the strength to compel them.

'*Carl.* And so, at most, you are founding a voluntary military state.

'*Friedrich.* You seem to reproach me for the same reason that Aristotle blamed some of the old lawgivers, namely that I think more about making the state great and powerful than about making the citizens wise and good, and that my design is more concerned with struggle and movement than with peace and leisure. You are not wrong as far as the beginning of existence is concerned—the epoch in which it is a question of the fight for independence. But gradually all the peaceful needs of human nature will prevail; then everything will necessarily balance out.'

Having thus relegated peace and leisure to the background, and resolutely brought struggle to the fore, Friedrich proceeded to expatiate anew upon the fact that 'every self-supporting state has its own primal life', until Carl conveniently remarked:

'In this sense you mean that states are individuals.

'*Friedrich.* Individualities, analogous one to another but essentially independent of each other. Instead of those transient conglomerations which rise like cloudy images from the contractual teaching [of the school of natural law], I see spiritual beings, original creations of the human spirit,—one might say, thoughts of God.

'*Carl.* I do not want to contradict you: your view seems to me to be too firmly grounded [for that], and I confess that I am prepossessed by it.'

Friedrich could not, however, avoid all discussion of the actual constitution of the divinely inspired struggling individuality. Carl said, 'But I cannot see how the fact that the government has no formal counterpoise can be rendered innocuous.' Whereupon Friedrich went off into a dissertation upon the 'spirit of the common being'. Carl brought him up sharp with the pertinent question: 'But why do you not further bring the spirit of the common being into perfect consciousness, to representation and expression?' Friedrich said that Carl must not misunderstand him; he did not oppose representative institutions as such, but he did not think them indispensable, and he quoted Heraclitus to the effect that 'hidden harmony . . . is better than open'. Friedrich was clearly more at home in maintaining that

'in our parts nobody is exempted from the fulfilment of military service; purely private life, indeed, no longer exists. Our activity belongs above all, in and for itself, to the community.

'*Carl.* But what does the private man receive in return for all his participation?

'*Friedrich.* It is its own reward in the just state; he does not think of evading it: he perceives the necessity; for him there is no purely private existence': a curt answer. But Carl persisted, 'You would demand patriotism even in everyday life.'

'*Friedrich.* It must be fostered in that way so that it does not fail on the special occasions; in a certain sense it must in general be the principle of activity.

'*Carl.* You turn the whole man into a political creation.

'*Friedrich.* I am convinced that the development even of personal characteristics depends upon the reality of one's participation, I do not say in the forms of the constitution, but in the progress of the general welfare, in the common being.'

The exuberant Friedrich was apparently somewhat nettled by Carl's rather spiritless observations and gave him a final lecture upon moral energy, adjuring him in particular to observe the stars in their courses. Carl broke in, 'Enough for to-day.' He was left with some doubts, but, as is sufficiently obvious from the extracts given, Friedrich had much the best of the argument throughout. Indeed at one point Carl asked

Friedrich not to smile if he compared himself to Eckermann sitting at the feet of Goethe.

The *Politisches Gespräch* is striking in its self-consciousness. The position taken up by the historical school is vindicated with full awareness of its implications. The new subjective German doctrine is set out with objectivity. To cast a retrospective glance over the earlier corpus of historical thought in the light of this dialogue is, as it were, to behold masses of brute matter piling up until a deft hand effortlessly moves a lever and, before one fully grasps what is happening, the scheme of things emerges, the cracks, spreading almost imperceptibly at first, suddenly run together and reveal a widening gulf; the whole mass of matter moves as one, with gathering velocity; German thought is swinging right out of the western orbit.

Glimpses of such vistas should not, however, be confused with appreciation of the immediate historical perspective. The *Politisches Gespräch* was probably no exception to the run of Ranke's balanced and rather academic articles in failing to evoke any very ready response from either of the two main political groupings which were then crystallizing in Germany as elsewhere. The course of this process is a measure of the trend which practical politics were taking, and some brief notice of it is necessary for an understanding of the further development of political thought in Germany.

Ranke was not altogether exaggerating when he wrote in 1832 that even the French had come to admit the greater depth of German thought. The period from 1815 to 1830 has been called the great European age of Germanism. In France Madame de Staël, Benjamin Constant, the Duchesse de Broglie, and the group of the *Doctrinaires* bore especial witness to the new enthusiasm for, and appreciation of, things Germanic. But the French revolution of 1830 largely reversed the trend despite Ranke's attempt to stem the turn of the tide. In Germany as elsewhere the two main political camps were beginning, though only beginning, to order themselves into standing political parties and to think in terms of conservatism and liberalism; and the bourgeois revolution of 1830 produced an immediate reaction from German liberals, disciples of men like Welcker and Rotteck of Freiburg. The princes of Brunswick and Hesse-Cassel were expelled and constitutional charters obtained from their successors; a charter was extracted from the king of Hanover. Things went far in Rhenish Bavaria, where Wirth and Siebenpfeifer edited radical newspapers and instigated a popular gathering at Hambach in May 1832 in order to celebrate the anniversary of the granting of the Bavarian constitution. Counter-measures were promptly taken. The German confederate diet forbade popular societies and meetings and the wearing of cockades; the Carlsbad decrees were renewed and the princes urged to withstand all popular demands. Next year an attempted radical *coup* at Frankfurt further strengthened the vigour of the forces of reaction; Austria, Prussia, and Russia jointly reaffirmed their right of giving aid to any sovereign who asked for it without any other power having reason to complain. The liberal movement had met with no popular response in Prussia and it was significant of the strength, or rather lack of strength, of liberalism in Germany at the time that its active manifestations were confined to the smaller states.

By the end of 1833 reaction was firmly in the saddle again in most places. The German liberals, vaguely reverencing watered-down notions of liberty and progress, turned largely to the Young German movement, a collection of mediocre *literati* led by Gutzkow the dramatist and Gervinus the historian. Significant for his relation to this group was Wolfgang Menzel, an uncouth scribe who grossly overwrote himself. Menzel had been among the keenest of the *Burschenschaften* and actually earned his living for a time as a gymnastic instructor. He reviewed favourably the early works of Heinrich Heine, who was among the most radical and much the most gifted of those affiliated to the Young German movement. But with time Menzel turned increasingly to reactionary religiosity, becoming an absolutist and a monarchist, an ultranationalistic francophobe. He stirred up the authorities against the Young Germans and particularly against Heine, that witty lover of liberty and the sea, an untypical German, a Jew, never generally popular in Germany either then or since. Heine spent the last twenty-five years of his life as an exile in Paris. This circumstance alone sundered him effectively from his countrymen. Some years after he had migrated thither, in 1840, a wave of patriotic indignation swept over Germany in response to the French threat of war. It showed that many of the so-called German liberals differed only in degree from the conservative nationalists; and often not greatly in that. Nor is this surprising when it is remembered that the demand for German national unity headed the liberal programme and, further, how men like Görres, Arndt, and Grimm, who were reckoned as liberals, equated national unity with Pan-Germanism. Constitutionalism itself came under the spell of the historical school, as was apparent from the chief liberal work of the time on political theory, Dahlmann's *Die Politik, auf den Grund und Mass der gegebenen Zustände zurückgeführt* (*Politics, reduced to the Basis and Measure of Given Conditions*), published in 1835. Dahlmann professed admiration for England and her institutions; but so, for instance, did Adam Müller.

The liberal movement was counterbalanced by a similar definition of attitude and organization of activity on the conservative side. Over against the *Burschenschaften* there stood, for example, the 'Cockchafer' movement which was supported in particular by patriotic and romantic young Prussian officers and civil servants. Thence there evolved the Wilhelmstrasse Club which comprised the immediate circle of the Prussian crown prince, prominent among whom were the brothers Gerlach, Radowitz, Haxthausen, and Jarcke, the first editor of the *Berliner Politischen Wochenblattd,* which propagated the views of this set and was regarded as being in the vanguard of the conservative movement.

The most important single influence upon the crown prince and his circle was that of Karl Ludwig von Haller, a Bernese patrician who was often bracketed with Adam Müller as the principal exponent of romantic reaction. Haller's first book, the *Handbuch der allgemeinen Staatenkunde* (*Handbook of General Political Science*), was published in 1808, the same year as Müller's *Elemente der Staatskunst.* The *Handbook* set out the theories which were later elaborated in more detail, and with much greater popular effect, in the *Restauration der Staatswissenschaft* (*Restoration of Statecraft*). The restoration took a long time, volume after volume appearing in the years following 1816, but it achieved prompt notoriety and was singled out by the *Burschenschaften* for ceremonial burning along with the Code Napoléon, a corporal's stick, a pigtail, and a pair of corsets, on the Wartburg bonfire of 1817.

The nature of Haller's theory is largely indicated in the foreword to the *Restoration*, in which he asserted that it is only with the aid of God that he has been able to produce the work 'which, according to my strong conviction, . . . is to extirpate, with all its branches and leaves, the fundamental error of a false and pernicious science, which has held sway in the schools for two centuries, and in its stead reveal the order of God'. Indeed Haller, more deliberately perhaps than any of his contemporaries, rejected the whole teaching of the school of natural law, upon which the political thought of Europe had been built. With crabbed erudition he traced its course from Grotius to Kant, trouncing each theorist in turn; for him Hobbes was 'a melancholic fellow' and 'the ancestor of all jacobins'; Algernon Sidney caused Haller to regret the time he had wasted in reading the *Discourses concerning Government*; Rousseau was dismissed as 'an ignorant sophist'. According to Haller the school of natural law 'began to distinguish the *historical* from the *juridical origin* [of states] . . . as if everything historical must necessarily be wrong or irrational, and only that could be legal or rational which had never existed and, according to more exact investigation, is not even possible'.

The cardinal error of the non-historical theory of natural law was found in the fact that the sovereignty of the people was implicit in it and that consequently princes were not divine rulers, but mere parties to a contract which could be revoked by the people. For Haller 'the state of nature has never ceased', since it is the natural thing that there should be subjects and rulers. 'Instead of basing the powers of the rulers upon rights which they are supposed to have *received* from their subjects, may they not be much more simply and more satisfyingly regarded as proceeding from their own (natural and acquired) rights.' This natural relation between ruler and ruled rests upon the 'eternal unalterable ordering of God that the more powerful should rule, must rule, and always will rule'. It is in accordance with this law of nature that 'only the poor obey the rich, only the weak obey the strong . . . the greater (more intensive), the more extended and the more lasting the power, so much the greater and more lasting is the mastery'. Haller made it quite clear that he was not thinking merely of intellectual or moral power; he urged his readers to 'observe the beasts of the field and the birds in the air, from the eagle and the elephant down to the insect and the worm which crawls upon the earth: everywhere the stronger class lords it over the weak'. This relation is so fully natural and unavoidable that 'the more powerful rules even if he does not wish to, and does not seek to do so; the needy serves or must serve even if nobody demands his service'.

Haller saw the direction which his theory was taking, but he indignantly denied that he was equating might with right. He proclaimed a 'law of duty' to the effect that 'men should benefit and not hurt one another, do good and not evil'. But he significantly went on to remark that this law 'certainly does not compel in the same way as the external law of nature', which decrees that might shall rule.

Haller's proclamation of the principle of sheer power pointed towards much that was to come; but he remained none the less a somewhat archaic figure standing outside the main line of historical thought. Indeed he actually disapproved of much that the historical school taught. For Haller, 'smaller states are the true, simple order of nature'. And he pertinently asked 'what profit is there in the theory —as unnatural as it is unchristian—of unconditional unity, of the absolute isolation and rounding off of every single state, setting all in hostility over against each other as it now does'. It should, however, be remarked that Haller himself wrote of 'the macrobiotics of states' and thought that 'in the world there can only exist individuals and communities, physical or so-called moral, i.e. collective persons'.

The political groups which Haller influenced stood like him somewhat outside the main stream of historical thought. For the crown prince and his romantic circle reverence of God forbade absolute reverence of the folk-state and the principle of nationalism; they stigmatized pure historicism as pantheism. But the main current was flowing strong now and began to sap the positions that held out against it. The position of these conservative idealists remained centred upon Haller's restatement of the divine right of princes, but new elements were making themselves felt, and they compromised the original simplicity of solidity of that position. Jarcke, writing in the *Berliner Politischen Wochenblatte* in 1831, talked of 'the spirit of the folk in its most secret depths and multiplicity', while Friedrich Julius Stahl, the Hebraic champion of the authoritative Christian state, the prime theorist of the group in the eighteen-forties, maintained that the state is 'the folk constituted as a personality'. But any liberal tendencies which such references to the folk might be held to imply were offset by the political acquiescence demanded by the doctrine which Wilhelm von Gerlach summed up in his remark that 'right grows out of wrong like flowers out of a hotbed'. In a speech which his brother Leopold prepared for King Frederick-William in 1847 this remark is rendered as: 'From wrong, which is the divine order here on earth, there proceeds a right which cannot be overlooked without new wrong'. This theory opened up considerable practical possibilities, particularly when viewed in conjunction with Haller's insistence upon the rule of might. There were some who, in one form or another, made this conjunction. In the eighteen-forties the Gerlachs were on intimate terms with Otto von Bismarck.

Frederick-William and his circle were evidently not very incisive or single-minded thinkers. These theorizing dilettanti bridged too much for that. They linked theories which were antique even in their own time with new trends whose full significance appeared only in 1848 and the years which followed. They looked back to the medieval idealism of the Holy Roman Empire, and forward to the power-politics of Prussia welding Germany to her second empire.

This group was not alone in Germany in heralding a fresh emphasis upon force as an instrument of policy. The Prussian army was making an alliance with the new power of history. Upon the appointment of General von Müffling to be chief of the Prussian general staff in 1821 military science was made a 'permanent intellectual possession' by the systematic study of military history. Some ten years later appeared the book which, more than any other single work, crystallized the Prussian attitude to war and determined the quality of her military theory and practice of the future. August Schlegel and Humboldt, Adam Müller and Hegel, the rising historical school extolled the place of war in the life of man and the state. New content had been given to the idea of the state; the same must be done for war, the great instrument of state-policy. The total nation demanded the total war. This need was met by the treatise *Vom Kriege* (*Of War*), written by General Carl von Clausewitz. This incisive thinker, like Ranke and unlike many other Germans, did not contort his knowledge with theoretical ingenuity. Clausewitz assembled the facts about war as he saw them. This plain statement carried corresponding conviction.

War was total for Clausewitz in that 'war is an act of force and there are no limits in the use of the same', while at the same time warfare is merely diplomacy by other means. 'Often wars are not much more than an armed neutrality, or a threatening position in support of negotiations, or a moderate attempt to put ourself in a slightly advantageous position and then to await events, or a disagreeable treaty obligation which one fulfils as scantily as possible'. Expedience is the only limit to the extent of warlike operations and the degree of violence employed.

War is force, the great exploiter of weakness. It is laid down that 'the whole of war supposes human weaknesses, and it is against these that it is directed'. It follows that 'the best strategy is *always to be thoroughly strong*, first in general, and then at the decisive point'. And this strength should be used at a dynamic tempo. Clausewitz bluntly remarked that 'no conquest can be completed fast enough'. It is likewise in accordance with the concept of total war that 'a standstill in the warlike act is strictly speaking a contradiction of the nature of the thing since both armies must ceaselessly exterminate each other like two hostile elements, just as fire and water never set themselves in equilibrium but continue to influence each other until one has wholly disappeared'. Clausewitz saw this war of extermination as an ideal which could not, however, be wholly realized since, as he went on to say, 'wild as is the nature of war, it yet wears the chains of human weaknesses'. He thought it beyond human power to achieve the perfect inhumanity of total warfare. Nevertheless things were moving in the right direction. The 'restricted shrivelled-up form of war' which had prevailed in the eighteenth century was a thing of the past, since during the French revolution and the Napoleonic era 'war had again suddenly become an affair of the people'. War must be the war of the folk, and sentiments of humanity must not rob it of its great prerogatives, slaughter and the shedding of blood. Clausewitz declared: 'we do not want to hear anything of generals who conquer without human blood. If the bloody slaughter is a terrible spectacle, it should only occasion a higher appreciation of war, but it should not cause the swords . . . to be made gradually blunter from [feelings of] humanity.'

The treatise *Vom Kriege*, and its influence upon the Prussian general staff, foreshadowed grim work in the future when the German nation should once more rise in arms against its enemies. Along with this new and sterner theory of warfare went the rise in population, which meant more men for the fight, and the inventions of modern science which were to facilitate the swifter and more deadly conduct of hostilities. Of these inventions the railway may be reckoned among the greatest. During the eighteen-forties and fifties Germany was building her railways; in the eighteen-sixties she made her wars. Accordingly the German who may perhaps best claim to stand alongside of General von Clausewitz is, significantly enough, a liberal Württemberger, a friend of the radical Heine, the man who as a youth was rebuked by his master for reading 'even the mad Schanschak' (Rousseau), who was expelled from his own state and worked for some seven years as an emigrant in the United States.

In the early eighteen-thirties Friedrich List, back from America, young, corpulent, and vigorous, constituted himself as something approaching a railway-promoter-general for Germany. In 1833 he published a pamphlet entitled *Über ein sächsisches Eisenbahn-System als Grundlage eines allgemeinen deutschen Eisenbahn-Systems . . .* (*Concerning a Saxon Railway System as the Basis of a General German Railway System*) and began an intensive propaganda campaign for the building of railways throughout Germany, starting the *Eisenbahnjournal* (*Railway Journal*) in 1835. But List was associated with yet wider economic trends, and in particular with the beginnings of the Customs Union in Germany. Prussia, while apparently allowing herself to be led by Austria in the field of politics, struck out a new line for herself and Germany in economics. She led the movement against the tariff barriers which hampered all trade between the German states, and created an economic union which was recognized at the time to be big with political significance for the future. By 1834 Prussia, Hesse, Württemberg, Bavaria, Saxony, and the Thuringian states were members of the union; Frankfurt and Baden were soon to join.

List's association with the Customs Union is the more important in that he was the leading German economist of his day. It is a further reflection upon the nature of German liberalism that the doctrines of this economist, a man of truly advanced ideas, should have had so much in common with those of Adam Müller. The title of List's greatest work, *Das nationale System der politischen Okonomie* (*The National System of Political Economy*), published in 1841, gives some indication of the general character of his theory. His position, like that of Müller, was based upon a negation of the teaching of Adam Smith and his followers, The School, as List called them. According to him

'the system of the school suffers . . . from three main defects: firstly, from boundless *cosmopolitanism*, which neither recognizes the principle of nationality, nor takes into consideration the satisfaction of its interests; secondly, from a dead *materialism*, which everywhere regards chiefly the mere exchangeable value of things without taking into consideration the mental and political, the present and future interests, and the productive powers of the nation; thirdly, from a *disorganizing particularism* and *individualism*, which . . . considers private industry only as it would develop itself under a state of free interchange with society (i.e. with the whole human race) were the race not divided into separate national societies.

'Between each individual and entire humanity, however, stands *the nation*, with its special language and literature, with its peculiar origin and history, with its special manners and customs, laws and institutions, with the claims of all these for existence, independence, perfection and continuance for the future, and with its separate territory; a society which, united by a thousand ties of mind and interests, combines itself into one independent whole, which recognizes the law of right for and within itself, and in its united character is still opposed to other societies of a similar kind in their national liberty, and consequently can only under the existing conditions of the world maintain self-existence and independence by its own power and resources.'

List found in the nation the sufficient answer to Adam Smith's cosmopolitanism and disorganizing particularism. His correction of Smith's other main defect, his materialism, is indicated in his denunciation of it, and lies at the root of his economic theory. Müller had stigmatized Smith's failure to appreciate the element of 'spiritual capital'; List likewise insisted upon 'mental capital' derived from the past. He followed Müller in introducing into economics the vivid romantic conception of the historical continuum roving down from the past, through the present, into the future. In economics, as in other spheres of human activity, it is a question not of statics, of being, but of dynamics, of becoming. Smith's theory of values is, according to List, a shopkeeper's theory based upon the concept of 'value in exchange'. But for List 'the power of producing wealth is . . . infinitely more important than wealth itself'. He rejected what he termed the theory of values in favour of his theory of productive powers. And the great agent and condition of the development of productive powers is the nation. List followed Müller in stressing the importance of dynamic 'national enrichment' over against static 'national wealth'. And the sovereign means of ensuring national enrichment was to establish vigorous manufactures. 'All the mental powers of a nation, its state revenue, its material and mental means of defence, and its security for national independence, are increased in equal proportion by establishing in it a manufacturing power'. This power must be deliberately planned. Internally as externally, planned economy, not *laissez-faire*, was wanted. 'A statesman will know, and must know . . . how the productive powers of a whole *nation* can be awakened, increased, and protected, and how, on the other hand, they are weakened, laid to sleep, or utterly destroyed'.

List's scope of vision was not, indeed, wholly limited by the nation. He criticized the mercantilist system, since 'chiefly owing to its utterly ignoring the principle of cosmopolitanism, it does not recognize the future union of all nations, the establishment of perpetual peace, and of universal freedom of trade, as the goal to which all nations have to strive, and more and more to approach'. But with List, as with other Germans, such ideals were for the distant future. Great Britain was the only country which was truly in a position to benefit from free trade at present, and 'instead of hoping and waiting and expecting the Messiah of a future Free Trade, it would be better that the cosmopolitan spirit should be thrown into the fire'.

List saw well enough that the logical complement to the prevalent free-trade doctrine of the Manchester school was international co-operation and disarmament. He deliberately rejected this, asking

'would not every sane person consider a government to be insane which, in consideration of the benefits and the reasonableness of a state of universal and perpetual peace, proposed to disband its armies, destroy its fleet, and demolish its fortresses? But such a government would be doing nothing different in principle from what the popular school requires from governments when, because of the advantages which would be derivable from general free trade, it urges that they should abandon the advantages derivable from protection.'

Free trade was all very well for Great Britain, but 'if any nation whatever is qualified for the establishment of a national manufacturing power, it is Germany. . . . If any nation whatever had the right to anticipate rich results from a protective system adapted to her circumstances . . . it is Germany'.

List made it plain that military and political considerations were preponderant factors in determining his economic outlook. According to him

'at a time where technical and mechanical science exercises such immense influence on the methods of warfare, where all warlike operations depend so much on the condition of national revenue, where successful defence greatly depends on the questions whether the mass of the nation is rich or poor, intelligent or stupid, energetic or sunk in apathy; whether its sympathies are given exclusively to the fatherland or partly to foreign countries, whether it can muster many or but few defenders of the country—

at such a time, more than ever before, must the value of manufactures be estimated from a political point of view.'

For List enlightened politics in Germany meant that the Customs Union should form the basis of a corresponding political union, that recognition should be given to

'the great requirements of the German nationality. . . . From day to day it is necessary that the governments and peoples of Germany should be more convinced that national unity is the rock on which the edifice of their welfare, their honour, their power, their present security and existence, and their future greatness, must be founded.'

Corresponding to this greater united Germany List envisaged a greater German economic system. He thought that

'the German protective system only accomplishes its object in a very imperfect manner so long as Germany does not spin for herself the cotton and linen yarn which she requires; so long as she does not directly import from tropical countries the colonial produce which she requires, and pay for it with goods of her own manufacture; so long as she does not carry on this trade with her own ships, so long as she has no means of protecting her own flag; so long as she possesses no perfect system of transport by river, canal or railway, so long as the German *Zollverein* does not include all German maritime territories and also Holland and Belgium.'

It should not be imagined that List contemplated only the economic union of countries like Holland and Belgium. On the contrary,

'we from a national point of view say and maintain that Holland is in reference to its geographical position, as well as in respect of its commercial and industrial circumstances, and of the origin and language of its inhabitants, a German province, which has been separated from Germany at a period of German national disunion, without whose reincorporation in the German Union Germany may be compared to a house the door of which belongs to a stranger: Holland belongs as much to Germany as Brittany and Normandy belong to France. . . . In her position Holland cannot nearly so well derive profit from her colonial possessions as if they became a constituent part of the German Union, especially because she is too weak in the elements which are necessary for colonisation—in population and in mental powers.'

And similarly, according to List, with Switzerland, Belgium, and Denmark. When List talked of a greater German union he, like other German liberals, envisaged a body which included at least those four countries in addition to Germany proper. He held that there would be a general 'gain if Germany, Holland and Belgium constitute together a common naval power; for while separated these last are mere satellites of the supremacy of England, but if united they strengthen the opposition to that supremacy of all nations at sea'. The full implications of this were made rather clearer when List went on to remark that 'it cannot be denied that a correct view of the wants and interests of the continent underlay the continental system of Napoleon'.

List, like Napoleon, looked beyond Europe. He thought that Germany needed supplementary territories [*Ergänzungsgebiete*] 'as much as breath'. This need of vital living-space was fortunately met by the fact that 'it is hardly subject to doubt that providence has by preference dedicated the Germanic races, by means of their nature and character, to the solution of the great task of leading world-affairs, civilizing wild and barbaric countries and populating those that are still uninhabited'. The practical implications of this mission are outlined in a passage in which List argued that

'emigration to Central and South America, if it were well led and undertaken on a large scale, offers in a *national* point of view much greater advantage for Germany than emigration to North America. What good is it if the emigrants to North America become ever so prosperous? In their personal relation they are lost for ever to the German nationality, and also from their material production Germany can expect only unimportant fruits. It is a pure delusion if people think that the German language can be maintained by the Germans who live in the interior of the United States, or that after a time it may be possible to establish entire German states there. We once ourselves entertained this illusion, but after ten years' observation in the country itself, on the spot, we have entirely given it up. . . .

What we contend is . . . that those Germans who emigrate to the west of North America give no important assistance in increasing the demand for German manufactured goods, and that in reference to that object emigration to Central amd South America requires and deserves very much more direct encouragement.

The above-mentioned countries, including Texas, are for the most part adapted for raising colonial produce. They can and will never make great progress in manufacturing industry. Here there is an entirely new and rich market for manufactured goods to acquire; whoever has here established firm commercial relations, may remain in possession of them for all future time. These countries, without sufficient moral power of their own to raise themselves to a higher grade of civilisation, to introduce well-ordered systems of government, and to endue them with stability, will more and more come to the conviction that they must be aided from outside, namely by immigration. In these quarters the English and French are hated on account of their arrogance, and owing to jealousy for national independence—the Germans for the opposite reasons are liked. Hence the states of the *Zollverein* ought to devote the closest attention to these countries.

A vigorous German consular and diplomatic system ought to be established in these quarters. . . . Young explorers should be encouraged to travel through these countries and make impartial reports upon them. Young merchants should be encouraged to inspect them—young medical men to go and practise there. Companies should be founded . . . and taken under special protection, which companies should be formed in the German seaports in order to buy large tracts of land in those countries and to settle them with German colonists—companies for commerce and navigation, whose object should be to open new markets in those countries for German manufactures and to establish lines of steamships—mining companies whose object should be to devote German knowledge and industry to winning the great mineral wealth of those countries. In every possible way the *Zollverein* ought to endeavour to gain the good-will of the population and also of the governments of those countries, and especially to promote by that means public security, means of communication, and public order; indeed one ought not to hesitate, in case one could by that means put the governments of those countries under obligation to us, also to assist them by sending an important auxiliary corps.

'A similar policy ought to be followed in reference to the East—to European Turkey and the Lower Danubian territories. Germany has an immeasurable interest that security and order should be firmly established in those countries, and in no direction so much as this is the emigration of Germans so easy for individuals to accomplish, or so advantageous for the nation. . . .

'In anticipation of the inclusion in the *Zollverein* of the German seaports and Holland, it would be desirable that Prussia should now make a commencement by the adoption of a German commercial flag, and by laying the foundation for the future German fleet, and that she should try whether and how German colonies can be founded in Australia, New Zealand, or in or on other islands of Australasia.'

This bold and ambitious oceanic and continental policy of List's, like much of his other teaching, looks two ways. On the one hand there is a ring in it that takes one back to the maritime exploiters and mercantilist economists of earlier centuries, while on the other it has so modern a flavour that one already seems to be among the commercial competition and bitter colonial and continental rivalries upon which pivoted the relations of the great European powers during the last two decades of the century.

No single theory points exclusively in one direction. But the double impression created by that of List, as by those of the Wilhelmstrasse Club, may fairly be taken as a surface indication of deeper currents which influenced political thought as a whole in Germany in the first half of the nineteenth century. In them the relation between old and new, backward-looking and forward-looking, is a peculiar one.

In Germany, as elsewhere on the continent at that time, conservatives and reactionaries reverenced a patriarchal order of society, looking for light to the splendour of princely thrones and noble houses, the true enlightenment of benevolent despotism; whereas liberals and radicals beheld a brighter radiance in the dawn of a constitutional era, strong with the strength of the people, sound under popular rule. But in Germany both these political outlooks came under the influence of the historical school which was by now almost assuming the proportions of a distinctive mode of German thought, above conservative, liberal, and other partial limitations, resolving them within itself. This it was particularly fitted to do owing, largely, to the stress which it laid upon the historical continuum in which the present was the nexus between the, conservative, past and the, liberal, future. For the German liberal the historical school gave to the popular notions of the people and the nation a newly conjoint significance in that of a united body, national and popular, the folk. These liberals, lacking for the most part any very substantial practical political experience, tended to look for realization of this new significance of the folk less in the acquisition and functioning of popular representative institutions, though indeed they sought that also, than in the aggrandizement and completion of the folk by its unification within Germany itself and by the incorporation within it of independent peoples of Germanic stock or past. For the German conservative the historical school gave fresh weight to the friendly authoritarian past, to the rule of the strong, and to the traditional use of power-politics in the interests of the state.

The balance was tilted in favour of the conservatives. This was indeed necessarily the case since the new mode of thought was avowedly historical and the past history of Germany was in the main one of feudalism, bureaucracy, and militarism. The opponents of liberalism enjoyed a further advantage which was to stand them in good stead for the future. The creation of an effective German unity stood at the head of the liberal programme. At first conservatives were largely suspicious of this policy of centralization, but with advancing years some, then many, and finally most of the German, especially Prussian, traditionalists could answer that they, too, sought this German unity, but that the liberals were doing their best to frustrate it by insistence upon parliamentary government which deliberately sanctioned the standing feuds of hostile parties; the greater German union would not be achieved if the constituent states thus squandered their energies internally, but only if they led the way by maintaining discipline and unity within themselves. The question of German unity affected every single German as such, but for the governments of the particular German states it was a question of foreign policy, that is, of power-politics. And so it was the duty of every German to lay aside personal differences and party squabbles, to close the ranks and march with the state-leaders towards a greater German future. This general trend of thought, this tendency to identify unity with uniformity, was to exert powerful influence upon very many Germans for very many years to come.

In most European countries in the decades after 1830 the dynamic driving-force of idealism generally came from the left. It can hardly be said that this tendency was thus early actually reversed in Germany. The events of 1848 forbid that. But thus early in Germany was dynamic purpose latent in the right. The years following 1848 were to reveal the import of this circumstance.

Chapter IV

UNIFICATION 1848–1871

It would be an easy matter to carry on placidly, reciting the names of German professors and summarizing their political theories, dwelling upon mediocrity for lack of other material in the middle years of the nineteenth century. But it is to be feared that such as would delve only into the solid works of Bluntschli and Holtzendorff, of the historical economists Knies and Roscher and their like, would emerge tired-eyed without having obtained any very clear vision of the underlying forces which were influencing the German outlook on society and opening up the sweep of new perspectives. We have seen how the political theory which had grown up in Germany was emphatic in its stress upon historical fact as the basis of theory, in its identification of being with becoming, in its conviction that a German theory of society must be rooted in German life and experience. Theory cannot be artificially divorced from fact and context. The formative years of German nineteenth-century history are at hand. It is necessary to observe how far events chimed with previous thought, and in what sense they determined the outlook for the future. We take up the skein of history which leads from Saint Paul's Church in Frankfurt to the Hall of Mirrors in Versailles.

The events of 1848 in Germany, like most others in which the passions of men in the mass are engaged, had a background that was both intellectual and material. Of the intellectual background something has already been said. Of the many factors which conditioned material circumstances two stand out in sharp relief. In the first place the play of social forces in Germany in the first half of the nineteenth century was quite other than that which underlay political developments in France, whence came the first stimulus in 1848. The July revolution of 1830 had knocked the nails into the coffin of the French nobility and had proclaimed the rule of the *bourgeoisie*. The revolution of 1848 carried matters a stage farther. It was the first modern challenge to the principle of plutodemocracy; it questioned whether moderate political democracy was of value unless it was accompanied by its economic counterpart. And so Louis Philippe stepped out, murmuring in bewilderment *Comme Charles X*, *comme Charles X*. But in Germany, and particularly in Prussia, the case was not far from being reversed. By the turn of the eighteenth century the nobility in Germany had fallen into serious disrepute. But the romantics first heralded a swing in the opposite direction, although their immediate political influence was probably restricted. Men like Friedrich Schlegel, Schleiermacher, and Adam Müller were united in their reverence for nobility as a social and political element in society. The nobles were the living links with the feudal German past, in the light of which the romantics were proclaiming Germanity anew. They were the props of monarchy, upon which all true political order must be based. Görres came to describe democracy as decomposition and monarchy as synthesis. Müller in a characteristic conceit maintained that the nobility represented age in the state, and equated this conservative force with the feminine element. The more liberal Arndt was at one with his master Stein in desiring a more popular type of cameral government and reform in the status of the nobility; but his outlook on society was none the less essentially feudal; he agreed with the majority of his romantic contemporaries in rejecting the concept of political equality, holding that each should contribute according to his several capacities in a system of government by estates. And economic facts went hand in hand with romantic theories. Stein's emancipation of the peasantry was an important and symbolic political action, but it is very doubtful how far it immediately improved their practical condition, while in some cases it actually redounded to their economic disadvantage over against the aristocratic landowners who in any case retained the all-important rights of local justice and police. The Junkers entered into their hey-day. The power of the industrial and commercial middle-classes was at the same time gradually increasing, and authors like List showed that they were becoming more articulate. But only moderately so. Up to 1850 Germany was still predominantly an agricultural country and since about 1820 her agriculture had, indeed, made rapid strides under the stimulus of Thaer and Liebig. On the other hand, when in the middle eighteen-forties Lord Westmorland, British ambassador at Berlin, referred to List as 'a very able writer in the employ of the German manufacturers' List retorted that 'unfortunately it was not true, for the manufacturers do not take sufficient interest in the matter to require a paid agent'.

But if social conditions in Germany thus differed fundamentally from those in France and other European countries, they were, in another and more immediate sense, similar. The eighteen-forties in Germany as elsewhere were in general hard years. The effects of the industrial revolution were already beginning to make themselves felt. In Prussia a proletariat was growing up. The small Silesian spinners, for instance, could no longer compete with the big manufacturers. In 1844 they rose in revolt and were suppressed with bloodshed. The harvest of 1846-7 failed. Upper Silesia was ravaged by famine and typhus. Such conditions lent themselves to political exploitation, and radical agitators were active. Karl Marx had a number of collaborators and sympathizers, men like Moses Hess, Arnold Rüge, and Karl Grün. The liberal Germanists were also on the move. In 1846 Arndt, Dahlmann, the two Grimms, Uhland, Gervinus, and a number of others foregathered at Frankfurt amid popular applause. Next year a more significant assembly was held. Frederick-William IV felt compelled to go so far as to call the first united Prussian diet. In opening the diet on the 11th April, 1847, the king admonished the deputies to give the advice asked of them and to present petitions but not to express their own opinions, which would be an un-German thing to do, conducive to political strife. He said that he would never have called them together if he had had any suspicion that they would wish to play the rôle of so-called representatives of the people. But this assembly was not so wholly acquiescent as the king had hoped, and its committees were still in existence in March 1848 when all Germany was shaken by the repercussion of events in France.

The German revolutionary movement of 1848 rings hollow. The cardinal flaw responsible for this circumstance is, typically enough in German history, deeply embedded in a complex of circumstances whose intricacy has sometimes tended to obscure its most significant features. Conditions had not materially altered since 1789 in that now as then Germany did not exist as a coherent unit; but they had altered in that very many more Germans now looked forward to a united Germany. For liberals a liberal Germany and a united Germany came to be almost one and the same thing. Popular attention, both then and since, was naturally concentrated upon the idealistic movement towards a greater liberal Germany. In 1848 the worthy professors and lawyers and well-to-do bourgeois came into their own, marching in solemn processions, making solemn speeches and cutting figures as party politicians. But behind this unsubstantial façade the really considerable efforts to achieve German unification were being made by quite other people, with quite another outlook, in quite a different way. The problem was treated by the German governments as a matter for settlement between state and state, belonging to the sphere of foreign policy, of power-politics.

How far this was the case is evident even from the beginning of this rather curious episode in German history. In March 1848 Duke Adolf of Nassau sent Max von Gagern on a tour of the courts of southern Germany with a view to obtaining their reactions to a plan, derived mainly from his more gifted brother, Friedrich von Gagern, which proposed the unification of Germany as a federal state under Prussian leadership. The southern states had been the first to feel the repercussions of the French revolution, and their answers were in the main favourable. It was primarily this circumstance which induced Frederick-William IV to put himself at the head of the popular movement on the 21st March by issuing the proclamation 'To my People and the German

Nation' in which he announced that Prussia was now merged in Germany and that he had adopted the federal German colours, the black-red-and-gold. This was much more than a successful expedient for calming the populace of Berlin; it was the opening of an international duel which was to end only upon the field of Sadowa. Although Austria was herself rent by revolution the Austrian government promptly protested in a circular note of the 24th March against any unilateral modification of the constitution of the old German Confederation, the diet of which was presided over by the Austrian representative. The danger that Prussian pressure would oust Austrian influence from Germany was brought home when the preliminary German parliament met at Frankfurt-am-Main on the 31st March, 1848. Of the some 500 deputies 141 were Prussians, whereas the number of Austrian representatives was 2.

It was in this atmosphere that the German liberals went to work. Any truly revolutionary spirit bent upon the emancipation of the masses was, as events showed, quite alien from the majority of Germans. In April some radicals like Hecker, Struve and Herwegh made forlorn attempts at popular *coups*. The troops of Baden and Württemberg, backed by public opinion in Germany at large, were sufficient to crush such futile risings: futile, but significant in that they brought out the tardy growth of social consciousness among the German *bourgeoisie*, who were so late in making their first attempt at even moderate revolution that right from the beginning they were challenged by small groups of proletarian extremists—a challenge which tended to drive the middle-classes in the opposite direction towards conservatism.

The radical disturbances having been satisfactorily disposed of, the men of forty-eight proceeded with the real work in hand. On the 18th May the constituent German parliament opened at Frankfurt with an act of homage to the aged Arndt. But the power-political duel continued to constitute the underlying reality. On the 29th June Austria secured an important advantage when the parliament chose the learned and popular Archduke John to be imperial vicar at the head of a provisional executive government for federal Germany. The Prussian reaction was as might have been expected, and found expression, in particular, in a pamphlet with the significant title: *The Central German Power and the Prussian Army.* It is indeed an odd reflection upon the nature of then German liberalism that so many of its exponents should have looked to Prussian militarism for a lead. While Prussia was seeking to derive profit from the turn of events in Germany, internal reaction to the liberal currents was already mustering in force. On the 1st July, 1848, appeared the first issue of the *Kreuzzeitung*, which represented the feudal outlook of the Prussian conservatives with great effect and soon became the most influential German paper of the time. In the middle of August the 'Junker Parliament' met at Berlin; there were assembled the pick of the Prussian large landowners—Kleist-Retzow, Below-Hohendorf, Puttkamer-Reinfeld, Bülow-Cummerow, and Otto von Bismarck. This was the inception of the organized conservative party in Germany. Special societies multiplied amain, societies like the Central Silesian Union for the Protection of Property and the East Prussian Union for the Preservation of the Interests of Landed Property. Prussia was a well-disciplined country. Municipalities and the Churches lent a hand, organizing 'Fatherland and Prussian Unions', 'Unions for King and Fatherland', and the like. These activities met with a real response from the average Prussian. The military tradition stood the conservatives in particularly good stead; the Landwehr veterans of 1813-15 foregathered to demonstrate their hostility to democracy, singing the uncompromising new popular tune, *Ich bin ein Preusse.*

Meanwhile the well-meaning parliamentarians at Frankfurt-am-Main deliberated upon the forms of constitutions. These enthusiasts did a great deal of excellent work. On 21st December, 1848, a set of basic laws was promulgated; these included freedom of movement, free exercise of trading occupations, equality before the law, freedom of emigration, removal of distinctions between social ranks, general military service, protection from arbitrary imprisonment, abolition of the death penalty, freedom of the press, religious belief and education, state schools, right of assembly, independence of the judiciary, and trial by jury. This was an impressive list of liberties, but it remained ineffective so long as the practical conditions of its application remained unsettled. In endeavouring to determine these conditions the Frankfurt assembly became inextricably involved in the opposition between Austria and Prussia. From the various groupings there gradually emerged the Greater German party which favoured the inclusion of Austria in the German federation, and the Lesser German party which aimed at her exclusion. The possible permutations and combinations were many and intricate, one of the most hotly debated being the proposal that the German federation should exclude Austria but should be bound to her by an indissoluble pact. While the parliament debated diplomatic negotiations proceeded apace directly between the different states and at the same time also through the provisional federal government under the imperial vicar.

In southern Germany a forlorn attempt was made to revive the 'triadic idea' under Saxon leadership, but the most considerable south German state, Bavaria, acted rather as an intermittent go-between in the main negotiations between Prussia and Austria. The vigorous reactionary Prince Schwarzenberg was now at the head of affairs in Vienna and he pressed home the Austrian viewpoint both directly to Prussia and also, through the Austrian agent Schmerling, to the federal government. This viewpoint was based on the contention that there existed not only a greater and lesser German problem, but also a greater and lesser Austrian problem. Austria would not allow herself to be excluded from Germany, but the Habsburg empire was now a unitary state and must unite with Germany as a whole or not at all—a proceeding which would have meant, in effect, that Germany would have become a satellite of the Habsburg dominions. And so the negotiations continued, each side putting up draft constitutions and turning them down, and both making *démarches* to the impotent federal government when they thought that a tactical advantage was to be gained. The crisis came in March 1849. On the 9th Schwarzenberg dispatched a note to Frankfurt demanding the admission of the whole Austrian dominion into the German federation, rejecting the liberal constitution which the parliament was on the point of taking in second reading, and proposing an alternative of his own. After considerable parliamentary manœuvring the Frankfurt assembly gave its answer on the 30th by sending a deputation of thirty-two, including Arndt and Dahlmann and led by Simson, to invite the king of Prussia to assume the dignity of German Emperor. The deputation passed through Cologne to the accompaniment of catcalls and arrived in Berlin on the 2nd April, 1849. Next day King Frederick-William IV informed the deputation that he would not accept the imperial crown without consulting the German princes with regard to the offer and to the proposed feudal constitution. The deputation declared that this answer constituted a refusal of the offer and departed forthwith. It was a refusal in that the Prussian king was determined to accept nothing from a mere popular assembly, and scorned a crown which had been trailed in the mud of democracy; he also feared a crown which, if it were accepted, would in all probability involve him in open conflict with Austria. But this refusal was a very different matter from abstaining from any attempt to utilize circumstances in order to strengthen Prussia's power-political situation in Germany. On the contrary, on the same day on which Frederick-William rebuffed the delegation from Frankfurt the Prussian government dispatched a circular note to missions in Germany stating that in view of the fact that the imperial vicar John had decided to resign office, and that difficulties might accordingly arise, the Prussian king was prepared to take over the conduct of affairs. The German governments were invited to send plenipotentiaries to Frankfurt to discuss the form and constitution of a federal state under Prussian leadership. On the 8th April the Austrian government issued a tart rejoinder stating that the Austrian emperor had requested the imperial vicar to continue in his functions, and that Prussian intervention would therefore be superfluous. On the 15th May the Prussian king issued a proclamation justifying his refusal of the imperial crown, recalling his envoy from Frankfurt, and demanding that the imperial vicar should resign his office into Prussian hands; this the Archduke John refused to do. On the 26th May the Pact of the Three Kings created a new German bloc over against Austria; the kings were those of Prussia, Saxony, and Hanover.

The realities in the situation had at last penetrated to the surface. The liberal movement centred on Frankfurt, unable to draw support from either Prussia or Austria, collapsed ignominiously. Radical risings in Dresden and Baden were suppressed by Prussian troops. The Frankfurt parliament disintegrated, an emaciated but persistent remnant wandering off to Stuttgart. In the afternoon of the 18th June, 1849, the government of Württemberg posted troops round the assembly hall in Stuttgart and forbad the deputies to meet. That was the end. Thus the soldiery of Württemberg broke up the liberals with even greater ease than they had dispersed the radical following of the poet Herwegh. Just one week later the outstanding liberals in Germany, headed by Dahlmann, the brothers Gagern, Mathy, Simson, Grimm, and Von Vincke, came together in Gotha. There 130 signed a declaration stating that 'they rated the ends which should have been attained by the imperial constitution of the 28th March more highly than rigid adherence to the form in which this goal is sought'. That is, they rated imperial unification more highly than its acquisition in a liberal manner. Here, then, did the German liberals throw in their hand.

The foregoing events have been given in some detail since they constitute a decisive turning-point in German history. From them it appears that the liberal movement in Germany had to face great odds; and that thus early it succumbed to them. Hereafter liberal parties continued and even increased in Germany; but liberalism was not destined to flourish there henceforth. And now it appears how the theoretical and the practical jumped together. Just as the liberal outlook was swallowed up by the historical school of German thought, so were the liberal politicians engulfed in power-politics.

Sombre stretches lie ahead. It is first expedient to observe what Prussia did in the twenty years ensuing. This is the necessary basis for an estimate of the trends in the German outlook on society.

By the 'Interim' arrangement of September 1849 Austria and Prussia jointly took over central power in Germany. Schwarzenberg could not yet afford to enter into open conflict with Prussia. But next year he enjoyed his triumph. Austria placed a veto on Prussian armed intervention in

Hesse-Cassel and imposed upon her the humiliation of Olmütz. Earlier that year the diet of the old German Confederation had reassembled at Frankfurt, under Austrian presidency as before. It was here that Prussia mostly fought out her quarrels with Austria in the eighteen-fifties, and it was here that Otto von Bismarck served his diplomatic apprenticeship as Prussian representative. The two powers nagged at each other about the fortifications at Rastadt, about the federal German navy (which was put up for auction), about the Customs Union. The ill-feeling came to a head in 1859 when Prussia tried to make capital out of Austria's preoccupation in her war against Italy in order to place herself in supreme command of the armed forces of the German Confederation. This pressure was not a little responsible for Austria's precipitation in making peace.

Meanwhile reaction was clamped down in most German states. Since December 1848 Prussia had, indeed, a bicameral constitution, but its revision in an anti-liberal sense was among the chief preoccupations of the government in the following years. Its most signal achievement in this direction was the institution of the three-class system of voting for members of the second, nominally popular, chamber. By this system the primary electors were divided into three classes according to the amount paid in taxes. Each class elected the same number of secondary electors despite the fact that those in the third, poorest, class greatly outnumbered those in the first two. This system, together with publicity of polling, effectively secured the domination of the ruling classes.

In 1858 liberals hailed the dawn of the New Era in Prussia when the reactionary government was replaced by a moderate one consequent upon Prince William assuming the regency for the now decrepit king. In the following year the constitution of the German National Union under the patronage of the Duke of Coburg-Gotha, brother to the British prince-consort, signalled a revival of liberal nationalism throughout Germany. The object of the union was the promotion of German unity under Prussian leadership. It sought to further its cause by means of a series of patriotic festivals, gymnastic, musical and the like—a form of activity especially to the German liking.

It is significant that this movement coincided with the revival of Prussia's power-political manœuvres against Austria, which created a considerable impression. It was these harsher and deeper forces that were to mould coming events, both in Prussia and in Germany at large. In Prussia in that the regent's accession as King William I in 1861 soon showed the liberals that they had been as mistaken in counting upon his support as had their predecessors twenty years before in the case of Frederick-William IV. In December 1861 the elections to the Prussian chamber showed a substantial liberal majority. In March 1862 the composition of the Prussian government was altered in a conservative sense. The clash came, tellingly enough, over the army reforms which the king and Roon, the minister for war, were determined to push through in order to increase the efficiency of the formidable military machine. On the 23rd September, 1862, the second chamber rejected the proposed allocation for the military reforms. On the 24th September the king made Bismarck minister-president. Thus began the rule of this stark Brandenburger, the forty-seven-year-old Junker from Schönhausen, Prussian to the marrow, of fighting stock. For nearly a generation first Prussia, and then Prussian Germany, was to pursue the arduous path to greatness indicated by the commanding genius of this autocrat who had tried to engineer a Prussian counter-revolution in the early days of 1848. At that time his king had sized him up thus: 'Red reactionary; smells of blood; will be useful later.' This last prognostication was now verified. In September 1862 the king of Prussia found it useful to be able to call upon a man who was prepared to venture upon the undertaking of deliberately governing against the wishes of the majority of the representatives of the people of Prussia. For that was what Bismarck set out to do. The Period of Conflict had begun.

Next year the nature of the prevailing trend emerged in wider issues. Bismarck succeeded in isolating Prussia morally from the rest of Europe. While the other powers were protesting to the Russian government at their ruthless suppression of the Polish insurrection, Prussia supported Russia. A few months later Austria was on the move in Germany. Schmerling, who was an Austrian member of the federal German government of 1848 had had some little experience in intrigues with regard to hegemony in Germany, induced the Austrian emperor to summon a conference of all the German princes to consider measures for the reform of the German Confederation. With considerable difficulty Bismarck managed to persuade the Prussian king to absent himself from this conference which met at Frankfurt in August 1863. This absence successfully wrecked the conference and foiled the Austrian move. Bismarck, with bland cynicism in view of the then basis of his power in Prussia, countered with a Prussian plan which maintained that the reconstitution of Germany could only be based upon popular representation derived from the direct participation of the whole nation. The plan served its turn, and indeed Bismarck played his cards so well that he managed to estrange Austria from the other German states and bring about a Prusso-Austrian *rapprochement*. Bismarck's very practical purpose in promoting this friendship was soon evident.

In the winter of 1863 the Schleswig-Holstein question loomed up again as a result of the promulgation by the Danish king of a new constitution which bound those equivocally situated duchies more securely to the Danish state. The diet of the German Confederation supported Frederick of Augustenburg, the German claimant to the duchies, and sent a confederate force of Saxons and Hanoverians to occupy Holstein on his behalf. But Bismarck and Roon held quite other views. In November 1863 Roon thought that 'the question is altogether a question of power, not a question of right'. In December Bismarck warned the Prussian parliament that 'war breaks all treaties'. Next month a joint force of Prussians and Austrians was marching through the sullen confederate troops in Holstein on its way to the attack of Schleswig. The event symbolized the importance of the small states, of the confederation itself, in the face of the ruthless will to power of the true arbiters of the German destiny. And as in Germany so in Prussia itself.

The years from 1861 to 1865 are among the very few that do some credit to the forces of liberalism in Prussia, while at the same time revealing their impotence. The new progressist party (*Fortschrittspartei*), under the leadership of Virchow,

Forckenbeck, Hoverbeck, and Twesten, led the parliamentary opposition to the government, steadily refusing to compromise with it and to sanction its budgets. Bismarck and Roon went their way undismayed. On the 22nd January, 1864, Bismarck harked back to the despotism of Frederick-William I and told the Prussian Chamber:

'This *rocher de bronce* is still standing; it forms the basis of Prussian history, of Prussian glory, of the Prussia which has become a great power and a constitutional royalty. You will not succeed in shaking this rock of bronze either by your National Union, or by your motion of today [refusing credits for the Danish war], or by your liberum veto!'

And so the Danish war proceeded, planned by Helmuth Carl Bernhard von Moltke, the Prussian chief of staff who had first seen service in the Danish army, who made of modern warfare a very exact science, who thought that 'war is a factor in God's plan of the world. . . . Without war the world would sink into materialism'. Thanks to Moltke's army the Danes at least were saved from such degeneration. They steeled themselves to the bitter and unequal struggle. Their gallant resistance was finally crushed by greatly superior forces. In the subsequent negotiations Bismarck proved himself to be a man who felt no pity and showed no mercy. The robbers divided the booty, Austria taking over Holstein and Prussia Schleswig. The confederate German troops were constrained to withdraw; in Prussian eyes this was the prelude to the eviction of the Austrians themselves. For Bismarck, having used Austria as his dupe, was determined that the total profits of the enterprize should accrue to Prussia, and that Holstein not less than Schleswig should be added to her dominions.

In the face of this power-political success the liberals in Prussia began to waver. Even Max Duncker, hitherto a close associate of the Crown Prince who headed the liberals in high places, came round and gave his approval. In 1865 Twesten, one of Bismarck's bitterest opponents in the second chamber, refused to attend a congress of German deputies, saying that he did not wish to participate in resolutions directed against the development of Prussian power. Nor was the movement confined to Prussia. In the same year Von Treitschke, a

Saxon liberal who disapproved of Bismarck's unconstitutional rule in Prussia, wrote to a friend that

'in this matter [of Schleswig-Holstein] positive law is irreconcilable with the vital interests of our country. We must set aside positive law and compensate those who may be injured in consequence. This view may be erroneous; it is not immoral. Every step in historical progress is thus achieved. . . . Positive law when injurious to the common good must be swept away.'

The Saxon government, under the direction of the ambitious and agitating count Beust, was not so sure. Nor, indeed, was Austria herself. For she came to realize that Prussia had used her as a tool, and feeling was further heightened by the strained relations which existed between the administrations of the two duchies where the mild and benevolent Austrian rule contrasted sharply with the Prussian repression. Manteuffel, the Prussian governor of Schleswig, had indeed favoured at first a milder régime, but Bismarck had overridden his views and insisted that the unwilling population be subjected to Prussianism in all its rigour.

Things were coming to a head. Bismarck rejoiced at the fruition of his deep-laid plans. At a later period he admitted that 'ever since my arrival to power I have had the firm purpose of bringing Prussia to war with Austria, but I was careful not to talk to the king about it before the favourable moment appeared'. The favourable moment had now appeared. Bismarck talked about it to the king, and to the other ministers. They made their preparations accordingly. Both sides began to mobilize. On the 8th April, 1866, Prussia concluded an alliance with Italy against Austria. On the 9th April Prussia followed this up with an appeal to the diet of the confederation proposing popular federal reform. That was the next move in the game. At the beginning of June Prussian troops marched into Holstein and Austria in her turn appealed to the diet.

The 14th June, 1866, is an important date in Germany's history. That it is not very generally recognized as such is perhaps a reflection upon the general character of that history. On that day the Austrian representative at the diet of the German Confederation moved that the diet should order the mobilization of the confederate army in the face of

Prussian aggression. The states voted upon this proposal: Bavaria, Saxony, Hanover, Württemberg, Hesse-Darmstadt, Hesse-Cassel, Nassau, Frankfurt, down to Reuss, Lippe, and Waldeck. They knew what was at issue. They voted for the mobilization of the confederate army. The Prussian representative stated that his government considered the German Confederation to be dissolved. Thus began what was not only the final struggle between Prussia and Austria for German hegemony but also, as is sometimes forgotten, a great civil war in Germany. For this once the rest of Germany dared to withstand the Prussian will to dominate, though only as a result of Austria's pressure from the other side. Apart from some inconsiderable northern satellites Prussia was isolated. King William bitterly remarked: 'I have no ally but the duke of Mecklenberg and Mazzini.'

But if Prussia was alone, she was also strong. This war had been long envisaged by Bismarck, long prepared by the remote, industrious Moltke. It was their war. On the 16th June Prussia launched out simultaneously at Hanover, Hesse-Cassel, and Saxony, and overran them. Bavaria, Württemberg, and Baden were marked down next. On the 3rd July the Austrian forces were crushed at Sadowa. Prussia proceeded to mop up Germany. Her troops triumphed into Frankfurt-am-Main, Nuremberg, Darmstadt, Mannheim, and Heidelberg. She had won her lightning war. Prussia had conquered Germany.

By his use of the Prussian victory Bismarck proved his true statesmanship. Prussia was content with the elimination of Austria as a German power; she claimed no territory from Austria and acceded to her strong plea for the preservation of Saxon integrity. Prussia was content to swallow up the little ones, Hanover, Hesse-Cassel, Nassau, and Frankfurt, and to set herself at the head of the North German Confederation. It was nearly all head. The troops of all the members of the confederation were under Prussian command. The natural forces of attraction would do the rest. In order to make sure of the south German states Bismarck exploited designs of the security-seeking French who coveted German territory west of the Rhine. With unscrupulous skill he employed the new weapon of popular press-propaganda. German public opinion against France was whipped up most satisfactorily. In August and September 1866 Prussia successively concluded treaties with Württemberg, Baden, Bavaria, and Hesse-Darmstadt. They were accompanied by secret military alliances by which the command of the troops of the southern states was transferred to Prussia. Essentially there was only one military power left in Germany. That power was Prussia.

In the face of these splendid successes there was a general tendency among liberals to acknowledge the error of their former ways. In Hesse-Cassel Max Duncker appeared in the wake of the Prussian troops as civil commissar for the conquered territory. The parliamentary opposition crumpled up. The Prussian chamber voted an act of indemnity sanctioning the government's high-handed levies during the past four years. On this issue the liberals split, Forckenbeck and Lasker heading the new national-liberal party which was Bismarck's mainstay for years to come. Bismarck had not previously enjoyed the whole-hearted support of the conservatives themselves, particularly those who looked to the feudal austrophil camerilla in which Manteuffel and the Gerlachs figured prominently. But now conservatives, too, modified their attitude, and the new free-conservative party joined the national-liberals in their support of Bismarck's policy. This coalition meant that the conservatives fully accepted the ideal of national unification while the liberals agreed to forgo the reality of democracy, provided that some formal semblance of it was maintained; but it was threatened even in form. Prussian jurists were heard to maintain that their country was now so greatly aggrandized that the old, too liberal, constitution was no longer applicable.

In February 1867 the first North German parliament met. The dutiful national-liberals were there in force—Simson, former president of the Frankfurt parliament, Twesten, the old opponent, Lasker, the reformed progressist, Sybel, Duncker, Bennigsen, the conquered Hanoverian and president of the National Union. The victims of oppression in Hanover, Schleswig, and Poland tried to obtain some consideration. Bismarck said that he would not tolerate resistance; he would crush it. Nor was liberal conversion to power-politics confined to northern Germany. Liberal elements had always been particularly strong in Baden. Now under Roggenbach they clamoured for closer union with Prussia. Bismarck was at some pains to hold them off until the time was ripe. It was ripening.

Moltke and his general staff had reason to be satisfied with the achievement of the Prussian army in July 1866. It was a good beginning. In August the Prussian generals set to work to plan the war with the French. France was the chosen anvil upon which Prussia would at last beat out German unity. It took a little time to get things in train. But the danger of a Franco-Austrian alliance was obviated, and in the autumn of 1868 a vacancy of the Spanish throne was seized upon by Bismarck, who pushed the candidature of the house of Hohenzollern, a move which, if it succeeded, would signally promote Prussian interests while also constituting a direct menace to those of France. As an object in itself the candidature was unsuccessful owing, largely, to a judicious lack of enthusiasm on the part of the Hohenzollern princes concerned. But as an instrument of policy it more than justified Bismarck's efforts; in 1870 the unclever arrogance of French diplomacy in this matter gave him his wanted opportunity. He used it with the same unscrupulous eye to effective publicity that he had shown three years earlier. Bismarck's faithful minions Abeken and Keudell had recently received a recruit in the person of the learned philologist Busch, who supervised relations with the press. Articles inspired by Bismarck appeared in the *Kreuzzeitung*, the *Nationalzeitung*, the *Norddeutsche Allgemeine Zeitung*, and other leading papers. Copy was even sent to the British and Belgian press. Public opinion was being satisfactorily manufactured. The publication of the doctored Ems telegram roused the passion of all Germany against the French. Mobilization proceeded to the strains of *Die Wacht am Rhein*. On the 19th July, 1870, came the declaration of war. Prussia led; Germany marched.

And so from Berlin to Sedan. When Bismarck, standing on the hill-side overlooking the battle-field, first heard of the capitulation of the French emperor and of his imperial army he said to the crown prince of Württemberg, 'This day assures and strengthens the German princes and conservative principles'. Then on again from Sedan to Versailles, where in the month of October Bismarck set to work to draw the proper conclusions from the victory and his evaluation of it. Now at last it was time for Prussia, in the hour of her triumph, to press for the unification of Germany. The negotiations were arduous and complex. In November the southern states fell into line one by one. The princes of Baden, Hesse-Darmstadt, and Württemberg signed treaties of accession to the confederation. Only King Ludwig II of Bavaria held out, inaccessible in fastness of Hohenschwangau. This moody romantic kept the Prussian negotiators waiting on his whims. They tried to cajole him out of his lackadaisical aloofness, preparing a fine royal train to carry him in triumph to Versailles, promising him an idyllic residence at Fontainebleau or Trianon. Still he kept them waiting. When at last this unpractical Wittelsbach consented, he secured considerable practical concessions as his price. Bavaria alone among the German states secured the right of maintaining her own diplomatic representatives abroad and of retaining her army as a separate entity within the federal army, subject only to occasional federal inspection. And her self-assertive spirit was not yet exhausted.

In December 1870 Simson for the second time in his life headed a parliamentary delegation to invite the Prussian king to become emperor of Germany. Much had happened since that first time in 1849. But the German rulers had not greatly changed in outlook. The enthusiastic deputies from the parliament of the North German Confederation were met with sneering frigidity at Versailles. The parliamentarians were made to feel quite out of place in this town which the princes and generals occupied by right of conquest. For the second time in his life Simson was told by the king of Prussia that he could only accept the crown with the consent of all the German princes. But this time the only real difficulty on that score came from the king of Prussia himself. King William was Prussian to the core and regarded the title of emperor as an unsubstantial pomp which would detract from his cherished status as king of Prussia. To win him over it was necessary that his fellow rulers should press him. Bismarck at last managed to engineer an invitation from the King of Bavaria asking William to assume the imperial honour. But at the same time the Bavarian government insisted that the Prussian king should not become emperor of Germany, but only German emperor. William said that he would either be emperor of Germany or else no emperor at all. He became German emperor. Nor had the Bavarians finished yet. Long after the other German parliaments had ratified the treaties of unification that of Bavaria delayed its sanction. For three weeks after the unification Germany and Bavaria were separate states. For three days the German emperor had no legal authority over Bavaria. On the 21st January, 1871, the parliament at Munich finally sanctioned the incorporation of Bavaria into the German empire. The president cried 'By this decision the work of German unity is finished.' Technically it was so, but the true climax had come three days before.

On the 18th January, 1871, William of Prussia was crowned German emperor in the Hall of Mirrors at Versailles. Thus, far from the German people, surrounded by the German princes, in the midst of war, on conquered soil, the German emperor was proclaimed to the blare of trumpets. The princes, obedient now to the greater might of Prussia, were her stays in erecting the second German empire upon the ruins of the second French empire. Such was this apotheosis of force and the will to power. Such was the unity achieved by Prussia and acclaimed by the peoples of Germany.

The story of the unification of Germany forms an integral part of an estimate of the development of the German outlook on society, for it was in the course of this process that the bulk of German liberals sacrificed insistence upon the general tenets of liberalism to the achievement of national ends. These ends were achieved not by the liberals, but by stark Prussians who looked to might for their righteousness and gloried in the element of force. And it was with them that the future lay. But liberalism was not the only alien force with which power-political conservatism in Germany had had to reckon. In that country, as elsewhere on the continent, socialism was beginning to assume proportions which demanded recognition.

The effect of the prompt repression of the scattered radical risings in Germany in 1848 and 1849 was consolidated by the economic expansion of the eighteen-fifties and sixties. The mesh of the network of German railways became ever finer; in 1869 the total length of the German railway union, including the Austro-Hungarian railways, was more than six times what it had been in 1850. The output of the mining industry nearly quadrupled. The receipts of the Customs Union rose steadily. Big business and the manufacturers were getting into their stride. Industrial and technical associations multiplied. Meanwhile the flourishing co-operative movement and lending societies inaugurated by Schulze-Delitzsch considerably allayed the immediate hardships of the small artizans.

This enterprize of Schulze-Delitzsch, and more especially the opportunity of acquiring practical experience in administration and social co-operation which it offered to the workers, won the approval, in particular, of Karl Johann Rodbertus, who was a Prussian social theorist, prominent in his own day, much respected by later Germans, but little known outside his own country. Rodbertus did not extend his approvàl to the economic basis of Schulze-Delitzsch's movement, which seemed inadequate in the light of his own copious social schematism. This schematism was historical in inspiration. Rodbertus sought in the first place to disentangle the origins of the economic system of the ancient world. According to him these origins were to be found in the Oikos and the Polis. For Rodbertus the Oikos was the self-sufficient stead, ruled by the lord of the family and almost entirely self-supporting in raw materials and consumption-goods, a complete economic microcosm apart from restricted imports of goods such as iron and salt, the beginning of luxury. The spatial propinquity of a number of these steads formed the basis of the ancient state, the Polis, which constituted a linguistic, religious, and military whole. Thus Rodbertus arrived at his basic concept of the total community by way of early Greek economy just as Friedrich Schlegel had done by way of early Greek culture. For Rodbertus this first, ancient heathen, period developed by way of Roman caesarism into the second, Christian Germanic, period. The great economic distinction between the two was that whereas in the first private property extended even to individuals under the system of slavery, in the second it was confined to land and capital. Since the Reformation the feudal order of society had gradually disintegrated, offering free scope for individual exploitation: but at the same time the central power of kings and other national rulers had steadily increased. Rodbertus held that this dual development would issue in a second age of caesarism in which the rulers would steadily increase their personal power and their restrictions upon free economy. Just as the first caesarism had betokened the transition of the first period of social history to the second, so did the second caesarism imply the transition from the second period to the ideal third. In this third period land and capital would cease to be private property, being nationalized in the interests of all in a controlled communistic national economy which would organize the national production and would reward the individual in proportion to his participation in the work of the national whole. The ordering of the third period would thus be the realization of Rodbertus' thesis that profit, rent, and wages are all constituent parts of a national income produced by the united organic labour of the members of the community. The affinity between this economic theory and that of Adam Müller is at once apparent.

Since the second social period in the schematism of Rodbertus was predominantly Germanic it was only to be expected that the German nation would be foremost in pressing forward into the golden age of national communism. Rodbertus announced to his fellow countrymen:

'We shall simply strip off the outlived form of the state, but shall take over with us into the new form the Germanic nationality which will be correspondingly the more refreshed; but in this process of stripping the Roman [nationality] will have gone to ruin. So do not let us cling obstinately with our hearts to 'the goods that are life's fleeting adornment', e.g. to bad social foundations; but let us all the more cherish the ethical and spiritual national kernel so that it may successfully stand the shedding of its skin.'

Rodbertus thought that this spiritualization of transcendental Germanic nationality would be partially effected by a rejuvenation of Christianity.

Such a conception of the nation as being the supreme social totality naturally brought Rodbertus into conflict with all class struggles and aggressively proletarian movements. His opinion was that the workers could only look for amelioration of their lot from a 'general law of state-authority', which should be 'granted in the deepest peace with the assent of all other classes'. For him the ideal was the reconciliation of all classes within the national community that was both popular and authoritarian. The stress upon authority was a reflection of the importance of the rôle which Rodbertus assigned to the Caesars. According to him

'Caesars are far more the children than the initiators of their age. Therefore they will never fail their age even though they may appear but rarely. Rarely, because these ages themselves are rare since they only constitute the transition to new state-orderings. . . . And rarely because the union of such characteristics is rare; for wonderful insight and rock-firm character, genius and greatness must further be sustained by the passions of an egoism which accomplishes for its own advantage that which redounds only to the good of society. No selfless virtue crosses the Rubicon or carries out an 18th Brumaire. Hence mankind should congratulate itself upon the fact that the ages of the caesars come but seldom; but when they are come mankind will again congratulate itself at being able to throw itself into the arms of a man who combines such characteristics.'

Rodbertus thought that the two truly caesarian spirits of the nineteenth century, the 'two giants', were Napoleon and Bismarck. But he was afraid that the social question would prove to be Bismarck's Waterloo. This anxiety was reflected in his estimation of the Prussian achievement soon after the foundation of the second German Empire:

'The former deeds of William I only put him on a par with Henry I, Otto I, Frederick I. If the imperial word were pledged in the social question it would set him by the side of Caesar and Charlemagne. These men were not merely great warriors, victors and conquerors; they were at the same time the creators of new kinds of states, the founders of newer and higher historical stages of development. Roman caesarism has only been discredited by students who loved their Cicero, and then by the Napoleonic counterfeit; it was precisely under it [Roman caesarism] that the greatest social reforms were carried out. . . . Charlemagne is the founder of the whole Christian Germanic order of the state which lasted for an epoch in the history of the world in the same way as the ancient heathen order of the state did. But the "social question" is in turn the initial letter of a new and different kind oi political epoch and it is quite impossible to think of any inauguration that it would be more magnificent for the new German Empire to undertake than the start of its solution. It is, without blasphemy, once more a piece of Christianity that seeks incarnation in law.'

Rodbertus, curiously prim and old-fashioned on the one hand, strikingly modern on the other, was, as has been indicated, decidedly a revisionist as far as immediate socialist policy was concerned. His own prescription for the solution of the immediate social problem appears to have been regulation by the state of all wages by means of authoritative arbitration between employers and workers. Wages would be periodically increased according as production increased. In order to ensure stability he proposed that currency based upon precious metal of fluctuating value should be done away with as soon as possible and that there should be substituted a currency based on work-coupons in accordance with his standard of work-time. At the same time a fixed quota system for production would be introduced. It was by means of such an organized economy, often reminiscent of Fichte's ideas, that Rodbertus counted upon eliminating the periodic economic crises and the general measure of pauperism which lay at the heart of the immediate social problem. But for Rodbertus this was necessarily short-term planning. He believed that it would be five hundred years before the ethical force of the people would be sufficient to achieve his ideal of the truly national socialist community.

In the field of German socialism in the middle years of the nineteenth century there stood alongside of Rodbertus, leader of the academic *Kathedersozialisten* (professorial socialists), a second important figure who shared a number of ideas with him but was quite his reverse in character, being a fiery agitator and a gifted popular orator who exerted great influence upon the German masses and was bent upon whipping them up to decisive action within a period considerably shorter than that of five hundred years.

Ferdinand Lassalle was an ostentatious and opportunistic Jew from Breslau. He was a friend of Marx, now in exile in

London, and mainly from him did he derive his radical theories based upon the class-struggle. But if these two largely agreed in their economic and social outlook which heralded the coming victory of the proletariat, Lassalle differed from Marx in remaining true to their common master Hegel with regard to political forms and to his idealistic outlook. Lassalle accepted the revelation of the Hegelian state and regarded Frederick the Great as an estimable revolutionary; nor did he fall so completely under the spell of the materialism of Feuerbach and Marx as to allow it to destroy his belief in that idealistic dynamism which underlay the transcendentalism of earlier German thought. In the middle eighteen-fifties Lassalle, under the influence of Hegelian dialectic, made a study of the obscure and far from democratic Heraclitus, a thinker highly esteemed by many Germans. According to Lassalle

'The centre of the philosophy of Heraclitus . . . is, then, nothing other than the true concept of the becoming, the unity of existence and non-existence, this absolute antithesis. And indeed—a point which should not be overlooked—this unity [is] conceived not as something still, but as a process. For him this unity is flux, as being active movement in process, and struggle or reflux as being the unity of the precise antithesis.'

Along with Lassalle's reverence for Hegel and for Heraclitus as interpreted via Hegel went high respect for the other great master, Fichte, who had been the first German to outline a politico-economic order of a socialist, national-socialist, kind. In a speech which Lassalle made in honour of Fichte in May 1862 he spoke of 'those Addresses to the German Nation which constitute one of the mightiest monuments of fame which our people possesses, and which, in depth and power, far surpass everything of this sort which has been handed down to us from the literature of all time and peoples'. Some weeks before he had proclaimed Fichte to be 'one of the mightiest thinkers of all peoples and ages'. This was in an address entitled 'Concerning the particular Connection between the Present Period of History and the Idea of the Working Class' which Lassalle delivered in the Oranienburg suburb of Berlin on the 12th April, 1862. This address, with its typically academic title, subsequently became known as the *Workers' Program*, and marks the true beginning of German Socialism in the theoretical field just as Lassalle's constitution of the General German Workers Union in May 1863 marked its inception in the practical. As a result of this address Lassalle had to stand trial in Berlin for endangering the public peace. In his lengthy defence Lassalle made much of the fact that his political system was based upon the might of the state.

'I ascribe to the state', he said, 'the high and mighty task of developing the germ of humanity, as it has done since the beginning of history, and will do for all eternity; and as being the organ which is there for all, [I entrust] to its protecting hand the promotion of the human estate of all. This doctrine, gentlemen, is no theory of destruction and barbarism; it is in the highest degree a *state-doctrine.*'

He then went into a diatribe against 'the men of Manchester' who in their crassly capitalistic materialism sought to disrupt the state: the invective culminated in the assertion: 'I, together with you [the court], am defending the age-old vestal fire of civilization, the state, against those modern barbarians!' Lassalle was justified in adopting this line of defence. In the speech which had occasioned his trial he had told his audience that

'the *bourgeoisie* conceive the object of the state as lying solely and entirely in protecting the personal freedom of the individual and his property. This, gentlemen, is the idea of a mere watchman. . . . The state is a unity of individuals in a moral whole, a unity which increases a millionfold the powers of all the particular persons who are included in this union; this unity multiplies a millionfold the powers which would be at the disposal of them all as individuals.'

While exalting the state, Lassalle did not neglect the element of nationalism. In another place he said:

'This national spirit itself is, with reference to its content, nothing other than the urge towards an ever deeper and more intensive mastery of the real world through the subjectivity of the spirit, an urge which proceeds from the innermost basis of reality in thought [*Gedankengrundlage der Wirklichkeit*], an urge towards an ever more intimate reconciliation of the spirit and the real world, proceeding from the most fundamental theoretical comprehension of that antithesis.'

With Lassalle, as with the main run of German thinkers, stress upon the unity and greatness of the national state was naturally accompanied by corresponding emphasis upon the element of force. In a speech to the workers of Berlin he said: 'So now, gentlemen, we have seen what the constitution of a country is: namely the *relations of power* which obtain in a country.' It followed that 'what is written on a sheet of paper is a matter of complete indifference if it contradicts the real position of things, the actual power-relations'.

The similarity between Lassalle's view of political relations and that of the then Prussian government is obvious. Lassalle stressed it himself. In a speech entitled 'What Now?' which he delivered in November 1862 he pointed out that Roon had only been expressing his, Lassalle's, own views when, in a speech to the Prussian Chamber on the 12th September last, he had said that 'according to his concept of history the chief content of history, not only as between individual states but also within each state, was nothing other than the struggle between the separate factors for power and increase of power'. Lassalle went on to associate Bismarck also with this outlook. They both of them equated all relations in terms of power, and both were ambitious to stand forth as leaders of men. Lassalle, unlike Marx and Engels, made no criticism of Bismarck's support of Russia against the oppressed Poles, and was content with the reflection that 'Russia has only been able to hold her ground by force of arms; Germany has often succeeded in germanizing provinces which she originally conquered by force and in turning them into conquests of German culture'. Next year he strongly advocated Prussian conquest and incorporation of Schleswig-Holstein. But perhaps the most immediate bond between Lassalle and Bismarck was their joint hostility to, and contempt for, the liberals who during those few years were, as has been seen, making something of a stand against the doctrine of authoritarian force in politics. The liberals were not behindhand in stressing the significance of this conjunction. In January 1863, for instance, the *Volkszeitung*, a leading progressist organ, remarked that 'anybody who, in his over-excitement, snatches at so-called power-politics on behalf of popular representation is, whether knowingly or not, performing very valuable services for the [cause of the] reaction'. Indeed it was widely put about that Bismarck was merely the pupil of Lassalle. Lassalle was at pains to issue a public denial in which he argued that in his political theory he had only taken due account of existing circumstances, but that he had never held 'that might *should* be preferred to right': an answer which carries limited conviction. In the great oratorical tour of the Rhineland which Lassalle made in the autumn of 1863 he took the opportunity of counter-attacking against the liberals. In a speech which he made at Solingen on the 27th September he said: 'Even if we exchanged shots with Herr von Bismarck, justice would demand that, even during the salvoes, we should avow him to be a man; but they [the liberals] are—old women!' The meeting was broken up by the local mayor, who was a progressist liberal. Lassalle at once telegraphed to Bismarck lodging a protest and demanding satisfaction. It was the real beginning of an association between these two men, who met together for a series of discussions. They were ostensibly an incongruous pair: the hard, ruthless Junker and the florid, wordy Jew. But they talked the same language. Both were manœuvring for power, for the furtherance of their ambitious designs. Some months earlier Lassalle had written to the Jewish radical Moses Hess that the speech which he had prepared for this Rhenish tour was 'a war speech, conceived in the spirit of a general addressing his army, and awfully trenchant'. That was the kind of spirit which Bismarck understood and approved. He later said of his discussions with Lassalle: 'Our conversations lasted for hours, and I was always sorry when they were finished'; and of Lassalle himself: 'He had something about him which attracted me extraordinarily as a private individual: he was one of the cleverest and most amiable men with whom I have ever had anything to do—a man who was ambitious in a big way'.

The main topic of these discussions was universal suffrage; Bismarck was attracted by the idea of a popular uniform vote throughout Germany which would counteract the particularist tendencies of the *bourgeoisie* and guarantee uniform submission to Prussian rule. The tone of the discussions may perhaps be gathered from a note which Lassalle sent Bismarck in January 1864: 'Above all I blame myself for having forgotten yesterday to impress once more upon you that eligibility for suffrage must be conferred upon positively all Germans. An immense means of power! The real "moral" conquest of Germany'. Thus was popular suffrage reckoned up in terms of power and conquest. And now the leader of German socialism, no less than the leaders of German liberalism, fell under the spell of the Prussian monarchy. Next month Lassalle, who had some time ago broken with Marx and Engels, wrote to a friend:

'Republican [as I have been] since infancy, I have never found anything as ridiculous, corrupt, and in the long run impossible as constitutionalism. It is organic self-destruction. As I have said, I have been a republican since infancy. And yet, or perhaps just because of that, I have come to the conviction that nothing could have a greater future or a more beneficent rôle than the monarchy, if it could only make up its mind to become a social monarchy. In that case I would passionately bear its banner, and the constitutional theories would be quickly enough thrown into the lumber room.'

Respect for constitutional safeguards was the real point at issue between Lassalle and the liberals. Where this unconstitutional social monarchy led Lassalle is evident from a passage at the close of his great speech of the 22nd May, 1864, delivered at Ronsdorf near Elberfeld. There he told the workers: 'We must forge our wills together into a single hammer, and must lay this hammer in the hands of a man in whose intelligence, character, and goodwill we have the necessary confidence, in order that he may be able to strike with this hammer!'

Hardly more than three months later he was dead. First his work and political ideals, and then his life, had been sacrificed for love of his fair Helen.

Such was the beginning of German socialism. Lassalle's politics were power-politics, his socialism was national-socialism, his object was dictatorship.

And now the picture is all but complete. Just as liberalism in Germany was informed by the current and peculiarly German trend of thought and action, so also was socialism. That trend was authoritarian, power-political, and nationalistic. The very various political events and combinations tended ever more to reflect, each in its own way, that distinctively German outlook which derived so much from the historical school of thought. During the historic years from 1848 to 1871 this school largely focused its attention upon history itself. It was the great age of German history. Sybel, Droysen, Ranke, and Treitschke flourished, drawing lessons from the German past and applying them to the present in terms of Prussian greatness and Bismarckian policy. At the same time theorists were elaborating the accepted tenets: men like Roscher, who urged that each nation must enjoy an economic system peculiar to itself, and Von Rochau who, in his treatise *Grundzüge der Realpolitik*, developed the familiar thesis that the state is might.

But the most important single new element introduced into the German outlook on society during this period was a foreign-derived elaboration of certain of the tentative speculations of the German romantics. In 1859 Darwin published *The Origin of Species*. The doctrine of the survival of the fittest was peculiarly congenial to the German outlook with its stress upon the vigour of the folk in the power-political struggle, and it had indeed been partially adumbrated in earlier German writers. But earlier in the eighteen-fifties another foreign work had appeared which attracted much less immediate attention, but which was destined to exert a far-reaching influence in Germany.

In 1853-5 Arthur de Gobineau published his *Essai sur l'inégalité des races humaines*. In this treatise Count Gobineau, a bold thinker, gifted and original, expounded a doctrine that was the expression of a frigid and sustained despondency. This aristocratic French diplomat, ethnologist, poet, and sculptor felt in general only contempt and hatred for the age in which he lived, its works, leaders, and ideals; but he did not doubt that they were strong and would prevail; and so he nurtured his despair. The *Essai sur l'inégalité des races humaines* was its manifesto.

The pervading undertone of the essay may be rendered by the opening of one of Gobineau's own poems: 'To the desert, to the desert, the wise and the strong!' For him human nature is essentially evil. 'Man is pre-eminently the wicked animal.' Human nature is not only wicked, but also weak. 'Poor humanity! It has never succeeded in inventing a means of clothing everybody and preserving everybody from thirst and hunger.' It is not only weak, but degenerating. Gobineau was 'tempted to assign to the domination of man upon earth a total duration of twelve to fourteen thousand years, divided into two periods: one, which is past, would [according to this view be taken to] have seen, to have possessed the youth, vigour and intellectual greatness of the species; the other, which has begun, will perceive the debile progression towards decrepitude'. This decay was the more lamentable in that life for Gobineau was struggle. He thought that 'when life is not a battle it is nothing'.

Gobineau thought man degenerate, but strictly speaking man as such did not exist for him. He wrote: 'There is no ideal man; *man* does not exist. . . . I know the possessor of the Finnish tongue, of the Aryan system or of semitic combinations; but absolute *man*—I know him not.' Union of all men in a common humanity was ruled out by the fact that 'the history of mankind proves that the destinies of people are governed by a racial law'. Gobineau's system centred in the exposition of this racial law, which he thus focused in relation to his general outlook: 'In order clearly to appreciate the intellectual differences of races the first care should be to establish to what degree of stupidity humanity is capable of descending.'

Gobineau based his racial doctrine on the fact that 'history . . . shows us that all civilization flows from the white race, that none can exist without the co-operation of this race, and that a society is only great and brilliant in proportion as it preserves for a longer period the noble group which has created it'. He spoke correspondingly of 'haughty despotism, the only sufficient check upon black peoples'. The superior white civilization centres in Europe, and there is 'no true civilization among European nations in cases in which the Aryan branches have not dominated it'. The Aryan is to the ordinary white man what the white man is to the black. 'Thus placed upon a sort of pedestal, and detaching himself from the background against which he moves, the Aryan-German is a powerful creature. . . . Everything that this man thinks, everything that he says, everything that he does accordingly acquires a major importance.'

In accordance with this theory the break-up of the Roman Empire by the untamed German barbarians was of major benefit to civilization, a view which had been earlier adumbrated by Görres. It is perhaps worth giving Gobineau's account in some slight detail since, in substance and in temper, it was to become increasingly prevalent among the modern descendants of those barbarians. Gobineau exclaimed:

'What is there more ridiculous than this opinion, consecrated however, which attributes to the invasion of the barbarians of the North the ruin of civilization! These poor barbarians! . . . The barbarians were not able to stifle anything for the conclusive reason that talents, spirit, elegant customs—everything had long since disappeared. What was, physically and morally, a Roman of the third, fourth, and fifth centuries? A man of medium size, weak of constitution and in appearance, generally dark-tanned, having in his veins a little of the blood of every race imaginable; believing himself to be the first man of the universe, and, in order to prove it, insolent, servile, ignorant, thievish, depraved, ready to sell his sister, his daughter, his wife, his country and his master, and gifted with an unequalled fear of poverty, suffering, fatigue, and death. . . .

'Over against this contemptible being, what was the barbarian? A man with fair hair, with a pink and white complexion, broad-shouldered, tall of stature, vigorous as Alcides, bold as Theseus, adroit, supple, fearing nothing in the world, and death less than the rest. . . . He had, in his nationality, nourished his spirit with the sap of a severe and refined religion, of a sagacious policy, of a glorious history. . . . When the vain and wretched Roman opposed his roguery to the rival astuteness of the barbarian, what decided the victory? The fist of the second. Falling like a mass of iron upon the skull of the poor descendant of Remus this brawny fist taught him to which side the force had passed. He wept and cried in advance to future ages to avenge the civilization that was oppressed in his person. Poor worm! . . .

'The Roman lied, and those who in the modern world have amplified these exaggerations from hatred of our germanic origins and of their governmental consequences in the Middle Ages have not been more truthful.

'So far from destroying civilization the man of the North has saved the little of it that has managed to survive. . . . It is his intelligent care that has transmitted it to us. . . . Without him, we should be nothing.'

Together with Roman civilization Gobineau condemned one of its chief products, natural law. He spoke of 'natural law, the law of peoples, the *jus gentium*. But this potpourri of positive doctrines . . . contained nothing that is evidently just and true'. To sum up:

'All in all and without exaggerating anything, almost everything good known to imperial Rome issued from a Germanic source. . . . The Germanic peoples' entry into possession was the legitimate work of a favourable necessity. . . . At that time God, in order to save the Church and civilization, gave to the ancient world . . . nations of tutors. . . . There is nothing more glorious in the human annals than the rôle of the peoples of the North.'

But the grandeur of these Nordic barbarians had since sadly decayed. In their descendants there still lived on, indeed, the last remnants of true life, but their position was becoming steadily more precarious. Gobineau saw the modern world thus:

'In sum the greatest abundance of life, the most considerable agglomeration of forces, is to be found today concentrated, and struggling with disadvantage against the infallible triumph of the Roman confusion, in the series of territories enclosed by an ideal contour which, starting from Torneo, embraces Denmark and Hanover, descending the Rhine at a slight distance from its right bank as far as Basel, encloses Alsace and upper Lorraine, hugs the course of the Seine, follows it to its mouth, extends as far as Great Britain and rejoins Iceland on the west.

'In this centre subsist the last remnants of the Aryan element. . . . It is also there that the heart of society, and consequently of modern civilization, beats. This situation has never been analyzed, explained or understood up to the present; nevertheless it is vividly felt by the general intelligence.'

It will be noticed that only a slender portion of modern Germany was included in this ideal contour. But Gobineau had early sensed a peculiar affinity with modern Germany and with Prussia in particular, though this narrower sympathy was later somewhat modified by his close friendship with Count Prokesch-Osten, the Austrian president of the confederate diet in the eighteen-fifties and the prime antagonist of Bismarck. As early as 1843 Gobineau had written significantly that in Germany 'ancient things subsist without too much difficulty in the midst of the modern movement'.

This observation may perhaps be viewed in the light of another remark of Gobineau's to the effect that 'all civilizations that assume democratic forms are speedily ruined'. And he further embraced that cardinal tenet of German thought, folk-unity, holding that 'a people, taken collectively, is, in its numerous functions, a being that is as real as if one saw it condensed into a single body'.

The essay on the inequality of human races enjoyed small immediate success. It was almost as isolated in the then European climate of opinion as was its lonely author in the society of his time, an arrogant and bitter man, very polite, destined to be a rover like the Viking Ottar Jarl whom Gobineau was at such pains to claim for his ancestor; and destined to find men contemptible wherever he ranged, from Persia to Brazil where he cut a poignant figure, miserable among the dagoes and finding solace only in Sunday *tête-à-têtes* with the emperor Dom Pedro.

One of the few people in Gobineau's own country who took detailed notice of the essay was his sapient and historically minded friend Alexis de Tocqueville who, as foreign minister in 1849, had first set him upon his diplomatic career by making him his chief of cabinet. Shortly after the publication of the essay, in November 1853, de Tocqueville wrote to Gobineau: 'Don't you see that from your doctrine naturally arise all the evils of inequality, pride, violence, tyranny, contempt of one's neighbour, and slavery in every form?' It was in some sense the cry of European civilization against a man who hated it. Such protests could not affect his outlook. Later he wrote to de Tocqueville: 'You see, I am one of those who despise.' In 1857 de Tocqueville returned to the charge, maintaining that Gobineau's doctrine was incompatible with Christianity. Gobineau retorted that he was a good catholic. Some considerably later correspondence throws light upon Gobineau's religious belief which is not without its significance in the line of theory into which his racial doctrine was to be incorporated. The year after Germany had finally crushed the France of Napoleon III, a defeat which Gobineau had foreseen and thought well merited, he became French minister at Stockholm, where at last he felt almost at home. In September 1873 he wrote to his sister: 'It is the difficulty of resuming the cult of Odin that holds up everything [in Scandinavia]. What would you say if you learnt that I had raised myself to the dignity of high-priest of Odin, Thor and Frey?' This might perhaps be dismissed as a passing fancy. Next February he wrote to his sister: 'I shall always be counted among the catholics. . . . Do you know why? Because I hate this age, and I shall do the impossible in order not to be [in agreement] with it.' He regarded his age as free-thinking, and so he did the impossible and plumed himself on his catholicism to spite it. He hinted at his real belief, however, in the same letter, in which he said: 'fundamentally I am returning to the religion of our fathers.' Some months later he wrote with reference to the Christian Church: 'I believe in something else; I do not believe in that.'

Thus did Gobineau sunder himself in outlook from de Tocqueville, from France, from that civilization of which France was the mainstay. Instead he dwelt upon the German element and exalted it. In Germany he found recognition, though even there not widely at the start; but presently the stormy composer Richard Wagner, then at the height of his powers, acclaimed 'Gobineau, who returned home weary and knowledge-laden from far wanderings through the territories of the peoples'. Wagner only met Gobineau for the first time in 1876, but for more than ten years before that he had been expounding racial theory. For Wagner the touchstone was racial purity. According to him

'the so-called romantic peoples, and indeed also the English, are praised as mixed races inasmuch as in cultural progress they have patently got ahead of the peoples of Germanic races who have kept themselves nearly pure. Whoever does not allow himself to be dazzled by the appearance of this culture and civilization, but seeks the welfare of humanity in the production of great characters, must on the other hand find that it is rather, indeed almost only, these races that have kept themselves pure which make their appearance; whereby it appears that the still unbroken generic force of nature in the first place compensates for [the lack of] all of the higher human virtues, which have not yet sprouted and can only be won through the hard proof of life, by *pride*. This peculiar pride of stock, which in the Middle Ages still furnished us with such prominent characters in the way of princes, kings and emperors, is probably at the present time still to be met with in the genuinely noble breeds of Germanic descent, even it it be in unrecognizable degeneration; we should seek to take earnest account of this [degeneration] if we wish to explain the decay of the German folk which is now exposed without defence to the penetration of the Jews.'

This passage is the index of much. In the first place it at once illustrates the change in the climate of opinion which conditioned racial theory when it crossed the Rhine; what had been astringent became almost cloying; the aloof and pessimistic scorn of the Frenchman gave way to the subjective pleading of the German. The racial doctrine became a counterpoise to outbalance the inferiority of German culture and civilization; and it found its practical expression in anti-Semitism. Anti-Semitism was indeed largely traditional in Germany. Luther, Fichte, Stein, Görres, and Müller had all of them been hostile to the Jews. The Junker party headed by von der Marwitz, Arnim, and Kleist had, as has been noticed, first erected anti-Semitism into a political principle. The racial doctrine now furnished this prejudice with a pseudo-scientific basis.

Wagner was diligent in his warnings against the Jewish peril. In 1865 he wrote:

> 'The Jew . . . took over the German head-work; and we see to-day a disgusting caricature of the German spirit held before the German people as its supposed reflection. It is to be feared that in time the people will believe that it sees itself in this reflection: in that case one of the fairest outlays of the human race may perhaps be killed for ever.'

In an essay entitled *Modern* Wagner vented his feelings against the three main dislikes of his maturity, the Jews, the press, and democracy. He wrote:

> 'I do not scruple to describe the revolutions which have occurred in Germany since then [i.e. the French revolution of 1848] as quite un-German. "Democracy" is in Germany a thoroughly transplanted affair. It only exists in the "press". . . . But the disgusting thing is that this translated French-Jewish-German democracy could really draw support, colour and a deceptive investiture from the mistaken and injured German folk-spirit.'

He further expatiated upon the fact that 'the astonishing unsuccessfulness of the movement of 1848, which made such a noise, is easily explained by this curious circumstance: that the real genuine German so suddenly found himself and his name represented by a kind of man that was quite foreign to him'. It was convenient for the sage of Bayreuth to forget the revolutionary of Dresden who had turned out in the streets in support of the bands of Bakunin in the spring of 1849.

The un-German nature of democracy was for Wagner one aspect of the general fact that the true German should be as pure and idiosyncratic culturally as he was racially. He once gave a description of the true old German life which summed up much of what Germans felt and much of that which stirred them most deeply in his heady operas:

> 'In rugged forests, in the long winter, in the warmth of the fire upon the hearth of his castle-chamber towering aloft into the air he [the German] indulges long in the memories of his forefathers, he transmutes his home-bred myths of the gods in legends manifold and inexhaustible. He does not oppose the influences which press upon him from abroad. . . . He translates for himself Roman, Romance and French legends and books. . . . But he is not content to gaze at the foreign thing as such, as something purely foreign; rather will he understand it "germanly".'

The German must understand foreign culture 'germanly'.

In a mature essay entitled *Heldenthum und Christenthum* (*Heroism and Christianity*) Wagner summed up his racial belief and faced up to the question of its compatibility or otherwise with Christianity. He began by avowing that 'the picture—uncommonly thoroughly worked out—which count Gobineau, in his work *Essai sur l'inégalité des races humaines*, offers us of this course of the decay of the human races strikes us with terrifying power of conviction'. He proceeded to recapitulate Gobineau's theory at some length. According to him it was now necessary to seek out heroes who were struggling against the debasement of their stock and its morals in order once more to establish themselves as godlike heroes. These heroes were apparently to free themselves from the lies and false principles of existing culture and civilization, which had developed since man lost the nobility of his blood, and to recapture the true spirit of martyrdom which had been destroyed in Christianity by the Church. These men who had reformed themselves in the spirit of truth were, in the ultimate event, to look less to a strictly racial doctrine than to a purified and germanized Christianity. At the last, then, Wagner took refuge in a nebulous piece of romanticism which idealized a heroic German Christianity, avoiding the full consequences of the racial doctrine. Gobineau once wrote to Wagner's wife: 'I am more Germanic than he [Wagner] consents to be.' But later Germans were to go the whole way with Gobineau.

We have now seen how Prussia at last carved the way to German unity, and how this establishment of German greatness was the complement of previous theory, and how the process made of German liberalism and socialism curious creeds included in the national whole, and how, with Germany set upon the path of power and prosperity, her outlook began to take increasing notice of a doctrine which in the name of science offered to the German folk the palm of pre-eminence among the peoples of the world. Stirring practical success had made straight the steep ways designated by the code of historical thought. The road lay open now. It was time for a concerted advance along it, out over the threshold of the Second German Empire.

Chapter V

EMPIRE

1871–1918

'In this [second] German Empire only one of the former states, namely Prussia, has preserved her sovereignty. The German Emperor is at the same time king of Prussia. . . . In war the German Emperor is War Lord. The right of arms has been transferred to the Empire, and it is in the same hands as the state of Prussia. . . . We find in the imperial law, as an extreme remedy, "execution", a shining sword which has never yet been actually drawn, only rattled once or twice in its scabbard. Fortunately the sense of loyalty among the constituent parts of the Empire is so strong that this means has not yet been employed. But it is there; the rebellious state may, by means of an "execution", be compelled to obey the laws of the Empire. It is the Emperor, however, who performs this "execution"; and the Emperor is not likely to inflict it on the king of Prussia. . . . The whole Empire is based historically and politically on the fact that it is (as Emperor William once said to Bismarck) "an extended Prussia", that Prussia is the dominant factor, both in fact and in formula. What is our German imperial army? Unquestionably it is the Prussian army, which . . . was developed into a nation in arms, extending over the whole Empire. . . . Every Prussian must feel it to be quite right that the best political institutions should be extended to the rest of Germany; and every reasonable non-Prussian must find cause for rejoicing that Prussia has brought the name of Germany into honour once again. The conditions are such that the will of the Empire can in the last instance be nothing else than the will of the Prussian State.'

These words came from a Saxon. The enthusiasm of Heinrich von Treitschke[1] for the Prussian hegemony illustrates something of the emotional and intellectual sway which that state exercised over the rest of the German empire. It was

[1]In *Politik* (2nd ed., Leipzig, 1899–1900), vol. ii, pp. 343–6. Quoted: H. W. C. Davis, *The Political Thought of Heinrich von Treitschke* (London, 1914), p. 104 f.

largely this influence which made it possible for Prussia to quell any insubordination by merely rattling the shining sword in its scabbard. But the more substantial guarantees of supremacy were ample. The state of Prussia occupied an area which embraced more than three-fifths of the empire. Nearly all the coal and iron in Germany came from Prussia. In the Bundestag two-fifths of all the votes were Prussian and it was never difficult for that formidable state to bring pressure to bear on her smaller neighbours sufficient to secure a Prussian majority. The Prussian prime minister was always chancellor of the German empire and in the ordinary way the Prussian Staatsministerium came to a decision on all laws before they were submitted to the Bundestag and the Reichstag.

After 1871 Prussia was thus, as Treitschke proclaimed, the dominant factor in Germany both in fact and in formula. But it was not enough. Treitschke set out to secure Prussian domination of German thought. He preached Prussianism to the youth of Germany, summing up the tradition of historical thought and restating it for the benefit of the second empire.

Heinrich von Treitschke was born in Dresden in 1834, the son of a distinguished Saxon officer. He was a keen scholar and passed from university to university. While he was at Leipzig he published, in 1861, his first considerable work, *Die Freiheit*, which was a critique of John Stuart Mill's *Essay on Liberty*. The subject accorded with Treitschke's then liberal outlook. But it was already evident that his liberalism differed sharply from that of Mill. Treitschke laid his stress upon the national state, attacking cosmopolitanism and holding that 'the thought of the fatherland brings us warning and guidance in the midst of our most private affairs'. It has already been noticed that in the years after 1848 liberalism in Germany largely meant the struggle for German unity, the exertions of Prussia. Treitschke was no exception. In the year after the publication of *Die Freiheit* he wrote an essay entitled *Das deutsche Ordensland Preussen* (*Prussia, the German Land of Order*). This vindication of Prussia and of her rôle in German history is an early illustration of the way in which history and political theory went hand in hand with Treitschke. This was but natural in view of his youthful enthusiasm for the teachings of historical theorists like Roscher the economist and Rochau who foretold that Germany could only be united by one state forcefully coercing the others. The other cardinal influence upon Treitschke's early thought was Machiavelli. Of him he wrote:

'Machiavelli sacrifices right and virtue to a great idea, the might and unity of his people. . . . This underlying thought of the book, its glowing patriotism, and the conviction that the most oppressive despotism must be welcome if it ensures might and unity for his mother country—these are ideas which have reconciled men to the numerous reprehensible and lawless theories of the great Florentine.'

The previous notice of Treitschke as a liberal who approved Bismarck's assault upon Denmark and ruthless conquest of Schleswig-Holstein now fits into place. While those doings were afoot Treitschke wrote to a friend that he would be happy if in his grey old age he saw a Prussian Germany. But under Bismarck's impulsion events moved faster than that. Just ten years later, in 1874, Treitschke became professor of history at the university of Berlin, three years after his election as a deputy to the Reichstag of the German empire. He remained in Berlin till his death in 1896. The two main products of this mature period were the *Deutsche Geschichte im . . Jahrhundert* and the *Politik*. This latter work comprised the substance of the lectures on politics which Treitschke delivered annually to large and eager audiences.

The *Politik* opened with the assertion that 'political science is applied history'; and Treitschke followed the earlier historical theorists in stressing the resultant opposition to the concept of natural law. For him 'the proper study of political science, such as was perhaps contemplated by Bluntschli, is still hampered by the consequences of the old doctrine of natural right'. It was necessary to delve back behind the period which respected this doctrine, for 'just as art and science recovered truth and greatness by digging in the youth-springs of classical antiquity, we too at the present day must abandon the standpoint of modern society in order to understand, as antiquity understood it, the importance and sublimity of the state'. Thinkers like Schelling and Niebuhr had already called attention to this antique understanding, and in particular to the estimable propensity of the ancients for identifying religion with the state. Treitschke indeed did not go that far, holding that the authority of the state should be subject to the creed of christianity. But where his veneration for the state tended to lead him in matters of religion is evident from his opinion that

'without community of religion the consciousness of national unity is impossible, for religious feeling is one of the primitive instincts of human nature. It was Jewish presumption which first undermined this truth when by a conjuring trick it displaced religion by denomination. Denominational differences may, of course, be tolerated by a great nation, though not without considerable difficulty. . . . On the other hand the co-existence within one nation of several religions involving totally opposed conceptions of the universe becomes unendurable for any length of time, and can only occur in a state of transition.'

Here was reflected the perennial concern of German thinkers over the fact that the religious life of Germany was split by the two great creeds of catholicism and protestantism. For Treitschke such a division might indeed occur in a purely legal state since this was only a transitional form in state-development which culminated in the truly cultural state. In the legal state unity was achieved by and in the common law; but the cultural state achieved the greater unity implied in the common ideology of a 'moral community'. This higher national unity of the cultural state did not, however, bring with it social uniformity. On the contrary, 'there can be no culture without its servants. It is self-evident that if there were no men to perform the menial tasks of life, it would be impossible for the higher culture to exist. We come then to realize that millions toil at the plough, the forge, and the carpenter's bench in order that a few thousands may be students or painters or poets'.

It would be incorrect to deduce from the above that Treitschke thought that the highest function of the state was to nurture a few beings of sensibility in the interests of higher culture. On the contrary, the state has a harsh way with it. 'The state declares: "It is quite indifferent to me what your feelings may be in the matter, but obey you must." That is the reason why fragile natures find it so difficult to understand political life.' In other words, the state is power and 'the theory of power, in which the first and highest obligation is to push forward with one's purpose completely and unconditionally, is a hard one'. Since 'the state is power . . . it is normal and reasonable that a great nation should, by its physical force, embody and perfect this power in a well-organized army'. In particular the power of the state is perfected in its army, in that it is by fighting for the state that the individual is most completely engulfed by it. According to Treitschke 'the individual must forget the claims of his own ego, and feel himself a member of the whole; he must recognize how trifling is his life compared with the welfare of the state. In that consists the grandeur of war, that trivial things are entirely lost sight of in the great idea of the state . But periods of peace are necessary in order to prepare for war. Treitschke taught that 'it is not necessary for an army to be always fighting; the silent work of preparation is continued in time of peace'. It was, however, hardly probable that such periods of peace would be very lasting, since 'to reproach a state for having a too irritable sense of honour is to fail to appreciate the moral laws of politics'; which meant that in practice 'if the flag of the state is insulted it is the duty of the state to demand satisfaction, and, if satisfaction is not forthcoming, to declare war, however trivial the occasion may appear; for the state must strain every nerve to preserve for itself that respect which it enjoys in the state-system'. The triviality of the occasion for war was of relatively small consequence since war was a good in itself. Treitschke affirmed that 'over and over again has it been proved that it is only in war that a people becomes in very deed a people'. So much so that 'any one with a knowledge of history realizes that to expel war from the universe would be to mutilate human freedom'. In fact 'war must be conceived as an institution ordained of God'. Treitschke realized that war brought horrors with it, but for him they only lent lustre to its glory. He wrote:

'Just where, to the superficial observer, war appears as something brutal and inhuman, we have learnt to discern its moral force. That, for the sake of the fatherland, men should stifle their natural human feelings, that they should murder one another, men who have done each other no wrong, who perhaps even respect one another as gallant enemies—at first sight this seems the revolting side of war; and yet herein consists its grandeur. A man must sacrifice not only his life, but also the profoundly just and natural impulses of the human soul. He must renounce his whole ego for the sake of the great patriotic idea. Therein lies the moral sublimity of war.'

War, then, is a very splendid Moloch; to it man must sacrifice not only his life, but also the profoundly just and natural impulses of the human soul.

Any attempt to deny war to Germans would be especial folly. Treitschke remarked that 'those who propound the foolish notion of a universal peace show their ignorance of the international life of the Aryan race. The Aryan nations are above all things brave'; brave, though indeed not necessarily supreme since Treitschke did not abide by any rigid racial doctrine. Still, the antipathy of the brave Aryans to any kind of ordered international society coincided most happily with the requirements of the omnipotent state; for 'the establishment of an international court of arbitration as a permanent institution is incompatible with the nature of the state'.

If the Germans were not positively supreme as a nation they were at any rate splendid in their intellectual isolation. Treitschke had already written in *Die Freiheit*:

'We Germans acquiesce in Paris fashions; we are bound to neighbouring nations by a thousand interests; yet our feelings and ideas are undoubtedly at the present day more independent of the intellectual world of the French and the British than they were seven hundred years ago.'

Since that was written Germany had further beaten France in war and had made her pay the price. In August 1870, even before the battle of Sedan, Treitschke was voicing the imperious demands of his nation. He asked:

'who, in the face of this our duty to secure the peace of the world, still dares to raise the objection that the people of Alsace and Lorraine have no wish to belong to Germany? Before the sacred obligation of these great days the theory of the right to self-government of every branch of the German race—the seductive battlecry of expatriated demagogues—will be ignominiously routed. These provinces are ours by right of the sword; and we will rule them in virtue of a higher right, in virtue of the right of the German nation to prevent the permanent estrangement from the German empire of her lost children.'

But defeated France never galled Treitschke in the way that Great Britain did. Treitschke held up the English people as an object of contempt and hatred; they were peace-loving and religiously minded, a decadent nation. As he put it:

'Cowardice and sensuality take shelter behind that unctuous theological rhetoric which, to us free German heretics, is the most repulsive of all the defects of the English character. We seem to hear the reverend snuffle when we see the English press turn up pious eyes full of indignation against the unchristian and warlike nations of the continent. . . . Oh, hypocrisy! Oh, cant, cant, cant!'

Furthermore

'the unchivalrousness of the English character, contrasting so remarkably with the simple loyalty of the German, is connected with the fact that in England physical culture is sought not in the exercise of noble arms, but in sports like boxing, swimming, and rowing, sports which have undoubtedly their value, but which obviously tend to encourage a brutal and purely athletic point of view, and the single and superficial ambition of getting a first prize.'

At the same time Treitschke did not condemn all English actions indiscriminately. For instance he recalled how

'at the time of the Indian Mutiny the English bound Hindus in front of the mouths of their cannon and blew them to pieces so that their bodies were scattered to the four winds of heaven, and, as death was instantaneous, we cannot blame the English for doing so. The necessity of employing means of intimidation is obvious in a case like this.'

But if this method of promoting British imperialism won Treitschke's approval the British Empire itself did the reverse. Here, indeed, we may perhaps trace the true source of his dislike of the English. He confessed: 'We realize now what we have missed. The results of the last half-century have been appalling; it was during this period that England conquered the world.' But he hoped that Germany would, as far as possible, recoup herself upon the continent of Europe. In order to facilitate this operation he sounded the call to internal unity, proclaiming that

'the horizon of German politics becomes freer and wider from year to year; if the nation once feels that the vital interests of the German state already extend into the Slav, the Scandinavian, and the Romance countries, that we are in the midst of the greatest and sternest revolution of the century, then our parties too will learn to rise above the disputatiousness of faction, above the pettiness of a doctrinaire programme to a great, strenuous and positive conduct of the affairs of the state.'

A number of Germany's immediate neighbours on the continent were small, weak states, contemptible as such. For example, 'Belgium is neutral; it is by its nature an emasculated state'. The way to deal with inferior peoples was simple. For Treitschke 'each dragoon who knocks a Croat on the head does far more for the German cause than the finest political brain that ever wielded a trenchant pen'. This was merely the practical corollary of Treitschke's belief that 'physical force is especially important in times like ours'. Similarly his opinion of small nations was the outcome of his conviction that 'the sin of weakness in politics is the sin against the Holy Ghost'.

Treitschke realized that not everybody could happily embrace his teaching. While still young he had written:

> 'Let us be grateful . . . to all those strong one-sided natures, who willingly sacrifice breadth of culture for a thousandfold gain in strength and depth. These men ask imperiously for either hate or love. Though their understanding be finally closed against many of the great blessings of humanity, their character is none the less harmonious, for it shows an exquisite adjustment between strength and ambition. How high they tower above those detestable mediocrities, who are becoming so terribly numerous at the present day.'

The strong narrow men were the men to promote the greatness of the state which is power.

The success of the lectures in which Treitschke expounded these ideas was enormous. For some twenty years the youth of Germany swarmed to hear this exposition of politics which in many respects accorded so closely to the traditional German outlook as to win ready acceptance while in others it betokened a new self-confidence and tough purpose which was calculated to inspire fresh enthusiasm. Treitschke spoke with the voice of the second empire. But when he began to lecture in Berlin the empire was still young. Bismarck realized the fact, and for twenty years his astringent realism curbed, in foreign policy at least, excesses of youthful vigour which might prejudice the most effective deployment of gathered strength when the time was ripe.

In 1872 Prince Frederick-William of Prussia said of Germany's international relations: 'We are not liked by anybody.' Bismarck knew that a young nation breasting its way as a lusty stalwart into the inner ring of the great powers was likely to receive the reverse of hearty welcome. And geographically Germany was set in the midst of great powers. So Bismarck bent his foreign policy towards exorcising the nightmare of coalitions against Germany. In the year of Prince Frederick-William's morose confession the Entente of the Three Emperors revived in some sort the grouping of Germany, Austria, and Russia which had distinguished the years after 1815. But even with such support Germany could not presume too far, as Bismarck found in 1875 when a 'moral coalition' of Europe headed by Russia prevented Germany from satisfying the wishes of its general staff and completing the good work of 1871 by attacking France again. Germany was steering a difficult course. The Entente of the Three Emperors did not last. Nevertheless Bismarck managed to maintain the balance all round. The dual alliance of 1879 between Germany and Austria was expanded three years later to include Italy, while, until the close of the Bismarckian era in 1890, Germany pursued her policy of reinsurance with Russia on the side in an uneasy effort to consolidate her international position and to derive the maximum benefit from that international tension that was the very condition of Bismarck's policy of peace in a divided Europe.

Bismarck's wary handling of foreign policy was offset by his imperious conduct of home affairs. The conditions of party-life in Germany at the inception of the empire have already been noticed. Power lay with the imperial chancellor, and he was resolved to use it to the full in order to weld the empire to firmer unity. His two most notable campaigns were both directed against elements whose foreign affiliations might weaken the all-important state-authority.

The declaration of papal infallibility in 1870 immediately preceded a revival of catholic political activity in Germany based on the centre party under the leadership of the Hanoverian Windthorst. Bismarck was not slow to define his position in the face of this development. The Prussian government supported the so-called old catholics who refused to recognize papal infallibility, and under the banner of culture it went out to fight the Catholic Church. The Lutheran confession was already identified with the state; but the catholic looked to supernational authority; the *Kulturkampf* was the necessary consequence. By a series of decrees culminating in the May Laws of 1873 and the further measures of 1875 Prussia sought to destroy or weaken catholic control over education, marriage, charities, clerical appointments and discipline, substituting that of the state. Resistance was chastised. The Catholic Church in Prussia was hard put to it. Bishop Martin of Paderborn fled to England; Archbishop Ledochowski of Posen, Bishops Eberhard of Trier, Melchers of Cologne, Brinckmann of Münster, and many others were evicted. By 1875 more than a thousand religious offices lay vacant. But Bismarck found in the Catholic Church an adversary whose resource and determination were a match for his own. The strife was allowed to subside and reconciliation was gradually achieved. This was the more desired by the chancellor since he was now embarking upon his second campaign against another body which also seemed to him to constitute a menace to the order of the state. Bismarck saw this other chief danger in the social-democratic party.

After Lassalle's death his docile pupil Schweitzer, together with Hasenclever, Hasselmann, and others, managed on the whole to develop the socialist movement on the nationalist lines laid down by its founder. In August 1869 the social-democratic party (S.P.D.) was constituted at Eisenach and put forward a programme of which the chief demands were universal suffrage, direct legislation through the people, controlled working-hours, abolition of indirect taxation, and state support for co-operative societies. But a split within the party was early apparent. Bebel and Liebknecht led the opposition against Schweitzer and his followers. They agitated for a more specifically communist and international programme. At the party-congress held at Gotha in 1875 this faction won the day. In the elections of 1877 rather more than 9 per cent. of the valid votes went to the social-democrats. The Prussian authorities had already been active against these undesirables and now Bismarck decided that it was time to act on a wider scale. Two attempts against the life of the emperor in 1878 provided the excuse for the regression of the socialists. The Reichstag passed a law banning societies which by social-democratic, socialist, or communist activity sought to overthrow the existing state and social order; meetings, pamphlets, and the collection of funds for such ends became illegal. Within a year 244 societies, 184 periodicals and 307 other publications had been suppressed. The law was renewed in 1880, in 1884, in 1888. The social-democrats were forced into underground agitation and to hold their conferences abroad. The anti-socialist laws were supported by the national-liberals. Meanwhile during the eighteen-eighties workmen's insurance against sickness and accident was introduced with the object of appeasing the populace with benefits bestowed from above. Thus did the German empire under Bismarck affirm its determination to maintain the authority of the state over against any tentative efforts to modify it on behalf of its humbler citizens.

These were the actions of a power-state, relished by Treitschke and the many who thought with him. But at the same time as Treitschke was affirming the splendour of power another thinker was doing likewise, though in a manner which gained him as little immediate popularity as Treitschke had won much. In time, however, he too won recognition and acclaim.

On the birthday of the king of Prussia, in 1844, a son had been born to the pastor of Röcken, a little village crouched upon the pool-strewn plains of Prussian Saxony. In joy he was named after the king. As a lad Friedrich Wilhelm Nietzsche hoped to follow in the clerical tradition of his family. Like so many other great Germans he endured the hard schooling at Pforta. Thence he pursued the same course as Treitschke, going first to Bonn and then to Leipzig. It was at Leipzig that this young man with the nervous voice, youthful despite his drooping moustaches, first met and paid homage to Wagner, then at the height of his reputation. It was a brave time for a German to be young in. Nietzsche thought that the Prussian conquest of Germany in 1866 was 'assuredly by no means moral, but, for him who contemplates it, sufficiently edifying and beautiful'. He said that he read Bismarck's speeches 'as though I were drinking strong wine'. (He retained his admiration of Bismarck to the last.) Nietzsche joined the Prussian artillery in 1867, but he fell from a horse, so that when the army went into action three years later he could only follow behind in a medical unit. But it is said that the sight of some crack German troops rushing up to the front largely inspired him with the basic principle of his future outlook.

Thus the beginnings of the second empire had an appreciable influence upon Nietzsche's youth, and yet much in that empire was quite alien to him so that he came to speak of 'that German grossness and thickness which, since the "Empire", goes growing and growing'. And if he did not think much of the empire few of its early citizens cared greatly for him. Thus the estrangement grew until finally Nietzsche delivered this judgement: in Germany

'a man must first and foremost be "German", he must belong to "*the* race"; then only can he pass judgment upon all values and lack of values in history—then only can he establish them. To be German is in itself an argument, *Deutschland, Deutschland über alles* is a principle; the Germans stand for the "moral order of the universe in history".... There is such a thing as the writing of history according to the lights of imperial Germany; there is, I fear, anti-Semitic history—there is also history written with an eye to the court, and Herr von Treitschke is not ashamed of himself.... I feel inclined, I even feel it my duty, to tell the Germans for once in a way all that they have on their conscience. Every great crime against culture for the last four centuries lies upon their conscience.... And always for the same reason, always owing to their bottomless cowardice in the face of reality, which is also cowardice in the face of truth; always owing to the love of falsehood which has become almost instinctive in them—in short, "idealism" '[1]

Nietzsche thought correspondingly that 'in the history of knowledge, Germans are represented only by doubtful names, they have been able to produce only *unconscious* swindlers (this word applies to Fichte, Schelling, Schopenhauer, Hegel and Schleiermacher, just as well as to Kant and Leibniz)'.

A man with such opinions must evidently stand somewhat apart from the main school of German historical thought. Indeed Nietzsche asserted that 'the Germans are a dangerous people: they are experts at inventing intoxicants. Gothic, rococo, ... the historical sense and exoticism, Hegel, Richard

Wagner'. These were more or less mature judgements, but in one of his earliest works Nietzsche had already taken up his position over against the historical school and its prime protagonist, holding that Hegel

'implanted in the generations whom he had thoroughly leavened that admiration of the power of history which practically veers round every moment into sheer admiration of success, and leads to divine worship of the actual. . . . He, however, who has learned to bend the knee and bow the head before "the power of history", at last nods "Yea" in mechanical Chinese fashion to every power, no matter whether it be government, public opinion, or a majority, and dances exactly to the measure which any power thrums on the strings. If every success contains in itself a rational necessity, if every event is the triumph of logic, or of the "idea"—then, just down on the knees at once and let the whole series of successes be adored!'

Overbeck, a friend of Nietzsche's, tried to secure Treitschke's interest in this early critique of historicism. Treitschke answered: 'How unlucky for you that you met this Nietzsche, this madman, who tells us so much about his inactual thoughts, and who has nevertheless been bitten to the marrow by the most actual of all vices, the *folie des grandeurs*.'

Treitschke's opinion is understandable since Nietzsche when young followed Wagner in his admiration of Schopenhauer, who was the opponent of Hegel, holding that for a philosopher history might stop at Herodotus and that the state was no guarantor of morality. But Schopenhauer mainly influenced Nietzsche, like others, by the precedence which he accorded to instinct over the intellect, his stress on the supremacy of the will, and his antichristian pessimism. For him

'inward discord is the very law of human nature, so long as a man lives. . . . Each must be a human being: that is, must be an unhappy creature, a fighter, a gladiator on the arena of life. Painless the battle of life cannot be: it may not end without bloodshed and in any case man must mourn. . . . *Haec est vivendi conditio*.'

Schopenhauer thought human nature pitiable and was pessimistic accordingly. Nietzsche thought human nature positively evil, but for him this was precisely a cause for optimism: 'the nature of man is *evil*, and this guarantees his *strength*!' This was joyful, since according to him the end of all human endeavour is not happiness, not virtue, not the good life, but power, power pre-eminent: 'only where there is life there is will; not however, will to life,—but—such is my teaching—will to power!' Thus was Schopenhauer's will to life transcended by the Nietzschean will to power. Elsewhere he asked 'would you have a name for my world? A solution of all your riddles? . . . *This world is the will to power —and nothing else*!' Nietzsche held that this natural and fundamentally right instinct for power had been robbed of its vigour by contemptible people who had erected their timidity into a code of morality. In this respect the Christians were the chief offenders. So Nietzsche went out against this costive creed which 'sided with everything weak, low and botched'. He maintained that 'one does well to put on gloves when reading the New Testament; the proximity of so much impurity almost compels one to do so. . . . There are only bad instincts in the New Testament'. Though he did allow one exception, remarking that 'in the whole of the New Testament only a *single* figure appears which demands our respect —Pilate the Roman governor. To take a Jewish affair seriously—he could not be persuaded to do so! A Jew more or less, what does it matter?' He closed with the affirmation: 'I call Christianity the one great curse, the one enormous and innermost perversion. . . . I call it the one immortal blemish of mankind.'

Nietzsche's breach with Wagner largely turned upon the latter's defection from the strict consequences of his racial theory and his championship of a germanized Christianity in Parsifal. Nietzsche once wrote: 'I frankly confess that I had hoped that by means of [Wagner's] art the Germans would become thoroughly disgusted with *decaying Christianity*—I regarded German mythology as a solvent, as a means of accustoming people to polytheism.' For Nietzsche Christianity was anathema because it promoted what he called a slave-morality; as he saw it 'the desire for *liberty*, the instinct for happiness, and the refinements of the feeling of freedom belong . . . necessarily to the domain of slave-morale and slave-morality'.

Nietzsche proclaimed a new code designed to destroy this slave-morality and to release the pent energies of the will to power. He harped upon the necessity of what he called the transvaluation of all values, the penetration beyond morality, beyond good and evil which were merely arbitrary standards serving the self-interest of conventional moralists. For Nietzsche 'morality is in itself a form of immorality', 'morality is the idiosyncrasy of decadents', 'morality must be shot at'. And he proceeded to shoot at it with boyish gusto.

In the new ethic all absolute values vanished: 'Our values are *interpreted into the heart* of things. Is there, then, any *sense* in the absolute? . . . All sense is will to power (all real senses may be identified with it).' All value is one, since 'value is the highest amount of power that a man can assimilate—a man, not mankind!' Accordingly truth itself is done away with. 'A strong temptation fights within us; the strongest, perhaps, that exists—the temptation of truth. . . . Truth? . . . I must repudiate this proud word. . . . We do not even want it—we shall be quite able to achieve our victory of power without its help.' Truth must go since ' "the will to truth"—is the impotence of the will to create'. From this Nietzsche drew the implication that 'a great man . . . would rather lie than tell the truth, because lying requires more spirit and *will*. There is a loneliness within his heart which neither praise nor blame can reach, because he is his own judge from whom there is no appeal'. The cultivation of the power-willing individual was Nietzsche's ideal; as he put it, 'not mankind, but *superman* is the goal'. This superman was conceived of in the light of Nietzsche's conviction that 'we are probably the first who understand what a *pagan faith* is . . .: to be compelled to value all higher existence as *immoral* existence'. For him this was indeed merely a reflection of actual fact since 'in *great men* we find the specific qualities of life in their highest manifestation: injustice, falsehood, exploitation. But inasmuch as their effect has always been *overwhelming*, their essential nature has often been most thoroughly misunderstood, and interpreted as goodness. The type of such an interpreter would be Carlyle': which puts Carlyle and his hero-worship in their place.

Nietzsche's supermen were to be the disciples of his creation, Zarathustra, of whose maxims the following are typical:

'This new table, my brethren, I put up for you: *Become hard*!'

'A man of enlightenment must be able not only to love his enemies, but to hate his friends.'

'Man must be trained for war, and woman for the relaxation of the warrior; all else is folly.'

'Ye should love peace as a means to new war; and the short peace more than the long. I do not exhort you to work, but to fight.'

'Ye say that a good cause will even sanctify war! I tell you, it is a good war that sanctifies every cause!'

It followed that 'the weak and defective are to go to the wall (the first principle of *our* charity). And we are to help them thereto. What is more injurious than any crime? Practical sympathy for the weak and defective—Christianity'. Might is right: 'the right of others is the concession of our feeling of power to their feeling of power. When our power is obviously broken down and quite impaired, our rights cease; on the other hand, when our power has greatly increased, the rights of others, as we have hitherto conceded them, are no longer binding upon us.' No rights for the weak, nor any pity. For it was laid down tersely that 'a man loses power when he pities'. Nietzsche identified his new code with the cult of Dionysus and wrote: 'Dionysus versus "Christ"; here you have the contrast.' And again: 'Dionysus: sensuality and cruelty.'

Nietzsche did not look forward to the appearances of isolated supermen here and there, but to a whole race of them. He wrote: 'My philosophy aims at a new *order of rank*: not at an individualistic morality.' He did not think this new order very likely to evolve of itself. On the contrary, he confessed that

'a certain question constantly recurs to us; it is perhaps a seductive and evil question: may it be whispered into the ears of those who have a right to such doubtful problems—those strong souls of today whose dominion over themselves is unswerving: is it not high time, now that the type "gregarious animal" is developing ever more and more in Europe, to set about rearing, thoroughly, artificially, and consciously, an opposite type, and to attempt to establish the latter's virtues? And would not the democratic movement itself find for the first time a sort of goal, salvation, and justification, if someone appeared who availed himself of it—so that at last, beside its new and sublime product, slavery (for this must be the end of European democracy) that higher species of ruling of Caesarian spirits might also be produced, which would stand upon it, hold to it, and would elevate themselves through it? This new race would climb aloft to new and hitherto impossible things, to a broader vision, and to its task on earth.'

These 'lords of the earth' were to behave in accordance with Nietzsche's opinion that

'the essential thing in a good aristocracy is *not* to regard itself as a function of either royalty or the community, but as the *significance* and highest justification thereof; it must acquiesce, accordingly, with a good conscience in the sacrifice of a legion of individuals, who, *for the sake of it*, have to be suppressed and reduced to incomplete men, to slaves and tools. Its fundamental belief must really be that society is *not* entitled to exist for its own sake, but only as a substructure and scaffolding, by means of which a select race of beings may elevate themselves to their higher duties, and, in general, to a higher *existence*.'

Nietzsche's views on the social structure bring one to his views on the state. But before considering this cardinal concept of German political thought it may be well to observe more closely how Nietzsche stood in relation to the main tradition of that thought. It is evident that the excesses of the cult of Dionysus were alien from that tradition, but that on the other hand Nietzsche's stress upon aristocracy, power and war were very germane to it. And in a number of more detailed respects Nietzsche was much more closely affiliated to the body-general of German thought than is sometimes supposed.

Nietzsche was an optimist, heralding the age of cruelty and holding that 'at the time when mankind was not yet ashamed of its cruelty life in the world was much brighter than it is nowadays when there are pessimists'. But he was only opposed to what he called the pessimisms of sensitiveness, doubt, and the will that is free. Ultimately his optimism resolved itself into the highest, pure form of pessimism:

'let us halt for a moment before this symptom of *highest* culture,—I call it the *pessimism of strength*. Man no longer requires a "justification of evil"; justification is precisely what he abhors: he enjoys evil, *pur, cru*; he regards purposeless evil as the most interesting kind of evil. . . . He now delights in a cosmic disorder without God, a world of accident, to the essence of which terror, ambiguity, and seductiveness belong. In a state of this sort it is precisely *goodness* which requires to be justified—that is to say, it must either have an evil and a dangerous basis, or else it must contain a vast amount of stupidity: *in which case it still pleases*.'

Besides which 'there is no such thing as the right to live, the right to work or the right to be happy: in this respect man is no different from the meanest worm'.

Nietzsche, then, denied not only goodness but happiness too. In this latter respect he was but the latest of a long line of German and germanized thinkers who deliberately rejected happiness: Kant, Holderlin and most of the romantics, Schleiermacher, Hegel, Schopenhauer, and Gobineau. Here German thought stands out in full contrast to that of the west. The theory of natural law had greatly stressed the goal of happiness in society, and its nineteenth-century projection, Benthamite utilitarianism, made a slogan of the greatest happiness of the greatest number.

The German school, with its antidemocratic bias, tended to see the finest example of sublime unhappiness in the lonely purposeful ruler of men who forewent all personal enjoyment in dedication to his high task: which was fitting in a country that looked back to Frederick the Great, who had cultivated the legend of his being, and perhaps in some degree was, a delicate artist-nature schooling himself to kingship and steeling himself to war in set renunciation of life's happiness.

Nietzsche often derided Hegel. But Nietzsche's superman might be not unfairly regarded as being in some sort an elaboration of Hegel's world-historical individual. For if the state was the form in which the Hegelian world-spirit found expression the means of it was the world-historical individual. Hegel remarked that

'if we further cast a glance upon the fate of these world-historical individuals who had the vocation to be the managers of the world-spirit, it is apparent that it has been no happy one. They did not arrive at quiet enjoyment, their whole life was work and toil, their whole nature was only their passion. . . . This shameful comfort, that the historical human beings have not been what one calls happy—a condition that is only possible in private life—this comfort can be drawn from history by those who need it.'

And furthermore

'a world-historical individual is not so jejune as to wish this and that and to take many things into consideration, but he is related quite ruthlessly to the One End. Thus it is also the case that they treat other great, indeed sacred, interests in a frivolous manner, which conduct is certainly subject to moral blame. But such a great form must trample underfoot many a guiltless flower, must destroy much in its way.'

Such as dared to champion the cause of morality against the ruthless world-historical individual only provoked Hegel's contempt. He considered that such historical persons

'are great men just because they have willed and accomplished something great, not indeed something imagined and presumed, but something that is just and necessary. This point of view also excludes the so-called psychological view which, as the best servant of envy, manages to refer all actions to the heart and to give them a subjective form in such a way that those performing them [are shown to] have done everything from some great or small passion, from a *mania*, and, on account of these passions and manias, to have been immoral men. Alexander of Macedonia conquered part of Greece and then Asia; accordingly [by this view] he had a mania for conquest. His actions were inspired by mania for glory, mania for conquest; and the proof that he was impelled by them lies in the fact that he did something which brought him glory. What schoolmaster has not demonstrated of Alexander the Great and Julius Caesar that these men were impelled by such passions, and were therefore immoral men? Whence it promptly follows that he, the schoolmaster, is a more admirable man than they because he does not possess such passions, and he gives as proof the fact that he does not conquer Asia, does not defeat Darius and Porus, but, to be sure, lives and lets live.'

Nietzsche's conception of the highest type of ruthless individual was thus not completely alien from that of Hegel; nor was his appreciation of the high function of the military state. Nietzsche thought that 'the future of German culture rests with the sons of the Prussian officers', and furthermore that

'the maintenance of the military state is the last means of adhering to the great tradition of the past; or, where it has been lost, to revive it. By means of it the superior or strong type of man is preserved, and all institutions and ideas which perpetrate enmity and order of rank in states, such as national feeling, protective tariffs, etc., etc., may on that account seem justified.'

In one of his notebooks Nietzsche jotted down the following succinct formula: 'The most favourable impediments and remedies against modernity. And first: (1) *Obligatory military service*, with genuine wars which put an end to all lightness of mind. (2) *National narrowness* which simplifies and concentrates.'

This chimed well enough with the main line of political thought in Germany as far as it went. But for many Germans the ideal state was now beginning to take shape as a more or less racial state. Nietzsche was properly speaking no racialist. Indeed he laid it down as a 'maxim: To associate with no man who takes any part in the mendacious race-swindle'. He had small use for Jews, maintaining that 'it was in fact with the Jews that the revolt of the slaves begins in the sphere of morals'; but Nietzsche was not an anti-Semite and he despised Wagner for being one, though recognizing that he was a typical German in this respect: Nietzsche once remarked that he had never met a single German who was well disposed towards the Jews. But if Nietzsche was not actually a racialist he wrote a good deal that was highly acceptable to those who were. He observed for instance that 'in the Latin *malus* (which I place side by side with *μέλας*) the vulgar man can be distinguished as the black-haired ("*hic niger est*"), as the pre-Aryan inhabitants of the Italian soil, whose complexion formed the clearest feature of distinction from the dominant blonds, namely, the Aryan conquering race'. And he went on to ask:

'Who can guarantee that modern democracy, still more modern anarchy, and indeed that tendency to the "Commune" . . . which is now common to all the socialists in Europe, does not in its real essence signify a monstrous inversion—and that the conquering and *master* race—the Aryan race, is not also becoming inferior physiologically?'

What this decline implied may perhaps be gathered from another remark to the effect that

'at the bottom of all distinguished races the beast of prey is not to be mistaken, the magnificent *blond beast*, roaming wantonly in search of prey and victory. It requires from time to time the discharge of this hidden source of its nature, the animal must again show itself, it must again go back into the wilderness. . . . It is the aristocratic races who have left the idea "barbarian" in all tracks in which they have marched.'

What Nietzsche mainly had in mind when talking of the magnificent blond beast appears from his observation that 'the profound, icy mistrust which the German provokes as soon as he arrives at power—even at the present time—is always still an aftermath of that inextinguishable horror with which for whole centuries Europe has regarded the wrath of the blond Teuton beast'. And Nietzsche looked forward to the revival of such barbarism, holding that 'a dominant race can only have terrible and violent origins. Problem: where are the *barbarians* of the twentieth century? Evidently they will only be able to appear and to impose themselves after huge socialistic crises'. He ventured to prophesy that

'there are now going to appear:

<table>
<tr><td rowspan="3">New barbarians</td><td>Cynics</td><td rowspan="3">The union of intellectual superiority and of an overflow of strength.'</td></tr>
<tr><td>Experimentalists</td></tr>
<tr><td>Conquerors</td></tr>
</table>

These new barbarians were presumably imagined as the products of Nietzsche's opinion as to

'*the means by which a strong species maintains itself:*—It grants itself the right of exceptional actions, as a test of the power of self-control and of freedom. It abandons itself to states in which a man is not allowed to be anything else than a barbarian. . . . Casuistry is carried to its highest pitch in regard to points of honour.'

This new barbaric aristocracy was to be racial, since according to Nietzsche

'the only nobility is that of birth and blood. (I do not refer here to the prefix "Lord" and *L'almanac de Gotha*: this is a parenthesis for donkeys.) Wherever people speak of the "aristocracy of intellect", reasons are generally not lacking for concealing something; it is known to be a password among ambitious Jews. Intellect alone does not ennoble; on the contrary, something is always needed to *ennoble intellect*—What then is needed?—Blood.'

Nietzsche's concept of race largely dictated his view of marriage. He thought that 'marriage, as understood by the old nobility, meant the breeding forth of the race—that is to say, the maintenance of a fixed definite type of ruler, for which object husband and wife were sacrificed'. This opinion conditioned his ideas

'about the future of marriage. . . . Privileges of all sorts for fathers who lavish boys upon the world. . . . A medical certificate as a condition of any marriage, endorsed by the parochial authorities, in which a series of questions addressed to the parties and the medical officers must be answered ("family histories"). . . . *Another commandment of philanthropy.* There are cases where to have a child would be a crime—for example, for chronic invalids and extreme neurasthenics. . . . The Mosaic law, "Thou shalt do no murder," is a piece of ingenuous puerility compared with the earnestness of this forbidding of life to decadents. . . . The latter must at all costs be *eliminated.*'

He went on to talk of castration, closing with the dictum: 'Compassion for decadents, equal rights for the physiologically botched—this would be the very pinnacle of immorality.'

Nietzsche realized that the German historical school, though it did not agree with him in everything, was in fact his forerunner and collaborator in the good work of promoting the n w race. For him

'the aim should be to prepare a *transvaluation of values* for a particularly strong kind of man . . . and, to this end, slowly and cautiously to liberate in him a whole host of slandered instincts hitherto kept in check: whoever meditates about this problem belongs to us, the free spirits. . . . To this order, it seems to me, belong, above all, the pessimists of Europe. . . . We should include in this group [of free spirits] all those critics and historians by whom the discovery of the Old World, which has begun so happily—this was the work of the *new* Columbus, of German intellect—will be courageously *continued* (for we still stand in the very first stages of this conquest). For in the Old World, as a matter of fact, a different and more domineering morality ruled than that of today. . . . Primeval forest creatures, the *Romans.*'

Nietzsche appreciated the history of the historical school more than its theory. Its theory was largely bound up with metaphysical speculation, whereas Nietzsche once said of his own philosophy: 'an anti-metaphysical view of the world—yes, but an artistic one'. In some sense, then, he was but the latest of the great German romantics, his main concern being not the good, but the beautiful, the beauty of power. He was an aesthete who proclaimed himself a moralist. And like the German romantics of the classical age Nietzsche was in general sympathetic to the historical school in so far as this was compatible with his individuality, which was of too high a calibre to allow the formulae of historicism to cramp his emotional style. Yet when Nietzsche did indulge in metaphysics he embraced the extreme of transcendentalism with a vigour which would have done credit to Fichte himself. Nietzsche thought that

'the foul blemish on Kant's criticism has at last become visible even to the coarsest eyes: Kant has no right to his distinction "*appearance*" and "*thing-in-itself*". . . . There is no such thing as a "fact-in-itself", *for a meaning must always be given to it before it can become a fact*. . . . In short the essence of a thing is really only an *opinion* about that "thing". . . . One may not ask: "*Who* interprets them?" for the act of interpreting *itself*, as a form of the will to power, manifests itself (not as "being", but as *process*, as *becoming*) as a passion. The origin of things is wholly the work of the idealizing, thinking, willing, and feeling subject.'

Here, then, did the will to power merge with Fichte's subjectivism and extreme egotism. And, as was logical, it did so in Nietzsche himself. The literary output of this lonely pensionnaire culminated in the autobiographical *Ecce Homo*. The chapter-headings are of interest: 'Why I am so wise', 'Why I am so clever', 'Why I write such excellent books', 'Why I am a fatality'. The third of these included blurbs for all his own books. For instance *The Twilight of the Idols* is described as 'altogether an exception among books: there is no work more rich in substance, more independent, more upsetting—more wicked'. As for *Thus Spake Zarathustra*—'before Zarathustra there was no wisdom, no probing of the soul, no art of speech. . . . Such things have never been written, never been felt, never been *suffered*: only a God, only Dionysus suffers in this way'. And in general

'no one has ever existed who has more novel, more strange, and purposely created art-forms to fling to the winds. The fact that such things were possible in the German language still awaited proof; formerly I myself would have denied most emphatically that it was possible. . . . The art of grand rhythm, of grand style in periods for expressing the tremendous fluctuations of sublime and superhuman passion was first discovered by me: with the dithyramb entitled "The Seven Seals", which constitutes the last discourse of the third part of *Zarathustra*, I soared miles above all that which heretofore has been called poetry.'

So self-conscious an ego is a very jealous thing. Nietzsche could not shake it off at night. He got no sleep. Drugs could not take him out of himself, until at last he knowingly took them in such quantity that they drove him out of his mind.

On the second or third of January 1889 Nietzsche went mad. A few days later his friend Overbeck found him in his humble furnished lodgings at Turin, ploughing the piano with his elbow, singing and shrieking in demented self-glorification.

It was a logical conclusion. For ruthlessness is a lonely thing, and if the void be filled by egotism, perfected and expanding within itself, then come megalomania, paranoia, insanity. Less logical was the fact that Nietzsche's friends and admirers allowed him to linger on as an imbecile for some ten years. Such was the end of the man who had written that

'the sick man is a parasite of society. In certain cases it is indecent to go on living. To continue to vegetate in a state of cowardly dependence upon doctors and special treatments once the meaning of life, the right to life, has been lost, ought to be regarded with the greatest contempt by society. . . . One should die proudly when it is no longer possible to live proudly.'

It was, however, during those last years in which Nietzsche was without his reason that Germans first really began to venerate the crudities of that immature philosopher. And at the same time as Nietzsche's ideas about the new race of superior men were first coming into their own, popular attention in Germany was increasingly fixed upon that more orthodox racialism which proclaimed the virtues of biological superiority. A certain Schemann succeeded Wagner as the chief German apostle of Gobineau's theory which he set out to popularize; in 1893 he founded the Gobineau Society. And the movement derived fresh impetus from Paul Anton de Lagarde, *alias* Bötticher, by profession a rather unsuccessful orientalist and biblical scholar, by inclination a conservative anti-Semite: he advocated a greater Germany whose racially pure inhabitants should embrace Christianity in a revised form which would correspond to the true being of the German folk. But the most influential exponent of racialism in the German empire was, like Gobineau, a foreigner and, like both Gobineau and Nietzsche, affiliated to Wagner's circle; indeed he became Wagner's son-in-law.

Houston Stewart Chamberlain was born at Southsea in 1855, the son of an admiral. His education was mainly foreign; in particular he studied a curious medley of subjects at Geneva—botany, geology, astronomy, and anatomy.

Thence he went to Germany; there he stayed, admiring Wagner, absorbing Germanism. The main fruit of this experience was published at the turn of the century under the title of *Grundzüge des XIXten Jahrhunderts* (*Foundations of the Nineteenth Century*).

Chamberlain himself described his general approach to his subject, asking:

> 'What is the good of "objective" phrases? . . . When it is a question of the dearest possessions of the heart I prefer, like the Teutons, to dash naked into battle with the sentiment that God has given me, rather than to march to the field adorned with the artificial armour of a science which proves nothing.'

And for Chamberlain the *Foundations of the Nineteenth Century* was a question of the dearest possessions of the heart, since it concerned the greatness of the Germanic race. The application of this peculiar method of approach to the central problem of race is seen in a passage in which Chamberlain asked:

> 'What is the use of detailed scientific investigations as to whether there are distinguishable races, whether race has a worth, how this is possible, and so on? We turn the tables and say: it is evident that there are such races: it is a fact of direct experience that the quality of the race is of vital importance.'

This in no way prevented the author from remarking four pages later: 'I think that we now have all the material that is necessary for a systematic analysis of our knowledge regarding race, from which we may then derive the cardinal principles of a conscious and appropriate judgement.' This conscious and appropriate judgement centred upon the principle of racial purity. According to Chamberlain

> 'horses and dogs give us every chance of observing that the intellectual gifts go hand in hand with the physical; this is specially true of the moral qualities: a mongrel is frequently very clever, but never reliable; morally he is always a weed. Continual promiscuity between two pre-eminent animal races leads without exception to the destruction of the pre-eminent characteristics of both. [Here a note refers to Darwin's *Plants and Animals under Domestication* and to his dictum: "Free crossing obliterates characters"—a favourite with Chamberlain.] Why should the human race form an exception? A father of the Church might imagine that it does, but is it becoming in a renowned natural investigator to throw the weight of his great influence into the scales of medieval ignorance and superstition?'

Thus summarily did Chamberlain dispose of the initial religious problem which had caused Gobineau and Wagner so much thought. If the racial theory was incompatible with Christianity it was further hostile to humanity itself. According to Chamberlain 'the notion "humanity" is, to begin with, no more than a linguistic makeshift. . . . I admit that the notion of humanity can acquire a positive purport, but only on condition that the separated race-individualities are taken as a foundation upon which to build.' Furthermore the concept of race itself must be narrowed so as to approximate to the nation. For Chamberlain

'the conception of race has nothing in it unless we take it in the narrowest and not in the widest sense: if we follow the usual custom and use the word to denote far remote hypothetical races, it ends by becoming little more than a colourless synonym for "mankind". . . . Here we begin to understand what nation signifies for race. It is almost always the nation, as a political structure, that creates the conditions for the formation of race or at least leads to the highest and most individual activities of race.'

Thus Chamberlain, working down or, for him, up from humanity to race to the nation, arrived at the Germanic folk-nation. He proclaimed that 'the races of mankind are markedly different in the nature and also in the extent of their gifts, and the Germanic races belong to the most highly gifted group, the group usually termed Aryan.' He followed Gobineau, to whom he acknowledged himself indebted, in exalting the Teutonic overthrow of the Roman empire. For him 'there is no doubt about it! The raceless and nationless chaos of the late Roman Empire was a pernicious and fatal condition, a sin against nature. Only one ray of light shone over that degenerate world. It came from the north. *Ex septentrione lux!*' 'The capture of the western Roman empire by the barbarians . . . works like the commandment of the Bible, "Let there be light"'. And he did better than Gobineau by claiming the renaissance also as a Teutonic event. He was certain that

'all those who from the sixth century onwards appear as genuine shapers of the destinies of mankind, whether as builders of states or as discoverers of new thoughts and of original art, belong to the Teutonic race. . . . The great Italians of the *rinascimento* were all born either in the north saturated with Lombardic, Gothic and

Frankish blood, or in the extreme Germano-Hellenic south. . . . From the moment the Teuton awakes the new world begins to open out.'

The great merit of the Germanic peoples was that by means of race they nationalized the state. Chamberlain wrote that

'the annihilation of that [Roman] monstrosity, the state without a nation, of that empty form, of that soulless congeries of humanity, that union of mongrels bound together only by a community of taxes and superstitions, not by a common origin and a common heartbeat, of that crime against the race of mankind which we have summed up in the world folk-chaos—that does not mean the falling darkness of night, but the salvation of a great inheritance from unworthy hands, the dawn of a new day. Yet even today we have not yet succeeded in purging our blood of all the poisons of that chaos. In wide domains the chaos ended by retaining the upper hand. Wherever the Teuton did not come forward in sufficient numbers to dominate the rest of the inhabitants physically, as, for instance, in the south, there the chaotic element asserted itself more and more.'

The mission of the Teuton, then, was to dominate physically. Chamberlain did indeed realize that it might be held that the Teuton had not fully accomplished his mission even in Germany itself. But he easily brushed aside such trifles, remarking that

'Renan shows how many Slavs have united with the Teutonic peoples, and asks somewhat sneeringly whether we have any right to call the Germans of today "Teutonic": well, we need not quarrel about names in such a case—what the Germans are today Renan has been able to learn in the year 1870; he has been taught it, too, by the German specialists, to whose industry he owes nine-tenths of his knowledge. That is the valuable result of the creation of race by nation-building.'

In the introduction to his book Chamberlain wrote with truth: 'I have . . . vigorously attacked whatever is unteutonic.' This attack naturally included warning as to the Jewish age and the Jewish peril. Chamberlain thought that

'thousands of side-branches [of the pure Jewish race] are cut off and employed to infect the Indo-Europeans with Jewish blood. If that were to go on for a few centuries there would be in Europe only one single people of pure race, that of the Jews; all the rest would be a herd of pseudo-hebraic mestizos, a people beyond all doubt degenerate physically, mentally and morally.'

But Chamberlain was not a conventional anti-Semite; he even censured 'the perfectly ridiculous and revolting tendency to make the Jew the general scapegoat for all the vices of our time. In reality the "Jewish peril" lies much deeper.' He admired the Jews for their racial consistency and held that Judaism was not evil in itself, but only quite alien to the great Germanic people. And since the good and interests of the Germanic people were paramount, those of the Jews must yield to them. In his desire to oust the Jews he even went so far as to entitle the eighth section of the third chapter of the first division of the first part of his work 'Christ not a Jew', though, typically enough, the text did not fully bear out the heading; but whatever Christ may have been, Chamberlain perceived well enough that the oecumenical Christian Church was a stumbling-block in the way of the supremacy of the Aryan race. As he saw it, 'from the ninth century to the nineteenth . . . it has been the same story. In the final instance the intellectual renaissance is the work of race in opposition to the raceless universal church, the work of Germanic thirst for knowledge, and Germanic national urge towards freedom'. But Chamberlain did not minimize the rôle of religion. On the contrary, it was among his chief preoccupations. He extolled German mysticism, holding that 'every mystic is, whether he will or not, a born antisemite'. In particular he revered 'the great Jacob Böhme', the 'dreamer of feeling'. But he was uncertain how far such mysticism might be able to provide a serviceable religion and he confessed that 'in the want of a true religion that has sprung from, and is compatible with, our own individuality, I see the greatest danger for the future of the Teuton. . . . A race so profoundly and inwardly religious [as the Teutons] is unknown to history. . . . The German stands apart and waits for a god to descend once more from heaven'.

But if Chamberlain was unable to say very much about this new tribal god, he was more specific with regard to the tribal hero, maintaining that 'just as important as a clear comprehension of the organic relation of race to nation is that of the organic relation of race to its quintessence, the hero or genius', which he explained as follows:

'Nothing is so convincing as the consciousness of the possession of "race". The man who belongs to a distinct, pure race never loses the sense of it. The guardian angel of his lineage is ever at his side. . . . Race lifts a man above himself: it endows him with extraordinary—I might almost say supernatural—powers, so entirely does it distinguish him from the individual who springs from a chaotic jumble of peoples . . .: and should this man of pure origin be perchance gifted above his fellows, then the fact of race strengthens and elevates him on every hand, and he becomes a genius towering over the rest of mankind, not because he has been thrown upon the earth like a flaming meteor by a freak of nature, but because he soars heavenward like some strong and stately tree nourished by thousands and thousands of roots—no solitary individual, but the living sum of untold souls striving for the same goal.'

Perhaps the racial genius soaring heavenward met the new god descending thence.

This prophet of the racial hero won ample recognition from the man who beheld in himself the heroic leader of the German nation. *The Foundations of the Nineteenth Century* was published in 1899, at the height of the Wilhelminian era. The age of the emperor William II was as distinct from that of Bismarck as Chamberlain's book was from Treitschke's *Politik*; and in something of the same way. In both cases the tough realism of the earlier period was superseded by grandiose pretensions.

For a century the throne of Prussia had been alternately filled by limited, unspectacular, very Prussian rulers, and by the more complex and less stable devotees of a more or less extravagant idealism. Frederick-William III and William I belonged to the former line; Frederick-William II, Frederick-William IV, and William II to the latter. William II was imbued with the magnificence of his destiny; for him it was a high thing to be an imperial autocrat, and higher and more anxious still to be ruler and warlord of the great German people, leading it towards the accomplishment of its age-old cultural mission in the world. Under him Germany would recapture her medieval splendour. These vaulting ambitions were pursued by William with authoritative vacillation and imaginative incapacity.

The emperor soon recognized a kindred spirit in the author of the *Foundations of the Nineteenth Century*. They met at Libenburg in East Prussia and again at the New Palace in Potsdam; there Chamberlain asked leave to express his thanks to the emperor in writing. He did not stint ink, paper, or enthusiasm. The massive epistle, written in November 1901, informed William that

'Your Majesty and your subjects have been born in a holy shrine. . . . I look back upon my past with terror. For though I had what must be called a happy childhood, there could be no true joy for me outside Germanism, and I tremble when I think how late I came in touch with the German language, and that to learn it was by no means easy. It is my innermost conviction—gained through years of study, gained in those solemn hours when the soul wrestles for knowledge with the Divine, like Jacob with the Angel—that the moral and spiritual salvation of mankind depends upon what we call German. In that "moral order of the world" of which your Majesty often spoke at Liebenburg, the German element is now the corner-stone; it is the central pivot. It is the language that convinces us irrefutably of this; for Science, Philosophy and Religion can today take no onward step save in the German tongue. . . . And because the German soul is indissolubly bound up with the German tongue, the higher development of mankind is bound up with Germany, a mighty Germany spreading far across the earth the sacred heritage of her language, affirming herself everywhere and imposing herself on others. . . . God builds today upon the Germans alone. This is the knowledge, the certain truth, that has filled my soul for years; to the service of truth I have sacrificed my repose; for it I will live and die.'[1]

The emperor thanked Chamberlain for 'the priceless jewel', and remarked that the Germans stood in need of a liberator like him who would reveal to them the sources of Indo-Aryan wisdom, continuing:

'You sing the High Song of the German, and, above all of our glorious tongue, and pregnantly summon the Germans to . . . take up the task of being God's instrument for the spreading of this *Kultur*, of His teachings. . . .

'And now I invoke God's blessing and our Saviour's strengthening upon my comrade and ally in the fight for Germans against Rome, Jerusalem, etc., in the New Year 1902. The feeling that one strives for an absolutely good, Divine cause holds the pledge of victory! You swing your pen, I my tongue. I grasp my guardsman's blade and say, despite all attacks and carpings: I stand my ground.'

[1]Quoted: H. Wickham Steed in *International Affairs* (London, September–October 1938), vol. xvii, pp. 667–8. Cf. *passim* for the account here given of Chamberlain's relations with William II.

In February 1903 Chamberlain sent William a 'birthday letter' which fills twenty-one printed pages; it exalted Germanism and the mission of kings while pointing out the defects of the English and the Americans. The emperor promptly replied invoking Chamberlain as a 'saviour in the hour of need'; he confessed that he had himself been producing a little literary work and wrote: 'I shall allow myself to lay my child also at your feet—you who are my spiritual midwife. In so doing I must ask your forgiveness if, in reading it, you should hear tones that seem familiar to you!'

This exchange of schoolgirlish fanmail continued up to and during the Great War when Chamberlain distinguished himself as the author of 'spiritual bombs' against England. In one of these he said: 'I found . . . everywhere in England, on my last visits in 1907 and 1908, a simply terrifying blind hatred against Germany and the impatient expectation of a war of destruction'. On the other hand, he assured his readers that *during the last forty-three years* [i.e. since 1871] *there has not lived a single man in the whole of Germany who wanted war, not one.* Whoever maintains the contrary is a liar.'

In view of this striking assertion it may be well to glance at political life in Germany during that period.

After 1871 the parties of authority held the field. The social-democrats were repressed. After the *Kulturkampf* and the Austrian alliance the catholic centre was on the whole remarkably prompt in regarding the feud as something past and in refraining from any decisive opposition which might compromise its important medial position in parliament. But the catholics were not immediately at one in this new policy and during the eighteen-eighties Windthorst was co-operating with Eugen Richter. Richter, the early friend of Schulze-Delitzsch, took over the leadership of the remnant of the progressist liberals after Hoverbeck's death in the eighteen-seventies. This was the only liberal force left in Germany. Honourably, persistently, the progressists rejected any compromise with the régimes of Bismarck and William II. They opposed the *Kulturkampf* and the antisocialist legislation; they voted against naval expansion and the imperialistic colonial policy. This firm line was largely a reflection of the unbending spirit of their leader: unbending and difficult to work with, for if Richter was liberal in conviction he was autocratic in temper. For twenty years his party dwindled and then in 1893 he split it altogether. Liberalism was broken as a force. In 1906 Richter died. In 1907 the last of the progressists were supporting Bülow's government. Outclassed and enormously outnumbered by its antiliberal opponents, the party had also been undermined by authoritarianism within. Virtually that was the end of liberalism in Germany.

There was in effect no gainsaying the men of authority. Autocratic rule could count on the support of the army, the aristocratic landed interest, the bureaucracy, and big business. This last was a new and growing force, particularly since political struggles tended ever more to turn upon economic questions in the face of the very general agreement of all the powerful interests upon purely political issues.

The second empire was the great era of German economic expansion. Unity was crowned with prosperity. Industrialization and mechanization proceeded at an almost dizzy pace. Germany crammed into a few decades an industrial transformation which had developed in the west in the course of a century and more. There was a suspicion of something unhealthy in the urgency of the drive. It is reckoned that during the four years 1871–5 the number of factories in Germany more than quintupled. The huge indemnity extracted from France came in very useful. In 1876 Wilhelm von Kardorff, a man of conservative principles and dubious connexions, founded the *Centralverband der deutschen Industriellen.* This Central Union became the corporate stronghold of big business, embracing iron, coal, chemicals, paper, textiles, food, luxury goods, and building estates. By 1903 it claimed to be maintaining relations with 35,000 industrial concerns whose output represented seven-tenths of total German production. Agrarian interests were to start with less comprehensively organized. But the temporary general set-back occasioned by the economic crisis of 1873 induced a common realization of the dangers of increasing foreign competition. The agrarians drew closer to the industrialists—Kardorff himself had agricultural as well as industrial connexions—and a joint push won Bismarck over to protection. The tariffs of 1879 were a conservative victory. In the eighteen-eighties the national-liberals, led by men like Heyl zu Herrnsheim, who was a large landowner besides being an important leather-manufacturer, approximated ever more closely to the conservative outlook until in 1887 they were actually united in the so-called cartel which supported the measures of military expansion demanded by Moltke.

The most considerable opposition to Bismarck's policy came, significantly enough, from the extreme right composed of those old Prussian conservatives, who thought it too imperial and not Prussian enough while particularly resenting the concessions which Bismarck made to the new industrialism and commercialism as typified by the national-liberals. This group centred round the Junker editor of the *Kreuzzeitung*, Baron von Hammerstein, who was once described as having

> 'a fox head on the neck of a steer, mighty muscles and small, crafty eyes, a short, broad-shouldered figure. He was of a centuries-old [Mecklenburg] family. . . . His education could hardly be called broad and his appearance seemed often hard and sharp. He could want more and want it harder, more untiringly than other men and so others followed him.'[1]

Affiliated to Hammerstein was Adolf Stöcker. Stöcker, a man of humble origin, was court-preacher; he set out to make conservatism a popular force by winning over the populace of Berlin through his Christian-social movement. He was so successful that in the early eighteen-eighties he was acclaimed as the 'uncrowned king of Berlin'. This success was not primarily due to the religious element in the movement, and indeed Christianity was perhaps not a very hopeful platform for a politician in the second empire. Stöcker whipped up the mob by his invective against Jews, bankers, and capitalists. While the intelligentsia of the German capital were listening to Treitschke the populace was fired by Stöcker.

The conservative socialism of the anti-Semitic Stöcker forms a fit background to the theories of the rather more intellectual Eugen Dühring, whose chief influence corresponded in time with that of Stöcker, and who, like Treitschke, held an appointment at the university of Berlin.

[1] *Kieler Zeitung*, 12 Oct. 1895. Quoted: P. R. Anderson, *Background of Anti-English Feeling in Germany 1890–1902* (Washington, 1939), p. 39.

Three out of Dühring's four main interests were indicated by the title of one of his books, the *Cursus der National- und Socialökonomie.* Dühring further dwelt upon the interconnexion between nationalism, socialism, and economics in his major work, the *Kritische Geschichte der Nationalökonomie und des Socialismus.* For the basis of his theory Dühring looked above all to

> 'Friedrich List, who is outstanding not less by reason of the significance of his views than on account of the range of his theory; he freed the German system of political economy from the British traditions and in a creative manner he acquainted it with new points of view, thereby rendering a service the chief effect of which is in part first entering into operation at the present time, but partly also still looking ahead into the future for its best result.'

Dühring wrote with particular approval of List's 'economic principle of nationality' which underlay his contention that

> 'every nation which is large enough to form a state that is suitably equipped in the various essential respects, and which includes besides within its scope the preconditions of an all-round economic development, must also become the basis of an economy that is to a certain degree self-sufficient. Over against other nations it must regard itself in an economic sense also as a solidary community [*solidarische Gemeinschaft*] whose interests centre independently in itself and are to be distinguished from those of the other national economic bodies.'

Dühring, in short, favoured the promotion of the self-sufficiency of the national community by means of a controlled economy. This national community, rather than the class struggle, was to be the basis of Dühring's socialism. This was the solution already propounded more or less by Rodbertus and his followers. But Dühring had a great contempt for the academic *Kathedersozialisten*, holding that socialism is an affair of the masses and that in socialist agitation

> 'the decisive thing is not knowledge for its own sake but will, which attains its more definite goal by means of knowledge. The necessity of making an impression upon great masses limits the utility of concepts to that which can be generally understood and partly also to that which lies near at hand or can be conceived of with certainty. Theories must here be stripped of all superfluous luxury, and it is essential every time to find the natural point of

contact through which they accord with the impetus of life as a whole.'

He went on to consider the relation between 'the theoretical compass' and 'the natural and justified passions'.

In view of this stress upon the adaptation of theory to popular politics it may seem curious that Dühring looked for his national socialism to List rather than to Lassalle. This was mainly owing to the fact that Dühring disapproved of class warfare and, even more vehemently, of Jews. Dühring, who claimed to be of old Swedish descent, spoke of Lassalle as 'the Jewish socialist agitator', and elsewhere he referred to 'intriguers and agitators like Messrs. Marx and Lassalle'. Indeed anti-Semitism came to rank along with Dühring's three other main interests. His chief anti-Semitic work was entitled *Die Judenfrage als Racen-, Sitten-, und Culturfrage* (*The Jewish Question as a Question of Race, Morals and Culture*). In view of the contemporary growth of anti-Semitism in Germany it may perhaps be well to glance at this exposition.

Dühring opened with the assertion that

'society is in many places so paralysed by moral poison that it can no longer stir its limbs to reaction. . . . Now what part have the Jews played in this corruption? . . . Where the Jews are to the fore, there is there most corruption. This is a basic fact of all cultural history and cultural geography.'

This basic fact was a reflection of 'the organization of the war of subjection and exploitation which the Jewish elements have for thousands of years waged against other peoples'; it was the expression of 'that tribal character of the Jews which has instituted an unforgettable world-historical memento of itself in the deed of Judas'. This racial critique was possible owing to the fact that

'we even have an artistic judgement with regard to that art which works in flesh and bone. Nobility and greatness are not merely recognizable in fashioned blocks of marble. The successes and failures in nature's fashioning truly do not elude us. Thus then we also have a gauge of folk-production. Happily we can distinguish not merely between cattle and man, but also between man and man.'

On this basis it was apparent that 'the Jewish skull is certainly no thinker's skull; in all time the Lord God and business affairs have claimed all the space in it insofar as it is not hollow'. In fact 'the fine arts and Jewry are opposites which exclude one another. After all the ways of the ordinary Jew make him an object of popular mirth. I will leave it to others to depict the angularity of the external figure of the Jew. . . . I only recall this corporal peculiarity in order to show that it corresponds to the spiritual'. Dühring followed this up with denigration of Jewish thinkers and savants from Spinoza down to 'the millionaire Ricardo', Börne and Heine.

In view of the mirthful ways and intellectual incapacity of Jews it was perhaps rather surprising that Dühring should have to deplore their predominance in the learned professions in Germany. According to him 'the Jews . . . have not merely swamped the legal profession, but are also already represented in considerable numbers on the judicial bench itself'. Similarly it was exasperating that 'the number of Jewish doctors has grown so excessively'. Furthermore, 'the Jews . . . exploit for themselves not merely the [political] parties, but also one of the most important branches of administration in which they are at their most harmful, namely that of higher education'.

One has the impression that Dühring's detailed denunciation of the Jews was largely overshadowed by the one great question:

> 'Why is Jewry proportionately far richer than the other social groups? The Jews themselves answer: on account of greater industry and thrift. But that is only the old fairy-tale. . . . I give the simple answer: it is the greater and less constrained adaptability which has caused the Jews to succeed in sucking gold out of all the human channels. . . . The doctrines of equalitarian free economics and of corresponding human rights in economics, as they were formulated in a humanely well-meaning way by the Scotsmen Hume and Smith, were used by the Jews in order to derive thence their own monopoly. . . . Essentially they want to be able to make of freedom a Jewish freedom, i.e. a Jewish monopoly.'

It was thus that Dühring harnessed his anti-Semitism to his dislike of free trade.

If the Jews were too rich for Dühring's liking they were also too articulate. He echoed Wagner's sneers at the press, remarking that 'one has only to look round in the Jewish press of the sixties and seventies in order to recognize how the litterateurs lived on Heine and Börne. . . . The most instructive form of this apparition in Germany was the social-democratic press. Here the semitization was most complete, namely in the Marxist strain of this press chorus.'

But that was only the most extreme instance: in general

'The Jews are in preponderant possession of the newspapers and other general periodicals by means of which the public is led and held in tutelage, mostly without noticing it. This possession of the press is almost exclusive in the field of the so-called liberal or radical organs. . . . In actual fact the traffic in the kind of goods which constitute the content of the newspapers is not any too respectable, and therefore it necessarily attracts Jewish competition like a magnet. It is a question of circulating about 95 per cent. of lies and distortions, and the remaining 5 per cent. is also cheap to come by and need in no way be of a particularly sterling quality. The conduct of a business of that kind has a specific charm for the people of the tribe of Judah. . . . Here is the confirmation of the thesis that corruption is a magnet which attracts the Jews.'

For Dühring the Jews were undesirable aliens not only in race and characteristics, but also in religion. He held that

'the text which, so to speak, still mostly affords the classic manifestation of the religion and morals of the Jews, is the Old Testament. . . . There is certainly small occasion for us Germans, artificially, by means of the affectations of Hebraic orientalism, to mislead the sensibility which has for thousands of years been stimulated in us by our nordic heaven and our nordic world. For us the Old Testament is a thoroughly foreign book, and it must become ever more foreign if we do not want to alter our peculiarity in the long run.'

Dühring further thought that

'one ought to bring out the contrast in the way in which Christianity as it is attested in the New Testament is regarded as being something that is still essentially interwoven with Jewish traits. One would then apply to Christianity itself a national critique similar to that applied to Jewry. What the newer, and particularly the German, peoples have made out of Christianity by their own manner of perception and feeling is something better than that original form which had a Jewish tinge.'[1]

It is evident from the above that the Germans were to be in the van of the attack upon Jewry. Dühring considered that 'in all respects the Germans still have to put up an especial fight for their nationality, and in accordance with the markedly Germanic quality of their original disposition they also have a corresponding vocation to enter in energetically with a view to liberating their nationality from the Jewish race'. The Germans would be spurred on to do their racial duty by bearing in mind the fact that 'when and where national policy in any countries is in decline the Jews are able to ascend and to gain a decisive influence in the destiny of the countries concerned. This is taught by France and England'. For Dühring the obvious targets here were Gambetta and Disraeli. Of the latter he wrote that

'in fact . . . Herr von Israel—we propose to give his name in the wholly German, not in the half-Hebraic, way—has been anxious to carry on the foreign policy of England in accordance with the principles of a private financial undertaking. He has tried gently to cash in on whole countries by deals in stocks and shares, in the course of which he has revealed a particular hereditary predilection for Egypt, the old home of the Jews. His forefathers loved the gold and silver of the Egyptians; but he wanted even to outdo the administrative system of Moses and to pocket the Egyptians themselves.'

The ascendancy of Jewish politicians in England and France indicated that those countries had failed to realize that

'in the first place . . . this general principle must be established over against the Jews, namely that every social or national-social group contains its particular code of law within itself and cannot therefore be compelled to embrace within its political bond everything which may please to make its nest among its [the group's] elements. Every political union, whether or no it be called a state, is, like every association, a positive creation. If one traces back historically the creation of the community one finds everywhere that it is a natural cohesion [*Naturzusammenhang*] that forms the basis of all communities.'

It was obvious, in particular, that the natural cohesion of a Gentile community would be completely undermined by sexual intercourse with Jews. Dühring considered that

'the unity and harmony of the family is upset by racially mixed marriages, even more than by those that are of mixed religion, when it is a question of the Jewish stock which is incompatible with all other folk-existence. . . . Under all circumstances only degeneration can result from an intermixture of Jewish blood. This corruption assumes its worst form when it falls to the lot of women who belong to the better peoples to serve as a means of propagating the Jewish stock and Jewish character. In the face of such a state of things the blood of the better peoples should, simply with regard to shame and honour, burst the veins of anger rather than tolerate even in the slightest degree such a debasement of their nationalities and such a semitization of their blood.'

Dühring went on to explain what he meant by 'even in the slightest degree', remarking that

'half Jews and quarter Jews or even three-quarter Jews are, however, a plague; for they have a better opportunity than the full-blooded Jews of penetrating into the rest of society. The improved understanding which the mongrels inherit from the element of the more highly qualified nationalities makes their portion of the Jewish character even more dangerous.'

Dühring's racial exposition culminated in the assertion that 'the destinies of peoples and of individuals are decided more by flesh and blood than by blood and iron; the training and rearing of men with a view to a nobler humanity and morality depends above all upon the breeding of the better type'. The community which was the social embodiment of the better type should make legal provision accordingly. As Dühring saw it

'every particular corporate body has its more restricted stipulations; and the whole political community, too, is a corporate body even though a very comprehensive one. Thus the political confederates can say simply: We who are united among ourselves do not accept such and such elements; at the outside we allow them to dwell and traffic among us under definite delimited laws. Now from such a concession there arises a definitely standardized legal relationship, perhaps even a half-citizenship. . . . If one applies this to the Jews it becomes apparent that the very expression "emancipation" is wrong. Here it is no question of liberation from a slave-relationship, but of positive admission into the full, special law of a political association of non-Jews. In view of the element of unsociability and of the harm to the members of the community which the insertion of Jewry brings with it, it would have been justifiable from the outset to keep the Jews off completely.'

Dühring went on to observe that, failing that, it was useless to imagine that one could deal adequately with the Jews by the indirect method of ostensibly general legislation instead of by legislation directed specifically against them. To adopt the first course would merely mean that 'one would impress upon it [the national legislation] the character of a set of decisions for a nation of criminals and one would thereby have to impose chains upon oneself' instead of upon the Jews alone. It is not surprising to learn that as regards the Jews Dühring thought that 'the banal and short-sighted pretext of toleration has . . . proved itself to be played out'.

Dühring's specific alternative to toleration for the Jews is conveniently summarized in the section-headings to the concluding chapter of *Die Judenfrage*. They read as follows:

'Preliminary reduction of Jewish advocates, officials, and judges according to the proportion of the Jewish population. . . .

'Necessity of a mediatization of the Jewish financial princes and Jewish financial institutes.

'Legal desemitization of the press. Similar treatment of other judaized trades. The Jews to be held off from the sphere of the state and of the community in general.

'Exclusion of the Jews from the public instruction of those belonging to other nationalities. Social defence against marriage with those belonging to the Jewish race. . . .

'Requisites of an effective agitation with the breaking of the power of the Jews as the final goal.'

It would be both unnecessary and unpleasing to trace in detail the measures by which Dühring proposed to implement this programme. A few examples will suffice. Dühring wrote:

'Now I consider the mediatization of the Jewish financial princes and corresponding financial institutes as that preliminary measure without which the power of the Jewish race cannot be effectively restricted. This mediatization would first of all consist of an arrangement whereby the financial principalities of the Jews would, in the interests of the state, be associated with curators whose duty it would be to supervise the operations and furthermore also to conduct them. . . . But this would indeed merely be a transitional measure tending towards full mediatization.'

The second great Jewish stronghold was the press. Dühring held that

'next to the power of the state the power of the press is the most important machinery, and in the external guidance of opinion the daily press at the present time ranks higher than the Church, which in earlier centuries had the monopoly of direct intellectual influence. On this point the nations must once more recall their racial honour [*Racenehre*] and should not tolerate the foisting of a Jewish opinion upon them as if it were their own opinion.'

Dühring thought that legislation as regards the press presented particular difficulties since the Jewish outlook had largely tainted non-Jewish journalists. More general press-laws might accordingly be necessary in addition to racial laws, particularly in view of the fact that there might be difficulty with the newspaper-readers themselves. Dühring maintained that

'the anti-Semitic element must be represented in all parties, and it goes with that that there should not be merely isolated [anti-Semitic] organs, but a whole new system of newspapers. . . . But . . . there is no evident possibility of achieving this by way of ordinary competition. Therefore here also society must decide to interfere as a state, and indeed with a direct racial law [*Racengesetz*].'

It followed that 'with the desemitization of the press the desemitization of literature in general will also be rendered possible'.

It was the same in education.

'It appertains in general to the racial honour of modern peoples that they should not allow those who belong to them to be taught by Jews. This point of view must also prevail in higher education and, for instance, the student should regard it as a matter of national honour that learning should not be served up to him or, much rather, squandered by a foreign, incomparably lower race [*ungleich niedrigeren Race*].'

Over and above such particular legislation Dühring proposed two main laws aimed at Jews in general. In the first place

'the corporations must at least have the right to forbid those who belong to the Jewish race to settle. . . . For the corporations, and also internationally for states, the general right of free movement and domicile must remain the rule with regard to all tolerable Races [*erträglichen Racen*] and nationalities; but just in order to preserve this liberty a thorough exception must be made against the Jews.'

Dühring considered that this provision should bring about a satisfactory diminution of the Jewish race; furthermore 'with regard to all kinds of direct taxation one could, from a similar point of view, effect the introduction of an additional charge in cases in which the taxed object is in Jewish hands'. Such legislation would merely be practical recognition of the fact that 'the final success of systematic restrictive measures must necessarily be the shrivelling of Jewish existence [*Zusammenschrumpfen des Judenwesens*] in numerical population and in wealth as also in general of their participation in state and society'.

Dühring was not content with theoretical exposition. He held that 'a systematic agitation against the Jewish influence is the immediate expedient [for clearing the way] towards everything further'. This agitation should be based on 'a powerful reawakening of the age-old, just folk-instinct' of anti-Semitism. Dühring further regarded this anti-Semitic agitation as a capital means of promoting that social solidarity which was to be the basis of his national-socialist community. He asserted that 'in a war the parties do not function, but their members enter the national host as fighters in general. . . . The agitation and the reform conducted against the Jewish race are to be conceived of in a similar way'.

The constant stress which this national-socialist anti-Semite laid on propaganda is very striking. In concluding he emphasized again that 'as the enlightenment about the Jews is propagated by the spoken and written word, so, above all, must independent speakers and authors do their bit': which brings one back again to the anti-Semitic agitator Stöcker. Indeed it is almost with relief that one turns from Dühring's cruelly systematic hatred of the Jews to Stöcker's more popular brand.

Gradually Stöcker drifted apart from the popular Christian-socialist movement and concentrated upon his following in court circles. After the accession of William II in 1888 this court party gained in importance. Two years later Bismarck found himself opposed by the emperor, the court party, and an increasingly vocal social-democratic party. Bismarck stepped down, constitutionally in favour of Caprivi, actually of William II.

Those who saw in the non-renewal of the antisocialist laws

and the general tendency of Caprivi's government a diminution of conservative influence were soon undeceived. Caprivi went in 1894. One by one the ministers who did not sufficiently fall in with the emperor's restless ambitions made way for men who did. The possibility of a *coup d'état* that would dispense with the Reichstag was freely canvassed. New men like Prince Philipp zu Eulenburg, German ambassador in Vienna, gained the confidence of William. It was largely thanks to Eulenburg's influence that Prince Bernhard von Bülow became foreign secretary in 1897; three years later he succeeded Prince Hohenlohe-Schillingsfürst as chancellor.

Bismarck thought that his epigoni were a set of incompetents and was angry with the Germans for accepting their government so tamely. But twenty years of Bismarckian rule had not made for popular initiative in political opposition. In middle-class and academic circles the cult of Bismarck spread, but no Bismarckian party was formed. Perhaps that was the measure of his failure. There was no weighty opposition to the conservatives who inherited Bismarck's system and scrapped his policy. For Junker conservatism was really getting into its stride; its strength steadily increased in the eighteen-nineties; it dominated the Reichstag. But now as earlier the Reichstag only constituted the political façade. The most significant event was the formation of a new pressure-group.

In 1893 the Prussian Junkers, particularly those east of the Elbe, founded the *Bund der Landwirte*, Farmer's Alliance, to protect their interests as large landowners which were threatened by the tariff policy of Caprivi, who tended to favour industry. But the significance of the *Bund der Landwirte* was much wider. At the period of the Stein-Hardenberg reforms, in 1848, and now again in the face of rising industrialism, the Junkers felt that their order was in danger. And each time they not only averted the danger but actually consolidated their position. The Farmers' Alliance now organized a propaganda campaign of quite exceptional vigour. They published their own journal and in 1900 they organized some 9,000 meetings. The protectionist arguments of List and Dühring were pointed with self-interest. One agrarian propagandist remarked:

'So much is perfectly clear to us, that in that moment in which old Europe, Russia excepted, did not know how definitely to free itself from the curse of English economic theory under the firm of Adam Smith, Ricardo, Malthus, Stuart Mill, Cobden its fate was sealed. It is true that Germany endeavoured under Bismarck in 1879 and 1887 to break away, but it did not go over completely to the List-Carey-Dühring ground.'[1]

In order to remedy this defect the cartel-coalition of 1887 was renewed as the *Sammlung*. The result of this log-rolling was the new tariff of 1902. The poor man had to pay more for his bread, but it was reckoned that rather more than 1,170,000[2] marks in additional profits would accrue to fifteen large landowners, all princes and dukes, in the six eastern provinces of Prussia.

While the Farmers' Alliance was thus looking after the interests of the Junkers the Central Union of German Industrialists was increasingly bent upon consolidating the position of the industrialists in opposition to the social democrats. The prime enemy of trade unionism and social democracy was Baron Carl Ferdinand von Stumm-Halberg, who manufactured iron and steel plating in the Saar and supplied the navy in the same way that Krupp did the army. 'King Stumm' exercised patriarchal sway over his factories and was convinced that 'social democracy can and must be suppressed'. His influence was such that the years from 1893 to 1896 have been called the Stumm Era.

The industrialists and Junkers steadily maintained that their political activities were designed to promote the interests of state and fatherland. The fact that they contrived to benefit themselves quite handsomely was, so far from being reprehensible, actually a proof of their patriotism. For they were the guarantors of the state, their interests were its interests. This situation was the practical counterpart to the antidemocratic and antiliberal tradition in German political thought. And if these landed aristocrats and captains of industry were a trifle ruthless in their methods they were only acting in accordance with the prevalent doctrine of power-

[1]W. Skarzynski, *Die Agrarkrisis und die Mittel zu ihrer Abhilfe* (Berlin, 1894), p. 12.

[2]For this figure, as for much other material in this section, I am indebted to P. R. Anderson, op. cit.

politics and displaying vigour and ingenuity in its application to home affairs.

In the face of these developments the social-democratic party largely succeeded in convincing itself that the class-conflict was diminishing in intensity and should be appeased. Eduard Bernstein led the reformists who advocated a policy of revisionism and rejected orthodox Marxism, about which many were in any case decidedly hazy. The reformists substituted evolution for revolution and preached the necessity of working for social reform by constitutional methods within the existing political order, the order of the Junkers. This reformist movement split the social-democrats into several factions, though only the extreme left under Rosa Luxemburg and Kautsky rejected outright the facile assumption that class-antagonism was growing fainter and revolutionary tactics were accordingly not to the point; but the left again was split within itself and its following was quite inconsiderable. In the field of theory the socialists, starting from historico-economic materialism, did much indeed to familiarize Germans with the idea of a post-capitalist planned economy, providing them with a popular critique of liberalism. But in parliament the social-democrats were mainly preoccupied in securing better conditions for the workers to the exclusion of any very considered policy towards the broad issues of state.

The conservatives did not, perhaps, talk so much as the social-democrats about the class struggle, but they were, if anything, more alive to its full implications. Despite the reformist movement the fear and mistrust with which the government and the ruling classes viewed social democracy increased if anything. But whereas many democrats tended to support Liebknecht's naïve view that 'the best foreign policy is none', the rulers of Germany thought to overcome difficulties at home by successes abroad. One of them said that Germany must pursue an expansive foreign policy 'in no small degree because there lies in this new, great, national task and the economic gain which is bound up with it a strong palliative against educated and uneducated social democracy'. The author of this remark was Admiral von Tirpitz, and his name became a symbol.

One of the first actions of Bismarck's successors was to allow the reinsurance treaty with Russia to lapse; soon after Russia and France were allies and the combination which Bismarck had striven for years to prevent was an accomplished fact. Germany was now thrown back on friendship with Britain and upon the Triple Alliance, which in practice meant mostly Austria. But this did not deter her from deliberately challenging Britain in her two most sensitive spheres of interest, the colonial and the naval. William had a personal penchant for the sea. German policy developed accordingly. With foolish arrogance Germany almost went out of her way to challenge, one after the other, those great powers which were subsequently united against her in the Great War. Having rejected Joseph Chamberlain's plan for an Anglo-German alliance, William, together with Von Tirpitz, pushed ahead with all speed with the formidable programme of naval armament. In the Morocco crisis Germany showed that she welcomed an opportunity of obstructing French colonial enterprise, not less than British; it was hardly surprising that the Anglo-French *entente* matured. At the same time Germany acted provocatively towards Russia in the Balkans, culminating in her support of Austria against Russia in the Bosnia-Herzegovina crisis of 1908. Henceforth European diplomacy became almost a series of crises, Germany keeping the others constantly on the jump. With the Agadir crisis of 1911 war was already looming up. At this period Austria was the one considerable friend left to Germany, whose position was now such that she felt obliged to cling to her, come what might. And so when on Sunday the 28th June, 1914, the Archduke Franz Ferdinand was murdered at Sarajevo the German government not only fully supported Austria against Serbia but actually encouraged her to war. Nor did William and Bethmann-Hollweg shrink from the heavy consequence of their policy. On the 1st August, 1914, Germany declared war on Russia. On the 3rd August, 1914, Germany declared war on France.

On the 4th August, 1914, as is notorious, Germany swooped upon Belgium in contempt of her international obligations and in particular of her signature of the treaty of 1839 which guaranteed the permanent neutrality of Belgium.

Germany herself admitted the brazen illegality of this act. On the 4th August the German chancellor informed the Reichstag:

'Our troops have occupied Luxemburg and perhaps are already on Belgian soil. Gentlemen, that is contrary to international law. It is true that the French government has declared at Brussels that France is willing to respect the neutrality of Belgium, as long as her opponent respects it. We knew, however, that France stood ready for invasion. France could wait but we could not wait. . . . So we were compelled to override the just protests of the Luxemburg and Belgian governments. The wrong—I speak openly—that we are committing we will endeavour to make good as soon as our military goal has been reached.'

It was, of course, unfortunate for the Belgians that the attainment of that goal necessitated a German policy of calculated frightfulness.

It is well known with what skill and tenacity Germany fought one of the greatest fights in history until at last she was beaten down, having held her own and much more than her own for four bitter years against the allied and associated powers. It was a very splendid war. It killed, it is estimated, nearly thirteen million people not counting the civilians.

William and his advisers had not planned the Great War or even desired it. But their whole policy tended towards it. It was a crude, swaggering, bullying policy. It was the power-policy of German dreams. At the beginning of his chancellorship Bülow declared in the Reichstag: 'I feel no embarrassment in saying here publicly that for Germany right can never be a governing consideration':[1] not right but might. The leaders of Germany did not wish war, but their thoughts were war-like and they wished to do things in the way that warriors do them.

These sentiments were not merely the aberrations of a governing clique. Bülow paid great attention to popular support. He deliberately set about stimulating nationalist feeling in Germany. As he saw it 'public opinion could only be brought into play when the national motive was emphasized and the national consciousness stirred up'. Accordingly 'to the government fell the task of awakening the patriotic feel-

[1] 13 Dec. 1900. Quoted: T. H. Minshall, *Prussian Influence in Germany* (London), p. 12.

ings which were asleep in all parties, of giving them life and of keeping them alive, unprejudiced and spontaneous, until they seemed strong enough for the practical work of fulfilling the national responsibilities of the empire'.

Bülow knew his German public. He and his colourless successor did not, indeed, achieve uniform success. There was, for instance, a wide sale for a book by a certain Quidde which, while ostensibly a serious historical analysis of the unbalanced emperor Caligula, was in fact a thrust at the emperor William II. In 1913 the Zabern affair seemed to indicate that there might be a limit to militarism even in Germany. The socialists steadily opposed militaristic imperialism; Bebel, for instance, spoke year after year against the naval expansion, which he castigated as an aggressive policy directed against Great Britain. The social-democrats won very substantial gains in the parliamentary elections of 1912, although they remained quite powerless to change the direction of policy even if they had wished to do so, which is perhaps doubtful since by that time they had largely become so tame that even their own leaders were disturbed and tried to revive the flagging movement by organizing a 'red week' of demonstrations. Nevertheless, in the main, Bülow knew his German public.

Two of the chief channels employed by the government to instruct public opinion were the press bureau of the foreign office, under Otto Hammann, and the Bureau for Publicity and Parliamentary Affairs which Tirpitz established in 1897. The object of this bureau was

> 'to enlighten and teach the German people its maritime goals and needs and to control the press. Furthermore, to influence publicity by word and picture, wherever possible by its [the *Reichsmarineamts*] own publications; to stimulate the important scientists and politicians to independent action, to supply them with materials; to work in associations, exhibitions and lectures as well as to provide prompt information on naval questions.'

Some indication of the quality of this enlightenment and instruction may perhaps be derived from the fact that Tirpitz was familiarly known among his officers as 'the father of the lie'. Tirpitz's bureau enjoyed the eager co-operation of the patriotic bodies founded by the private zeal of German citizens, and particularly of the two largest. Of these the oldest was the Colonial League, started in 1887. It was supported by big industrialists like Krupp, Hammacher, and the prince of Wied, and it sponsored the *Kolonialzeitung*, of whose views one sample will suffice. In 1899 it wrote: 'The time is not far distant when a foothold in the Mediterranean for Germany as a point of security for her civilizing activity and commercial power will be necessary. Cyrenaica would be quite suitable.' This was only an extension of Bülow's remark the year before when he professed himself 'convinced that the taking of Kiao-Chou will be a blessing to the Christian faith and culture and that it will further the economic development and the political power of the German people': a happy conjunction.

The Navy League like the Colonial League had big industry behind it. Indeed its founder, the journalist Victor Schweinburg, was an associate of Krupp's. It carried on extensive propaganda and in connexion with the naval law of 1900 it sponsored more than six million books and pamphlets. In that year it had 600,000 members and the circulation of its organ, *Die Flotte*, rose to 750,000. The league's director of propaganda was a certain General Keim, who was also a prominent figure in the Pan-German League.

The All-German Association, from which the Pan-German League developed, was founded in 1891 by a group of idealists including a certain Alfred Hugenberg. The league actively supported colonial and naval expansion, but its primary purpose was 'to work for all citizens in the sense of creating a *national morale*'. In practical terms this was the familiar goal, the achievement of Germanity, the union of all German stocks within the German Reich, an exciting word, more exactly realm than empire since it includes the spiritual realm of pure Germanity. The implications of this doctrine were brought out in the *Alldeutsche Blätter*, the organ of the league, which wrote, for instance, in 1899:

> 'Germany will never win Germandom [*das Deutschtum*] in the East March as long as there are Poles, this people whom fate had unfortunately given us as the irreconcilable enemy at our side. . . . The premise that there is equality of nationality must be given up in the East March.'

In the same year the league published a map showing the boundaries of Greater Germany in about the year 1950; they included Alsace-Lorraine, Dunkirk, Flemish Belgium, the Netherlands, southern Denmark, German Switzerland, north-eastern Italy with Trieste and Istria, Hungary, Bohemia, Slovakia, part of Lithuania with Memel, and most of Poland—more than Germany then possessed. In the year in which this map appeared the league had 159 local branches throughout Germany. The propaganda was directed by Ernst Hasse until his death in 1908 when he was succeeded by the even more violent Heinrich Class, who had come to the league by way of Friedrich Lange, editor of the *Tägliche Rundschau* and author of *Reines Deutschtum* (*Pure Germandom*). Class was an early pupil of Treitschke's and he found it 'impossible to describe the impression which Treitschke made on my cousin and me. . . . It was as if everything noble, great and strong had taken form in this man'. Later he read Lagarde, Gobineau, and Chamberlain and he did not know 'from which of these three great men I had profited most'. Thus the ideas of force, nationalism, and racial superiority were ever more widely propagated. After 1899 the Pan-German League published a special fighting organ significantly entitled *Odin*.

The Pan-German League spread, as was fitting, beyond the confines of Germany proper. Doctor Fick, a prominent member, lived in Switzerland. In Austria pan-Germanism assumed a particularly virulent form under the leadership of the anti-Semitic Schoenerer and the inspiration of Chamberlain. It was largely this latter influence, Chamberlain's religious opinions being what they were, which brought the Austrian pan-Germanists into conflict with Lueger, the burgomaster of Vienna, who led an anti-Semitic Christian-social movement much as Stöcker had done earlier in Berlin.

The membership of the Pan-German League refutes any idea that it was merely a band of inconsiderable fanatics. It included Ernst Bassermann, the leader of the national-liberal party, Kardorff, the founder of the Central Union of German Industrialists, Liebermann von Sonnenburg, the anti-Semitic agrarian, and Count Udo Stolberg-Wernigerode, the president of East Prussia.

Meanwhile the intellectual life of Germany was subject to like influence: not wholly subject, indeed; scholars like Dilthey and Troeltsch did not allow it to infect their work. But there were others like Driesmans, who gave full vent to his anti-Semitic and anti-Latin pan-Germanism; in the sphere of science Wilser set out to prove the superiority of the nordic dolichocephalic blond while Doltmann specialized in biological interpretation of intellectual and moral facts. In history Curtius had, rather earlier, turned like the romantic forerunners to ancient Greece, tracing in its rise a parallel to that of Prussia. But in this field it may be enough to notice how at the university of Leipzig the youth of Germany were being impregnated with pan-German doctrine by Karl Lamprecht, one of the most considerable historians of his day.

Writing in the early nineteen-hundreds Lamprecht proudly traced the growth of German economic might and rejoiced that 'the economic power-instinct has transformed itself into the political, and the movement for [German] unity has been followed in most recent times by world-politics'. It followed that 'one thing above all is clear: today the [German] Empire, even as a political body, does not stop short at its frontiers. . . . One can indeed describe the empire, in a good sense, as the Germanic *État tentaculaire*'. According to Lamprecht it was particularly desirable that Germany should spread her tentacles westwards, round Holland, Belgium and Switzerland, which formed part of 'central European Germanity' [*mitteleuropäisches Germanentum*]; he specifically approved the answer which Arndt had given to his question: what is the German fatherland? And for Lamprecht, as for others, the German realm was spiritual as well as territorial. He wrote: 'but who would wish to deny that even down to the present time there is a Germanic Christian God?'

In formulating his concept of Germanity and its work Lamprecht paid considerable attention to Germans living abroad, asking 'and should not the German living abroad participate in the propagation . . . of the universal-historical pride of our history? . . . Thus then let it go forth into the whole world, this German culture.' He boasted of the strength of this cultural Germanism abroad, expatiating upon the countless 'German clubs and casinos . . . the German skittle-clubs, smokers-unions and drinking-clubs' with which foreign countries were happily adorned. Education was excellent national propaganda; as Lamprecht put it,

'what a means for incomparable propaganda are the German high schools of every kind, from the hoar-old universities down to the most recent institutions serving technical and commercial ends! All of them, taken as a whole, constitute an incomparably weighty phalanx of the national intellectual life, whose present forward march puts the scientific strategy and tactics of every other nation to shame. And [they constitute] an armed power which is actually called upon to fight upon international territory! . . . These lines are remote from any chauvinism. They speak only in passing of the "pure Germanity" of Lagarde and Friedrich Lange; they recognize no cult, be it of Wotan or Tuisco.'

In order to prove that he was not a chauvinist Lamprecht said that he was not a pagan: which shows how far matters had already gone.

For Lamprecht economics, even more than culture, should be exploited in the supreme interest of national power.

'Today', he wrote, 'every nerve is strained in order to maintain, while at the same time increasing, the latest acquisition, the position of Germanity in the world. But to this end internal unity of economic life is above all necessary: in external affairs, in tariff and commercial policy as in other cases, it must be possible readily to employ the economic forms as a whole, like an army. Yes, just like the army and the navy: for in this connection these [instruments of policy] directly draw close to the national economy as being other forms and instruments of the expansion of the national existence.'

Lamprecht had an acute perception of whither this expansion was tending and realized that the means was in a fair way towards enveloping the end, that expansion might supersede nationalism itself. This was what he wrote in his *Zur jüngsten deutschen Vergangenheit* of the coming expansionist state:

'Now how does the expansionist state, . . . a new phenomenon, stand in relation to the national state, the bearer of the internal and external history of the nineteenth century? It is clear: it has in itself no specific relation with the concept of the nation, indeed not even with that of race; it merely presupposes a great mass united as a state. And thus already at the present time it is possible for the question to arise, whether it [the expansionist state] will not finally press back the nineteenth-century ideal of nationalism and, along with it, the liberal-democratic orientation and the superintendence of internal relations in the sense of regard for the masses. However, no more thorough treatment of internal policy can as yet be given here. But as regards external policy there is no doubt that the new state has brought and will further bring a new ideal of power which is rooted in an aristocratic-absolutist existence and is anchored in fanatical belief in the power of the single leading personality. For what is needed above all in order to carry through the establishment of the power of a given state-imperialism? It is clear, and no state demonstrates it more simply and plainly than the United States: the most decisive concentration of domestic forces with a view to great external effect of a permanent character; the most powerful extension of state-territory until internal economic self-sufficiency has been attained; and, as a manifestation, but, much more, with a view to the attainment of these goals and the position of world-power automatically derived from them, the most unitary leadership, even outside the boundaries [of the state], such as can only be guaranteed by a personality who towers above [his fellows] both in deed and right.

'Thus then, expansion into a superstate [*Grösststaat*], concentration of all the forces of state-society with a view to unitary effect abroad, and to this end the leadership of a man and a hero: these are the most immediate demands of the expansionist state.

'But can they now already enter fully into life and can they anywhere develop into full bloom? Hardly.'

Hardly. Such developments were indeed for the future, but meanwhile the spirit of aggressive imperialism took firm hold upon Germany. Popular publicists vied with each other in matching the prevalent mood. In 1905 Josef Ludwig Reiner elaborated a plan for extinguishing France, while allowing part of it, as a transitional phase, to retain some measure of autonomy although it would be included in Germany's economic territory.[1] In 1911 Taunenberg published his *Grossdeutschland: die Arbeit des 20sten Jahrhunderts*. Next year Daniel Fryman brought out his *Wenn ich der Kaiser Wär'* which maintained that 'the victorious German nation will have to demand that menace from France shall cease for ever: France must be destroyed'. It went almost without saying that puny states like Holland and Belgium had no right to exist. In 1913 Eduard Weber, in his *Krieg oder Freiden mit*

[1]Cf. E. O. Lorimer, *What Hitler Wants* (London, 1939), p. 133, as also, *passim*, for the following quotations from Fryman, Weber, etc.

England? confessed that 'to snatch world domination from the English appears to us an aim worthy of honourable toil. Our aim is the creation of a powerful, world-embracing German Empire. . . . If England stands in the way then let the cannon speak!' Germany was out to conquer, and she would fight for conquest, and she would show mercy neither in war nor in victory. A current German *mot* said of war that it should leave the conquered with nothing but their eyes wherewith to beweep their total loss. As early as 1877–8 some articles by General Julius von Hartmann had appeared in the *Deutsche Rundschau* under the title of 'Militärische Notwendigkeit und Humanität' ('Military Necessity and Humanity'). In them humanity came off second best. Hartmann wrote: 'It is a gratuitous illusion to suppose that modern war does not demand far more brutality, far more violence, than was formerly the case. . . . The enemy state must not be spared the want and wretchedness of war. These are particularly useful in shattering its energy and subduing its will.' Thus the line of militarist thought inaugurated by Clausewitz was carried forward until it reached a new highpoint, both in substance and in popularity, in the writings of General Friedrich von Bernhardi.

Bernhardi's major work, *Deutschland und der nächste Krieg* (*Germany and the Next War*), was published in 1911. By 1913 it had run into six editions. The title-page of this book bore a quotation from *Also Sprach Zarathustra*. Nietzsche's teaching, vulgarized, was falling on fruitful ground. Bernhardi set out to prove 'that war is not only a necessary element in the life of peoples, but also an indispensable factor in culture, indeed the highest expression of the strength and life of truly cultural peoples'. For him 'war is in the first place a biological necessity, a regulator of the life of mankind which is quite indispensable'. Furthermore, 'it has been the fight itself, which made Prussia significant . . . which forged that steel-hard Prussia upon which it was possible to base the growth of the new Germany as a mighty European state and a future world-power'.

This pre-eminence of war greatly simplified questions of right and wrong. For Bernhardi 'might is at the same time the highest right, and the lawsuit is decided by the dynamometer, war, which always decides correctly according to biology, since its decisions proceed from the very being of the thing'. Since war was the only way of settling a dispute Bernhardi quite logically denied the existence of any common standards of right and wrong. As he saw it

'each people derives from itself its own concepts of law, each has its peculiar ideals and endeavours which proceed with sure necessity from its character and historical life. These various views bear their living justification within themselves, and can come into the harshest contradiction with those of other peoples without one being able to say that one people has a better right than the other. There never has existed and never can exist a general law for humanity.'

Accordingly it was only natural that Bernhardi should be indignant because

'it is proposed that the great disputes of peoples and states should be settled by courts of arbitration, that is by arrangements; it is proposed that one-sided, circumscribed, formal law should be substituted for historical decisions, that the same right to exist should be accorded to the weak folk as to the strong, vigorous folk. All this constitutes a presumptuous encroachment upon the natural laws of development, an encroachment which could only lead to the worst results for the whole of humanity.'

The happy occasion for war was, as with Lamprecht and so many other German theorists, the need for expansion. Bernhardi observed that

'strong, sound and flourishing peoples increase in population; accordingly from a given moment they have need of a constant expansion of their frontiers, they need new land in order to accommodate the surplus population. But since the earth is colonized almost everywhere new land can in general only be won at the expense of the possessor, i.e. by conquest which therewith becomes a law of necessity.'

Accordingly Bernhardi thought it unfortunate that the Triple Alliance was only defensive, and particularly unfortunate for Germany whose population had risen from rather over 36,000,000 in 1855 to more than 60,500,000 in 1905; besides which

'present-day Germany is geographically speaking only a mutilated torso of the old imperial power; in general it includes only a fraction of the German people. A large number of German compatriots are attached to other states. . . . Germany is robbed of her natural frontiers; even the source and the mouth of the German river, of the much-sung German Rhine, lie outside the German sphere of power.'

Bernhardi like Lamprecht regarded Germans living abroad as an important political and cultural factor, but like Treitschke he was more concerned at Germany's late and comparatively modest entry into the colonial field. He strongly resented the fact that the power which had been defeated in 1870 should have acquired the second largest empire in the world. But after all it was only second largest, second to that of Great Britain; which meant that for Bernhardi Britain was first enemy. He thought that

'a peaceful settlement with England is . . . a will-o'-the-wisp which no serious German statesman should undertake to pursue. Much rather must we constantly keep in view the possibility of a war with England and arrange our political and military measures accordingly, untroubled by possible peaceful demonstrations on the part of English politicians, publicists and utopians.'

Bernhardi did not have to wait long for his war. And his feelings had been those of many others. For instance, the prominent publicist Maximilien Harden, who thought of France as female and Germany as male, wrote, upon the outbreak of the Great War: 'Why not admit what is and must be the truth, namely that between Vienna and Berlin everything was fully prepared. We should be mere slaves, unworthy of the men who achieved predominance in Germany if . . . things could be otherwise.' And again: 'Not as weak-witted blunderers have we undertaken the fearful risk of this war. We wanted it.' At about the same time Paul Rohrbach, a publicist not quite so well connected as Harden but no less prolific, maintained that:

'The war which we are now conducting must be called a "ripe" war. The friends of peace in the pacifist sense will suspect us of having wished that the crisis should ripen into war. . . . I openly admit that in the days in which the decision—war or peace—hovered as if upon a knife-edge I trembled at the sinking not of the scale-pan of war, but at that of peace.'

The nation accepted war with enthusiasm and party strife was hushed. For Germany the war was ripe; and ripeness lends relish.

Even Rainer Maria Rilke acclaimed the war-god in his *Fünf Gesänge August 1914*:

> *Zum erstenmal seh ich dich aufstehn,*
> *Hörengesagter, fernster unglaublichster Kriegs-Gott.*[1]

With him, however, lament exceeded praise; the war was alien to this poet who loved Russia, solitude, and the personal death. But over against Rilke stood George, his peer in poetry or nearly so. Soon after the outbreak of war the French author Romain Rolland appealed to the leaders of German thought to urge the sparing of historical cities, and particularly of Rheims Cathedral. In effect, Stefan George refused this plea. In November 1914 he was asked reproachfully if he regarded the destroyers of Rheims and Ypres as his children and followers. He retorted savagely: 'Yes, that they are and if there were more of them then they would win! And if all fought as they do they would have victory for reward!' George, indeed, regarded the Great War as a terrible yet inadequate affair; for him it was the 'first world-war'. It was only the prelude to his dream of the new empire, of the race of heroes, of the day when the people would at last rouse itself and would perceive:

> '. . .*Die göttliche Deutung*
> *Unsagbaren Grauens . . . dann heben sich die Hände*
> *Und Münder ertönen zum Preise der Würde,*
> *Dann flattert im Frühwind mit wahrhaftem Zeichen*
> *Die Königsstandarte und grüsst, sich verneigend,*
> *die Hehren, die Helden.*[1]

But perhaps after all the esoteric heroics of *Das Neue Reich* are of less immediate significance than the cult of Maximin. And the significance of that also is largely relative to the post-war future; whereas as yet the war continued.

Among the most thoughtful, certainly among the most interesting, books produced in Germany during that war was Friedrich Naumann's *Mitteleuropa* (*Central Europe*).

[1]'For the first time I see thee arise, most distant, incredible war-god of hearsay.'

[2]'The divine meaning of unspeakable horror. . . . Then hands are raised and voices intone in praise of the majesty, then, with the token of truth, the regal standard flutters in the early wind and greets with obeisance the august ones, the heroes.'—*Das Neue Reich.*

Naumann had begun life as a Lutheran pastor and a follower of the court-preacher Stöcker. Later, and in particular in his book entitled *Demokratie und Kaisertum*, he sought on his own account to reconcile conservative authority with social reform. To this end he founded a national-socialist party. It was a failure and Naumann drifted into connection with the *petit-bourgeois* radicalism of the south German *Volkspartei*. When war came he thought he saw his opportunity. *Mitteleuropa* opened with the assertion:

'I write deliberately in the midst of war, for it is only in war that minds are prepared to entertain transforming thoughts. After the war is over the everyday spirit very soon emerges from its hiding again, and the everyday spirit is incapable of fashioning central Europe. Just as Bismarck founded the German empire during the war of 1870 and not after the war, so must the foundations of the new form be laid by our statesmen during war, amid the flowing of blood and the surge of peoples.'

This new form, as appears already, was based upon the reorganization of central Europe as a coherent unit. Naumann's eyes were

'first turned towards the land of central Europe which stretches from the North and Baltic Seas to the Alps, the Adriatic and the southern edge of the Danubian plain. Take up a map and behold what lies between the Vistula and the Vosges, what lies extended from Galicia to the Lake of Constance! These expanses should be thought of as a unity, as a many-membered brotherland, as a defensive union, as an economic territory!'

This was the nucleus to which accessions might subsequently accrue. Naumann said that 'in the following elaboration we leave the French outside the affair, whilst always hoping that in the more distant future they will just rank themselves along with central Europe'. Not France but Austria was the foreign state mainly concerned. By his central European construction Naumann tried to solve a practical problem:

'The question is, then, whether the German empire can go to meet the future with confidence if it has not a union with Austria-Hungary, whether it is even true perhaps that we are stronger without Austria-Hungary than with her. That is what we deny. . . . The German empire by itself is too small to defy the assaults of all the others in the future and in the long run.'

Naumann, then, sought to give a more comprehensive form to the Austro-German alliance upon which the foreign policy of Germany had for years been based. The prime object of this closer union was avowedly the benefit of Germany. Naumann said frankly that

'whoever seriously tries to think himself into the historical feeling of the dual monarchy will understand without more ado that the creation of a firm bond with the Prusso-German empire is thought of as a very serious step since despite all the necessary regard for self-determination it comprises without doubt a bond which it might be hard to tolerate under certain circumstances. To put it quite frankly, Austria-Hungary finally subscribes to the shift of preponderance which resulted from the year 1866. Thereby it renounces [its design of] being once again, as in the splendid days of old, the first dominating power in central Europe. That constitutes no formal dependence, no restriction of sovereignty, no surrender of inherited power, but what it does constitute is an actual recognition of existing power-relations. . . . The Bismarckian foundation of the Empire and its confirmation in the world-war has created a situation in which in Central Europe the German Empire has become the first of the two leading states in population, military strength and uniformity.'

Thus did the judicious and well-mannered Naumann explain to the Habsburg empire, politely but firmly, that it was now time to move toward from Prussian control of Germany to Prusso-German hegemony over central Europe. This would be effected with a minimum of inconvenience to Austria-Hungary. Over constitutional details Naumann was more politic than precise. But in any case Austria was a constituent element in Germanism and 'the culture of central Europe grows round about Germanism'. Naumann realized that other peoples might not see it quite that way, and he did not minimize the strength of national particularism or the consequent need for compromise. In mentioning the 'preaching of the "German idea in the world"' he remarked that

'no nationally minded Hungarian or Czech will think evil of us national Germans if we sing, dream, ponder and work for *Deutschland, Deutschland über alles*. We need that. That is our life-blood. Only we should not thereby fail to remember that the non-Germanic confederates also possess a life-blood and also want to know what they are prepared to strive for. At the same time as we exalt our nationality we should treat theirs tenderly.'

It is apparent that Naumann crowned the long line of German expansionists and to some extent blended the aspirations of the pan-germanists with those of the geopolitical school, men like Ratzel and Dix, who maintained that Germany's destiny as an expanding continental power was prescribed by the geopolitical imperative. It is equally evident that Naumann's treatment of the problem was exceptional. His central concept was a bold one and his vision was often of surprising penetration, but his grasp of reality was hardly less keen; he seldom ran away with and from his subject. That this should mark him as almost an exception is a reflection upon the prevalent trend of political thought in Germany.

Naumann based his scheme for central Europe upon three main grounds. The first, as has already been suggested, was military. The setting of the new central European system was post-war Europe as Naumann saw it. This is what he saw:

'After the war frontier-entrenchments will be constructed everywhere where there is a possibility of war. New Roman walls arise, new Chinese walls made of earth and barbed wire. The consequence of this policy of defensive trenches is that when the military fortifications are laid out in the first place one is under a compelling necessity of being clear as to the people with whom one counts upon living in friendship in all circumstances. Europe acquires two long ramparts from north to south, one of which goes roughly from the lower Rhine to the Alps, and the other from Courland downwards, either right or left of Rumania. That will be the great and unavoidable trisection of the continent. The central European question now is whether between the two great north-to-south ramparts it will be necessary to have another intermediate rampart between Germany and Austria-Hungary. It becomes necessary as soon as the uniformity of their future policies does not seem to be guaranteed; but if it should become necessary it would be in the highest degree harmful and fatal for both parties.

'The future policy of defensive trenches means that small states will only be able to maintain their independence with the utmost difficulty. . . . Higgling for neutrality will be made much harder by the approaching policy of defensive trenches. It is possible that the defensive trench is the greatest means employed by providence in order to make war illusory by means of its own technique. But first the long trenches have to be built, paid for and manned. In this process central Europe will either be constituted or else its unity will be made impossible for all measurable time. It is upon these grounds that a decision must be taken.'

Naumann evaluated the future entirely in terms of power-politics. He asserted that 'all the participants in the world-war have a definite feeling that in present and future times no small or medium-sized power will any longer be able to carry out high policy. Our concepts of size have mightily altered. Only thoroughly large states still have any significance on their own account'. He did not ignore the possibility of a league of nations, but he rejected it. Like George he thought that the post-war world would also be a pre-war world, and he remarked that

'even an expansion of a peaceful frame of mind among the [various] populations can do little to alter this continual preparation for coming war since the historical moment in which mankind will merge into a single mighty organization is not yet present by a long way. Before there can come into being the organization of mankind, the "United States of the Globe", it is to be expected that there will be a very long period in which groups of humanity, exceeding the dimensions of a nation, will struggle for the leadership of the destiny of mankind and for the proceeds of the work of mankind. As such a group is central Europe proclaimed, and indeed as a small one: strong but lean!'

Small, thought Naumann, in comparison with Great Britain, the United States, and Russia.

Thus Naumann no less than Lamprecht proclaimed the advent of the superstate. And like Lamprecht he was of the historical school. History was the second cardinal foundation upon which he reared the edifice of central Europe.

According to Naumann

'the German Emperors of earlier times are central European figures in the full sense of the word and for that reason they are now for the first time becoming fully recognizable again. . . . Today during the war which extends from the North Sea to Anatolia, today Barbarossa rises aloft from out of the river Selef in the distant land of the Turks. . . . In the whole of central Europe and out beyond the boundaries of the German language, penetrating deep down into the people, there is a notion *that in those days central Europe already existed as a world-power*.'

One is given a vivid picture of how

'the [medieval] Germans occupied central Europe in the midst, but on all their margins drew the neighbouring peoples to them: the Holy Roman Empire of the German nation. Now during the world-war this old Empire is striving and pushing beneath the earth, for it is in glad advent after long slumber. All the longing after unity in the mouldering centuries that lie between was the after-flicker of its light.'

Thus did Naumann stir the recesses of historical romanticism which lived on in Germans from generation to generation; thus did he hark back to the dawn of historical thought in Germany, to the visions of the great romantics. And on the way back thither he saluted the chivalry of German history, Treitschke, Sybel, Droysen, Gervinus, and Arndt. He praised them as useful and most patriotic men. But now their scope was not enough. New historians must arise who would do for central Europe what they had done for Prussian Germany.

Economics were the third factor in the triple basis of the central European order. Naumann, again like Lamprecht. paid particular attention to economic questions and it was in this field that he was at his most original. Here also the starting-point was war and the psychology of Germany at war. Naumann singled out this fact for special notice:

'In this war we are all pondering [and trying to understand] why we Germans and in particular we Germans of the empire are so unpopular in the rest of the world. Many well-meaning compatriots find this international aversion quite horrible and they rack their brains to discover what we must do in order to find peace at last. In this attempt they often look for the source of the ill-will of the other peoples to points of very secondary importance such as the lack of social good form shown by loud-voiced German tourists who travel abroad clad in homespun, or the theatrical sabre-rattling of a few discharged generals; but they do not look for it in the national economic type itself. . . . It hardly occurs to them that we are unpopular because we have discovered a method of labour which, both now and for a further future period, no other European people can imitate and which consequently seems to the others to be unfair. This is precisely what we have described as the transition to the impersonal capitalism of the second stage, a proceeding which with us is the result of about a century and a half of work and education.'

In order to illustrate the difference between the first and the second stage he contrasted shrewdly, though perhaps not quite accurately, the organization of the docks at London and Hamburg, stating in conclusion that

'London's shipping still exceeds that of Hamburg in quantity, labour, cash value and goods; but as regards unity and articulation, as an organism, it is already an older form of life. Hamburg learnt from London, but quite on its own it introduced into its study something quite peculiarly German which at first appeared to be merely an additional characteristic in the shape of more rigid policing and order but which grew in the course of time to be the essential trait.'

The same process was occurring in German agriculture and in industry, which Naumann described as

'full of organizational ideas and regulations for combines. Since I wish to speak of the economic syndicates and cartels in various other places I would only call special attention here to the bare fact that in the last twenty years our German industry has assumed an entirely new aspect. At the same time as it grew it interpenetrated. By means of employers' federations, payment-cartels, zonal compacts, and price-agreements there arose a multi-articulated apparatus of spheres of business and dependencies in which the outsider can hardly find his bearings; but this structure was created bit by bit according to requirements and by means of it the old-style private *entrepreneur* was, in the course of a generation, quite quietly led over into the ordered industrial joint-economy even though originally he may have been thoroughly opposed to it. He is becoming a federated *entrepreneur*. If the first and second generations of *entrepreneurs* were resistant in accommodating themselves to this course of development and prefer to remain individual capitalists in the western European sense, yet the *entrepreneur* of the third generation is mostly born as a federated being to start with. . . . Therewith the basic industrial form of the age has been found and now it continually penetrates deeper. Another twenty years and we shall have before us the most comprehensive distribution of labour and plans for domestic economy. The regulation of production is on the march. What appeared forty years ago to be the ideologies of socialist and state-socialistic dreamers, remote from reality, now appears with incredible certainty as a form of reality which has become an accomplished fact in the meantime. Germany is on the way to becoming not only an industrial state but especially an *organizational state*.'

Naumann was quite aware of the deeper implications of this development.

'Everything', he wrote, 'now follows the same path: the technicians, teachers, senior teachers, scholars, doctors, even the artists. The guilds of artisans are adapting themselves to the altered conditions of the time. Despite all the strife between the many associations of opposing interests we are yet a uniform folk, grandly uniform in this method of constituting practical life and work. To this end national schools, universal conscription, the police, science and socialist propaganda have worked together. We hardly knew that fundamentally we all wanted the same thing: the regulated labour of the second capitalistic period, which can be described as the transition from private capitalism to socialism provided only that the word socialism is not taken to mean the phenomenon of purely proletarian big-business but is broadly understood as folk-ordering with the object of increasing the common profit of all for all.

'This new German being is incomprehensible to the individualistic peoples since he seems to them to be partly a reversion to past times of constraint and partly an artificial product of coercion which denies and rapes humanity. In the cultivated circles of Paris and London people's feelings towards this German type are compounded of pity, shyness, respect and aversion. Even if they could produce the same thing there they would not want to since they do not want this disciplined soul, they do not want it because that would be the death and surrender of their own soul. Only the person who had occasionally tried to view Germany from outside with the eyes of a foreigner will be able to understand that fully. The inner force of this contrast must necessarily remain hidden from the German who only knows Germany; he does not feel at all how foreign he has already become even to the best people in the western nations, not through anything particular that he does but simply through being what he is.'

Naumann further drew attention to what lay at the bottom of this new German order, remarking that

'the war [of 1914] was only the continuation of our life with other means, but fundamentally with the same methods. Therein indeed lies the secret of success. . . . If our adversaries like to describe this inner connection between the work of war and the work of peace as the "militarism of Germanism", we can only regard it as just since in fact the Prussian military discipline has its effect upon us all from the captain of industry right through to the navvy.'

And Naumann observed that the circumstances of the war, and particularly the blockade, had powerfully reinforced the prevalent trend in German economic life. He thought that after the war

'only we central Europeans will have learnt and experienced something positive, something particular . . ., for we have experienced the "closed commercial state", the bold dream of the German philosopher Fichte, which thanks to fate and folk-tendency realized itself with us in war. The enemy thought to do us evil but God, the God which Fichte believed in and taught, thought to do us good.'

Naumann urged that after the war the lesson of the blockade should be laid to heart and provision made accordingly.

'When the war is finished," he wrote, 'we wish to lay out official or state-controlled storehouses for the most essential materials. . . . But this storage policy is by nature an interference with private economy. . . . Thus here also the preparation for the economic war leads to a kind of state-socialism, and in truth to a very obscure and unexplored kind.'

These last words may have indicated a certain misgiving, but Naumann asked bitterly, 'How in the world could we do otherwise in order not to have anxieties again about being starved out?'

Naumann summed up the effect of the war upon German economy as follows:

'In the war our self-knowledge is this: that we Germans have slipped into this state-socialism or folk-economic activity in the strict sense of the word. When we emerge from the war we shall no longer be the same economic beings as before. Past, then, is the period of fundamental individualism, the period of imitation of the English economic system which was already more or less in decline; but at the same time past also is the period of an internationalism which boldly vaulted beyond the present-day state. Upon the basis of wartime experiences we demand a regulated economy; *regulation of production from the point of view of the necessity of the state.* Such movements will also manifest themselves elsewhere in the world among other peoples, even among the English, but with us, in our cut-off state, they are riper than anywhere else. . . . That is a world-economic occurrence of the first rank which, in its far-reaching significance, will presumably be much better and more clearly understood by later generations than it is by us who first experience it.

'Therein there is a sure reconciliation between the bourgeois-nationalist and the socialist concept of economy. Already before the war we knew that the opposition between them was diminishing.'

Naumann foresaw the foreign reaction to the post-war development of German economy, and prophesied that 'abroad they will talk even more than before about German economic militarism, but we are convinced that the conversion forced upon us in time of war will not suit us badly.' He summed up the German economic outlook thus:

'On all sides state-socialism or national-socialism grows up; "regulated economy" grows up. Fichte and Hegel nod approval from the walls; after the war for the first time the German becomes an economic state-citizen body and soul; his ideal is and remains the organism, not free-will. . . . That is our freedom, our self-expansion. Therewith shall we experience our day in history. . . .Germany foremost in the world!'

And for Naumann Germany was the nucleus of central Europe. He laid it down in italics that '*the German economic creed should in future become even more the characteristic of central Europe*'. One example will perhaps suffice to illustrate the German itch to take over and organize the activities of neighbouring peoples more efficiently and profitably than they could do themselves. At one point Naumann exclaimed,

'What might the Hungarians not do with their land! . . . According to the varying years thirty-five to thirty-nine thousand square kilometres are tilled as cornland. Just think of what might grow there! What a splendid golden harvest, double as thick [as the present one]! Of course one ought not to blame the people by reason of the climate, but nevertheless the fact remains that it is conceded on all sides that there is a painfully deficient yield to be deplored. Hungary with her magnificent land produces about half as much as Germany per hectare.'

But Naumann was quite aware that the

'romantic tempers [of south and central Europe] are opponents of the modernization of economy. They will not have their old-fashioned souls cleaned and repaired, for—what does it profit a man if he gain the whole world and lose his own soul?

'Come here, dear romantic, we will talk that over as friends.'

Naumann proceeded to explain to the worker that under the old order he had been exploited by the capitalist; he contrasted the 'upper side' with the 'needy underworld', pointing out that 'indeed the beautiful old culture hardly belonged to you at all'. He concluded upon a more ominous note: 'After the war there will be much to pay. With higher prices one just cannot wish to be an economic romantic without sinking in the social scale': sober words and a sombre outlook.

It is fitting that a survey of the political outlook in Germany during the second Reich should close with this notice of the work of Friedrich Naumann; for by his self-consciousness and his critical acumen Naumann, like Ranke before him, affords a vantage point whence one may take a circumspective view of the ground already covered. Naumann like Ranke perceived the full magnitude of the issues involved in the further development of the German way of life and mode of thought. But with him there was even less hesitation. He stood by Germany and exhorted her, conscious of the implications.

We have seen how with Ranke German thought was already swinging out of the western orbit. We have seen how after Ranke, decade after decade, remorseless Germans widened the gulf between themselves and their fellow-Europeans of the west. We have seen what was done for German thought by List, Rodbertus, Lassalle, Wagner, Treitschke, Nietzsche, Schemann, Lagarde, Dühring, Chamberlain, Lamprecht, Bernhardi, and the rest. And now Naumann called upon the German people to take cognizance. At a time when Germany was at war with the west he brought out the fundamental incompatibilities which sundered her from her enemies more surely than the trenches and the no-man's-land in Flanders; and he showed her how it was good. Now there was a no-man's-land of the spirit. Between the two parties there was both distance and conflict. Fraternization there might still be from time to time; but familiarity was absent.

Those who find that Naumann's thought, and particularly its economic kernel, is unfamiliar and distorted would do well to recall his bitter cry: 'We are a folk; we have learnt and found our folk-economy in an economic prison amid a world of foes. That remains as the background of everything which may subsequently befall'. That was a cry which pierced right home in Germany: we are a folk; we have learnt and found our folk-economy in an economic prison amid a world of foes. That remains as the background of everything which may subsequently befall.

The degree in which Naumann's preoccupation with economic questions and his central European ambitions were shared by the German leaders was amply illustrated by the settlements which victorious Germany imposed upon the east.

In the autumn of 1917 Russian resistance collapsed under the pressure of the German armies and the Bolshevik revolutionaries. At Brest-Litovsk a Bavarian nobleman, a Knight of the Golden Fleece, and a Prussian major-general[1] discussed terms of peace with a band of unkempt terrorists under the leadership of the Jew Braunstein, *alias* Trotsky. The peace of Brest-Litovsk was signed on the 3rd March, 1918. By the terms of this treaty, as amplified by supplementary agreements, Russia renounced sovereignty in favour of the central powers over Russian Poland, Estonia, Courland, Livonia, and Lithuania; in Lithuania a Württemberger, Prince William of Urach, ruled as Mindove II, an ephemeral puppet. Russia recognized the independence of Georgia, the Ukraine, and Finland, satellites which gravitated into the Teutonic orbit. The German forces extended their occupation to Odessa and the Sea of Azov. Russian reparation payments were fixed at 6,000,000,000 marks. These payments were to be made by a country which had been deprived of 34 per cent. of her population, 32 per cent. of her agricultural land, 85 per cent. of beet-sugar land, 54 per cent. of her industrial undertakings, and 89 per cent. of her coal-mines. Of this settlement the *Norddeutsche Allgemeine Zeitung* wrote: 'The significance of the treaty with Russia lies in the fact that the German Government has worked only for a peace of understanding and conciliation.'[2]

This satisfactory situation was further enhanced by the fact that Serbia was crushed and Bulgaria an ally. Austria herself was dependent upon Germany from whom she had had to entreat soldiers and supplies and in deference to whom she accordingly renounced any independence of action as regards the Russian settlement. It only remained to deal with treaty-shirking Rumania. On the 7th May, 1918, she was dealt with. By the peace of Bucharest Rumania ceded territory to Hungary along the whole length of the strategic Carpathian border; she ceded the whole of the Dobrudja to the central powers; territorially she was cut off from the sea; her

[1]This description of the representatives of the central powers, together with other particulars concerning the eastern settlement, is derived from J. W. Wheeler-Bennett, *The Treaty of Brest-Litovsk and Germany's Eastern Policy* (Oxford, 1939).

[2]Quoted: J. W. Wheeler-Bennett, op. cit., p. 11.

oil-wells were leased to Germany for ninety-nine years; her economic life was co-ordinated with that of the central powers and exploited for Teutonic benefit.

Such was the situation in the spring of 1918, and it augured most happily for the establishment of Naumann's central European realm. Ludendorff, first quartermaster-general of the supreme command, began to envisage Germandom in the most expansive terms; and it was Ludendorff who was then the real dictator of German politics behind nondescript chancellors like the Prussian bureaucrat Michaelis and Hertling the aged Bavarian. Germany was mistress of all central Europe: that was the beginning. When a Rumanian diplomatist ventured to remonstrate at the harshness of the peace of Bucharest a German staff-officer answered: 'You call it a *harsh* peace? Just wait till you see what we are preparing for France and England.' And it may well have seemed that he would not have to wait very long. Ludendorff's great offensive in the west was rolling forward. The German forces drove through to Soissons and Montdidier. By the middle of July the Germans, thrusting to Dormans and Château-Thierry, crossed the Marne; their line was within forty miles of Paris; they captured 2,500 guns and 225,000 prisoners; they inflicted nearly a million casualties upon the enemy. It was Germany's supreme effort, supreme in force, but also supreme in time.

Autumn closed in, and Germany was spent. Her armies were in full retreat, and its generals suing for an armistice. Meantime the admirals, as a result of politic calculation, resolved upon a most heroic action. They decided that the whole German navy should go upon its death-ride, steaming out to engage the enemy's superior fleet. But just as the German navy had been the symbol of the militaristic imperialism of the second empire, so now did it signal its collapse. On the 4th November, 1918, mutineers seized the port of Kiel and thereby inaugurated the German revolution. On the 10th of November the emperor William II fled across the border into Holland. At eleven o'clock next morning the war concluded.

That was the end of the Second German Empire.

Looking back upon that empire one sees a vigorous, ruthless and aggressive society, more expert than wise, more arrogant than noble, a braggart nation and a brave one. There were indeed exceptions, but they were exceptions.

Looking deeper and trying to discern what that empire stood for, one is struck, as so often in German history, by the degree in which her national structure accorded with her geographical position. Germany was the node of east and west. In organization, in industrial technique, in economic enterprise, she more than held her own against her western neighbours, gaining steadily upon them. Whereas in social and political structure she was archaic, approximating far more closely to absolutist Russia than to the liberal régimes of France and Britain. Forms of constitutions might sometimes obscure, but never alter, the fact that Germany was ruled by an imperial autocrat and lorded over by a hierarchy of princes and dukes, by a landed nobility and a military caste. The true source of their hold over the people was not to be found in democratic suffrage or popular politics, but in the vigorous efficiency of the dominant order, in power, prestige, and propaganda. In this feudal society, as in its prototypes, the Jews became increasingly prosperous and disliked. The importance of the great capitalists and industrialists grew, but in the last resort they were the ministers, not the managers, of the prevailing system. That transformation in the economic make-up which Naumann noticed meant that it was the economic system which was accommodating itself to the political. The second stage of anti-individualistic capitalism was the counterpart to modernized feudalism; furthermore advances in German science had enormously increased the power behind that politico-economic order. In Germany classes which were elsewhere obsolescent were in control of techniques and resources vastly in advance of anything previously conceived of.

Thus once again the practical had kept pace with the theoretical. In both spheres Germany was divorced from the west. The historical school remained true to itself. The union between historical fact and political theory is most impressive. It was with justice that Naumann wrote: 'Even we ourselves hardly noticed how very much our philosophers were practical prophets.' That was true of what had passed, but events to come were to give it yet more urgent meaning.

Chapter VI

REPUBLIC

1918–1933

The November Revolution was not in the first instance a spontaneous uprising of the German people. The impetus was military. The war-lord had failed. The army was beaten. The soldiers and sailors of the home forces mutinied. They were war-weary, and the war and the army and the old order went together. That left a void, and the obvious people to fill it were the people themselves, as had happened in Russia. And so they followed the soldiers and sailors, followed and joined with them. There was popular enthusiasm for the revolution because it was under way; it had not got under way because of popular determination. New forces were liberated since the German war-machine had crumpled up: even in dissolution it swayed the fortunes of the nation. The revolution happened and the people said they wanted it to happen.

That was the beginning of the Weimar Republic.

The duality of impetus and effect was clearly mirrored in political organization. The revolution found its first expression in soldiers' and workmen's councils on the pattern of Russian Soviets. These simple bodies exemplified the organizational and social breakdown; they were the inchoate expression of incipient and partial popular will, and it was through them that the proletariat of Germany first tried to fumble its way from collapse to collective security. It did so by calling upon the other and more authoritative political product of the revolution. On the 10th November, 1918, the workmen's and soldiers' councils of Berlin foregathered in the Busch Circus, the rotunda where wild beasts were exhibited; there they elected the first republican government of Germany.

This Council of the Representatives of the People was composed of socialists under the leadership of Friedrich Ebert and Philipp Scheidemann. These two came from the majority socialist party, whose socialism was of a more or less opportunistic brand. Associated with them were independent socialists like Hugo Haase and Wilhelm Dittmann, whose more doctrinaire and purely Marxian creed had led them to split from the majority and to maintain a steady opposition to the war. It might seem that this government was a logical extension of the revolutionary councils. In reality it was far otherwise.

The one political party which was truly fired with the spirit of revolution was the relatively small Spartacus Union, a group of left-wing independents led by Rosa Luxemburg and Karl Liebknecht, son of that Liebknecht who had headed the revolt against the tame and Lassallean Schweitzer in the early days. This pep-group worked for revolution on the Russian model, power being vested in workmen's and soldiers' councils. But now as early as November they saw the revolution slipping through their fingers. The councils, instead of proclaiming full solidarity with the Spartacists, pledged support to the majority socialists, the Kaiser's socialists as they were derisively called. Many of these parliamentarians and trade-unionists, who were in any case often more *bourgeois* than proletarian in outlook, had come to think of themselves as the permanent opposition. Under the old order they had been mainly concerned with the immediate care of improving the workman's daily lot. Their activities had been conducted within the framework of authority. Of the burden of government they had no experience whatever. Now suddenly all was changed. These humdrum socialists found themselves with a revolution on their hands, with chaos to cope with, with a nation to rule.

Ebert and his followers were not glad and resolute in their new responsibility. Their first care was not to promote the revolution but to curb it, Ebert himself remarking that he hated revolution as he hated sin. The republican government did not represent a radical departure, but merely a shift to the left in the coalition of the centre, liberals, and socialists which had been formed in 1917 and had provided the basis for the short-lived liberal government of Prince Max of Baden after the collapse of Ludendorff's armies and dictatorship in October 1918. But although that government itself had not lasted, the introduction of the régime which it stood for was the real and lasting German revolution. Constitutional parliamentarianism and the abolition of the Prussian three-class suffrage was quite enough for most Germans. Therefore the rôle of Ebert's government was to preserve the form of the November revolution while liquidating its reality and perpetuating that of the October revolution.

The socialist ministers turned at once to such of the past as survived. They leant upon the two main pillars of absolutist tradition in Germany: the bureaucracy and the military caste. The imperial civil service was left substantially untouched; popular representatives made a few excursions into its labyrinthine depths, but the results which they produced were often more laughable than laudable; the old officials carried on and a man like Solf, the secretary of state for foreign affairs, was allowed to manifest his open hostility to the independent socialists in a cabinet meeting. Meanwhile Ebert was in close touch with the military high command under Hindenburg and Groener. A private telephone line led from Ebert's room in the Foreign Office to army headquarters at Cassel. The generals eagerly promised Ebert support against the radicals. To this end ex-officers trained free-corps, recruiting them from the stampeded middle-classes and from counter-revolutionary adventurers and desperadoes. These free-corps were sworn in to Ebert on the 17th December. Thus behind the political divisions there already loomed up the sinister shapes of hostile paramilitary bodies. The free-corps stood over against the soldiers' councils.

Action was not slow to follow. A series of disputes and affrays between the supporters of the councils and of the government culminated on the 29th December in the resignation of the independent socialists from the government. Next day the Spartacus Union widened the breach by reconstituting itself as the German Communist Party. The Spartacists were still in association with workers' and soldiers' councils led by the revolutionary foremen (*Obleute*) of Berlin.

It had taken less than two months to convince these councils that they had been betrayed by the Government of the People's Representatives. The immediate occasion of the clash was, significantly enough, the question of the control of the Berlin police; the chief was an independent socialist who sympathized with the foremen; he refused to resign his post. The Spartacists came out on the streets in support. The government appointed Gustav Noske, a majority socialist, to be commander-in-chief of its troops. Noske called in the generals and the free-corps. A staunch Prussian conservative, General von Lüttwitz, was in command; under him served units which had been raised by General Maercher, General von Wissel, General von Roeder, General von Held, General von Hülsen, and General von Hoffmann. The free-corps did their work with savagery and expedition. By the middle of January 1919 the Spartacists were crushed, and troops with artillery and machine-guns paraded through Berlin. On the 15th January the free-corps captured Karl Liebknecht and Rosa Luxemburg and beat them to death. Four days later elections for the national assembly at Weimar took place.

On the 6th February the assembly met. The central council of the workmen's and soldiers' councils protested, but its power was now hardly more than nominal and the free-corps could be trusted to deal with inconvenient radicals. After their success in Berlin the free-corps formations were expanded. In the first half of 1919 the government sent off trained bands on punitive expeditions to Bremen, Halle, Leipzig, Brunswick, Thuringia, and the Ruhr. Suspects were taken into protective custody and there was ugly work in the prisons. On the occasion of a strike in Berlin in March Noske issued an illegal decree ordering his troops to shoot at once all persons found in arms against them. The free-corps interpreted this instruction with liberality and executed it with alacrity; a certain Lieutenant Marloh, in particular, distinguished himself even in that company by his butchery.

Hitherto Bavaria alone had been exempt from strife, thanks largely to its forceful prime minister Kurt Eisner, who favoured conciliar organization rather than military repression. In February Eisner was murdered and after a period of communist confusion the central government in Berlin resorted as usual to the free-corps. On the 1st–2nd May, 1919, Munich was taken by free-corps and Bavarian volunteers drawn from the reactionary *bourgeoisie*. Hundreds of people were shot, out of hand, in batches. Henceforth Bavaria remained a stronghold of reaction.

Thus did Ebert and his colleagues establish their authority throughout the land by means of a brutal soldiery. Thus six months after the collapse of the German army militarism was again rampant in Germany, and the revolution was looking to reaction for its strength. In 1918, just as seventy years before, the moderates who were in control of the revolution feared that the extremists would overtake them, and accordingly resorted to repression. The representatives of the people had instituted a white terror.

That was the setting to the debates of the national assembly at Weimar, a seat chosen, ironically enough, with a view to emphasizing the humanist tradition of Goethe and Schiller in contrast to Prussian militarism. Ebert was elected president of the German republic, Scheidemann becoming chancellor and Noske minister for the Reichswehr, as the army was now called. The new constitution was passed on the 31st July. It was based on the principle of parliamentary democracy and on the authority of the Reichstag. But, as events were to prove, the new régime rested merely upon a constitutional transfer of sovereignty, important but not decisive in itself. The government showed no inclination to establish a firm and practical foundation upon which a new order might be built in a country where power-politics were the tradition. This neglect was exemplified not only in the handling of the bureaucracy and the army, but also in the refusal to abandon federalism, to socialize big industry and, above all, to redistribute the latifundia of the Junkers.

The temper of the socialists was illustrated at their party meeting held in June 1919. One of their spokesmen, Bernstein, ventured to criticize the old imperial leaders and to raise the question of their war-guilt. His remarks provoked great indignation and he was accused of being antinationalist. It was at the same meeting that Wissel, the new minister for economy, spoke as follows:

'We have not yet done anything but carry on the programme which had already been begun by the Imperial German Government of Prince Max of Baden. The constitution had been prepared without any real and active participation on the part of the people. We have not been able to satisfy the dull resentment with which the masses are imbued because we have had no real programme. Essentially we have governed according to the old forms of our state life. We have only succeeded in breathing very little fresh life into these forms. We have not been able so to influence the Revolution that Germany seemed filled with a new spirit. The inner structure of German civilization, of social life, appears little altered. And even so, not for the better. The nation believes that the achievements of the Revolution are simply negative in character, that in place of one form of military and bureaucratic government by individuals another has been introduced, and that the principles of government do not differ essentially from those of the old régime. . . . I believe that the verdict of history upon both the National Assembly and ourselves will be severe and bitter.'[1]

Wissel saw clearer than most, but he faithfully reflected the general gloom and disillusion. And hunger sharpened the exasperation—hunger which Germans ascribed to the maintenance of the allied blockade throughout the winter. Illicit traffic in food, the so-called Schieb system, was rife. Corruption grew apace and already began to eat away the dignity of the republic. The canker tainted men in high places, and most notably Erzberger, the energetic orator of the catholic centre who was the driving force behind the government after Scheidemann had resigned in June because he could not stomach acceptance of the treaty of Versailles, a revulsion which was shared even by the Spartacists on the extreme left. The government tried to keep order by sporadic bursts of violence, as when in January 1920 the Berlin police brought out their machine-guns and mowed down independent socialists who were demonstrating outside the Reichstag. Meanwhile German militarism was finding an outlet in the Baltic states where so-called volunteers were fighting the Russians and forming a reactionary nucleus which drew support from the wide lands of the Junkers in the east. The Letts and Esthonians themselves finally had to fight their nominal supporters and the free-corps withdrew under threat of an

[1]Quoted: Arthur Rosenberg, *A History of the German Republic* (Trans. I. F. D. Morrow and L. M. Sieveking, London, 1936), pp. 125–6.

allied ultimatum. On their return to Germany they were not slow in making their presence felt.

Reactionary nationalism was already coming out into the open. The sinister Erzberger was being denounced as the epitome of republican corruption in a campaign conducted by the equally sinister nationalist financier Karl Helfferich. On the 12th March, 1920, Erzberger resigned. This was the signal for the Kapp *putsch.* Kapp was a nationalist politician and a former governor of East Prussia. He now sought to seize control with the support of free-corps units who had lately returned from the Baltic and resisted all attempts to demobilize them. On the 13th March the Ehrhardt brigade, the most famous of them all, marched into Berlin under the old black-white-red colours. The government fled to Dresden and then on to Stuttgart. But the rising was premature and failed. So far was it, however, from being crushed that the troops which had sponsored it were actually used by the government to suppress a radical agitation among the workers in the Ruhr. The free-corps, baulked of constitutional success, took it out of the workers with peculiar ruthlessness.

In June 1920 elections for the Reichstag were held. They constituted a defeat for the democrats and showed that the majority socialists had lost half their following in eighteen months. A catholico-capitalist government was formed under Fehrenbach, but the most significant member was the nominal democrat Gessler who was minister for the Reichswehr. He worked in with General von Seeckt, the very able chief of the army command. Gessler was the man for the Reichswehr generals, and therefore though governments came and governments went he was in them all right up to 1928: a proof of the power of the Reichswehr. The German army was now limited to 100,000 men, but General von Seeckt and his associates planned and organized and hoped for the day when this potent nucleus should rally the nation and lead it into its own once more. In politics the Reichswehr was naturally on the right, and such was its power that it came near to being the government behind the government. The political governments were many and transient, but the Reichswehr was a permanent force.

At the same time as military reaction was discreetly making good in Berlin, Munich was the centre of a parallel movement, parallel but peculiar, more evident and yet more complex.

Simultaneously with the Kapp *putsch* the Bavarian government was taken over by Von Kahr, a conservative civil servant. But Kahr succeeded where Kapp failed. In Bavaria the reactionaries angled for popular support and had themselves duly elected to office. This support was largely a reflection of the two main currents of opinion which then predominated in Bavaria. The first was anti-communism. The bitterness left by the communist experiment of 1919 was heightened by the fact that for the small man with something to lose communism vaguely meant insecurity; and as the years of inflation made his struggle for security more desperate, so did they intensify his hatred of communism. And with anti-communism went anti-Semitism. Just as the Prussians had tried to make a scapegoat of the Jews after the disaster of Jena, so now after the humiliation of Versailles did the Germans turn upon them. The Jews were hated because of their radical tradition in Germany and because of their financial hold; and because they were Jews. The leading anti-Semitic review, *Auf Vorposten*, inflamed Germans against the two Jewish internationals, the financial and the Marxist-socialist. The bogus Protocols of the Elders of Sion did good propaganda. Their author, Gottfried von Beck, *alias* Baron von Haussen, shared with Ludendorff visions of a Russian ghetto for all European Jews and of Europe itself subject to Germany and to a German religion. Ludendorff was further connected with the review entitled *Judentum und Freimaurerei* (*Jewry and Freemasonry*), which was under the direction of Major Henning, a former staff-officer.

Anti-Semitism was among the main planks of the *Völkischer Schutz- und Trutzbund*, an organization which maintained the tradition of extreme nationalism upheld during the Great War by the Fatherland Party of Admiral von Tirpitz. This organization was doing well in Munich in 1920, and a kindred spirit of anti-Semitic nationalism inspired the *Deutsche Arbeiterpartei*, which the narrow-chested, narrow-minded locksmith Drexler had founded the year before. A particularly useful member of this group was Captain Ernst Röhm from the Epp Corps, a swashbuckler who brought in the soldiers and police, maintaining close liaison with the free-corps and paramilitary bodies, prominent among them the Einwohnerwehr and Orgesch formation, illegal by now but actively encouraged by the Bavarian government. The chief theorist of the German Workers Party, particularly on the economic side, was a disgruntled civil engineer named Gottfried Feder. It was he who denounced the tyranny of interest (*Zinsknechtschaft*) and established the distinction between creative, industrial, Aryan, capital (*schaffendes Kapital*) and rapacious, financial, Jewish, capital (*raffendes Kapital*). Feder delivered a lecture along these lines in June 1919 which captured the imagination of a house-painter from Vienna called Adolf Hitler. Next month he joined the party. This highly strung ex-corporal was an admirer of the Austrian anti-Semites Schoenerer and Lüger; he was also a good orator despite the fact that his voice had been affected by severe gassing during the Great War.

In 1920 the German Workers Party was reconstituted as the National-Socialist German Workers Party (N.S.D.A.P.). The Nazi programme, dated 24th February, 1920, contained twenty-five points, of which the main were: the ideal of Greater Germany and of free self-determination for the German people, entailing the abolition of the treaties of Versailles and Saint-Germain, full equality of Germany with other nations, and the return of the former German colonies; a racially regenerated Germany free from Jewish influence; a strengthened executive and a single parliament; a new German common law free from Roman taint; abolition of the professional army and formation of a national army; cultivation of national fitness by means of physical education and compulsory games and gymnastics; work for all in the interest of the common good which takes precedence over individual good; abolition of unearned income; nationalization of large concerns; communalization of large shops to the benefit of the small tradespeople; suppression of speculation and profiteering; agrarian and educational reform; culture and office within the reach of all; suppression of newspapers transgressing against the common weal; respect for the rights of the two great religious confessions in so far as they constitute no menace to the morale or ethical sense of the Germanic race or to the existence of the state.

In order to implement this programme the Nazi claque and party toughs were organized as the *Ordnertruppe* under the ex-convict Maurice. Among the Nazis were idealists like Gregor Strasser, but Hitler's closest associates were for the most part a dubious crew—men like the homosexual Röhm, Christian Weber the chucker-out, the perverted debauchees Hermann Esser and Julius Streicher, Hanussen the magus, and Hoffmann the unsavoury photographer. While the party toughs were developing their terror-tactics against opponents in Munich Hitler was extending his relations elsewhere. He spoke to the National Club in Berlin and negotiated with Counts Behr and von Wartenburg, leaders of the conservative party and the old Prussian upper house. He stayed with Siegfried Wagner at Bayreuth, where he established contact with Houston Stewart Chamberlain, to whose theories he had been introduced by Dietrich Eckart, editor of the *Völkischer Beobachter*, a paper which the Nazis bought in December 1920. By 1923 Chamberlain had deserted the ex-emperor for Hitler. In the October of that year he wrote to Hitler:

'You have mighty things to do; but in spite of your will-power I do not take you for a violent man. You know Goethe's distinction between violence and violence. There is a violence that comes out of and leads back to chaos, and there is a violence whose nature it is to form a cosmos. . . . It is in this cosmos-building sense that I wish to count you among the up-building, not among the violent men. . . .

'The ideal of politics would be to have no politics. But this non-politics would have to be frankly professed and imposed upon the world by force. Nothing can be done as long as the Parliamentary system rules; God knows that the Germans have no spark of talent for this system. Its prevalence I regard as the greatest misfortune, for it can only lead again and again into a morass and bring to nought all plans for restoring the Fatherland and lifting it up. . . .

'My faith in Germanism had not wavered an instant, though my hope—I confess—was at a low ebb. With one stroke you have transformed the state of my soul. That in the hour of her deepest need Germany gives birth to a Hitler proves her vitality; as do the influences that emanate from him; for these two things—personality and influence—belong together. . . . May God protect you!'[1]

Ludendorff, not less than Chamberlain, was attracted to Hitler. In 1921 the *Völkischer Beobachter* took up his pet notion of joint European action against Soviet Russia and ran a series of flaming russophobe articles by Arnold Rechberg, the potassium magnate. But those were aspirations, and meanwhile there was immediate work on hand. At the end of July 1921 Hitler wrested the party-leadership from Drexler and his followers, and on the 3rd August the *Sturm-Abteilungen* were created. These storm-troopers purported to be the expression of the defensive idea of a free nation. They were one more symptom of the rampant growth of cryptomilitary formations in Germany. The nominal prohibition of free-corps and kindred bodies did nothing to impede their spread. In April 1921 the Bavarian secretary of state estimated that the Orgesch formation comprised 320,000 men, 240,000 rifles, 2,780 machine-guns, 34 mine-throwers, and 44 field-guns. The free-corps—Ehrhardt, the Iron Division, Löwenfeld, Oberland, Aulock, Rossbach, and the rest—were scattered as units throughout Germany, maintained on the estates of Junkers and supported by the Reichswehr. The Ehrhardt brigade went underground as the Consul Organization; the ramifications of the free-corps, or Black Reichswehr as they were called, extended through a network of semi-sporting societies and gymnastic associations such as the Olympia Sport Association, the Steel Helmet League, the Viking Society, Blücher Union, Bismarck Union, Young German Order. Membership figures were not easy to come by, but it was estimated that they totalled not less than three-quarters of a million. These sinister formations spread secret terror throughout the country. Members who told too much were marked down for death and these Vehm murders were generally committed with impunity. For the free-corps and defence associations had the Reichswehr behind them; it foiled attempts to deal with them; if members were tried for murder the courts regularly accepted the evidence of expert witnesses put up by the Reichswehr; those who protested

[1]Quoted: H. Wickham Steed, op. cit., vol. xvii, p. 669.

against this secret army were imprisoned as traitors or, more simply, murdered themselves. In June 1921 Garreis, a socialist deputy who had been particularly active against the defence associations, was assassinated in Munich. In August two of Ehrhardt's men did away with Erzberger. Next year Walter Rathenau followed. This politically minded and scholarly industrialist favoured the policy of fulfilment towards the allies, and he was a Jew. That was enough. His murder created a stir and the government set up a special court to try conspirators against the republic: but the Reichswehr soon penetrated there also and deflected the zeal of the judges from the free-corps to the communists. It was not a very creditable chapter in the history of the German law.

Towards the end of 1922 the free-corps became the focus of further turgid intrigue. Tiring of the slow methods of the conservative party, renamed the German National People's Party, the free-corps broke with them and formed the German Racist Liberty Party with the support of elements of the Völkische organization and notably of the deputies Graefe, Wulle, and Henning. The Nazis came to an understanding with this group while at the same time keeping themselves before the notice of the military reactionaries in Berlin. Early in 1923 Class of the Pan-German League was exercising himself over the possibility of a national government based on the Reichswehr and headed by himself and General von Seeckt; Hitler would represent Bavaria. But meanwhile the Reichswehr had other things afoot. As a result of the Franco-Belgian invasion of the Ruhr in January 1923 the Reichswehr, while recognizing that immediate resistance was useless, decided that loose affiliation with the defence associations was not enough, and it proceeded to expand its regular units behind the subterfuge of labour detachments (*Arbeitskommandos*). It wished to incorporate free-corps formations, thus depriving them of their individuality. The free-corps reacted against this attempt and concentrated their forces under Lieutenant Rossbach. Rossbach and Graefe went to Cuno, the managing director of the Hamburg-Amerika line who now headed a government based on capitalist support. They proposed to Cuno that all the defence associations should be united under General Ludendorff in support of the government against the social democrats and communists. The chancellor shelved this suggestion, and in March the Reichswehr secured the arrest of its rival Rossbach.

The feud simmered through the summer until the autumn, when it assumed a new and sharper form. In Bavaria, as distinct from the rest of Germany, the free-corps and the conservatives were still in firm alliance. The defence associations accordingly fell back on Munich, always their surest stay. On the 26th September, 1923, the Bavarian government decreed a state of emergency and what amounted to a dictatorship of the right, vesting supreme powers in Kahr. The central government was now under Gustav Stresemann, the leader of the German People's Party, the new name which masked the old national-liberals and big industry. In the face of developments in Bavaria the Reichswehr induced Stresemann to invest it with full executive authority in the Reich. The Reichstag authorized the government to promulgate orders with the force of law in the spheres of industry, finance, and social policy. On the other side General von Lossow associated the Bavarian Reichswehr with Kahr in defiance of General von Seeckt. Civil war seemed imminent and defence associations under Ehrhardt mobilized on the northern borders of Bavaria. But between Bavaria and Prussia lay Thuringia and Saxony, both of which enjoyed democratic governments at that time. At the end of October the Reichswehr from Berlin arbitrarily deposed both governments, an action conspicuously devoid of any legality. But Kahr still hesitated to take the decisive step. The racial extremists decided to force his hand. On the evening of the 8th November, 1923, the Bürgerbräu Keller in Munich witnessed the first example of the Nazi technique of co-ordination. After a curious scene Hitler and Goering induced Kahr and Lossow to associate themselves with them and Ludendorff. But the Bavarian leaders backed out overnight and next day the Nazi demonstrators were shot up and dispersed. Ehrhardt declared for Kahr. The *putsch* had failed. Hitler and his followers were condemned to short periods of detention. Kahr and Lossow had tacitly aligned themselves with the main body of reaction by turning against the racist formations. Nothing further was heard of Kahr's treason and

Lossow's mutiny. They were continued in their posts, and the Reichswehr enjoyed its victory without ostentation.

It was just five years since the institution of the republican régime in Germany. It had made a pitiful beginning. Five years only and democracy was discredited, the country a prey to strife between rival groups of nationalist reactionaries. The sinister story of this development was completed by its sombre background. The republic meant humiliation—Versailles and the occupation of the Ruhr; it meant hunger, and unemployment and insecurity, fortunes for some and ruin for more; it meant wild speculation and dizzy inflation—money melting away hour by hour and values gone crazy with noughts, 12,000,000, marks to frank a letter, 4,200,000,-000, in exchange for a dollar. The *petit bourgeoisie* was largely proletarianized. Disintegration was moral as well as economic. Latent instincts came to the top; sexual excess became almost commonplace; Berlin was the home of debauch, and, together with Cologne, it was the chief focus of the Dada movement. Those were the conditions in which the youth of post-war Germany grew up. In an official pamphlet on conditions in Berlin at the beginning of 1923 the chief burgomaster stated that

> numbers of children, even the very youngest, never have a drop of milk. . . . They have dry bread, sometimes spread with mashed potatoes. The children frequently go to school with no shirts or warm clothing, or are kept from school owing to lack of underclothing. Want is gradually strangling every feeling for neatness, cleanliness and decency, leaving room only for thoughts of the fight with hunger and cold.'

Conditions in Berlin were, perhaps, hardly typical of those in Germany at large; but they were at least indicative. Many of the German youth either nurtured their resentment or sought escape how best they might, often through the romantic vagabondage of the Wandervogel and the like.

Such were the political events and social conditions which moulded post-war Germany. Without some appreciation of this pungent setting it would be difficult to form any very accurate estimate of the contemporary outlook on society.

In thought as in politics continuity with the past found its clearest expression in the military sphere. For instance the pre-war author of *Germany and the Next War* became the post-war author of *Concerning the War of the Future*. Such tenacity of purpose inspires something akin to awe. Bernhardi began his new book with the words:

'There is no longer a German army at all. For the few men whom we are still permitted to maintain by the peace treaty cannot count as such. Our colonies are gone. Our fleet lies at the bottom of the sea.'

For Bernhardi this bleak prospect was but a spur to action. The old German fleet might rust in the depths, but a new fleet should make the deep its own.

'Despite the stipulations of the peace the U-boat weapon must be developed as far as possible. The fact that that and the extension of the army can be carried out is proved by the years following 1806 in which, instead of the allowed 42,000 men, 200,000 were drilled under the very eyes of the French garrisons':

a fact which had not escaped the generals of the Reichswehr. Bernhardi closed with the affirmation—

'I know very well that for the moment we depend entirely upon the will of our enemies. . . . I know very well that the interest of our opponents requires at the present moment that we should be rendered defenceless for as long a time as possible; but I know also that a people of approximately 70 millions, which can considerably increase its numbers if the Germans of Austria join it, will not be suppressed in the long run, that it cannot be degraded to being a slave-people as is at present apparently the case.'

He looked forward to the time when the German folk would

'show itself worthy of its great forefathers and further envisage war as it is fashioned by reality. I myself shall hardly live to see this great time. My existence is past in that I helped to build the state which is today broken in pieces; but I write in confidence of the future. . . . Germany will arise; she still has a great future before her!'

But Bernhardi was an avowedly militant spirit, and in order to redress the balance it may be well to turn to a man who was held to be so liberal and unpatriotic that he was murdered for it.

The thought of Walter Rathenau is important not only in itself, but also in that he was an outstanding example of the German conjunction of technique and idealism. Well versed in philosophy and a student of Fichte and Nietzsche, he also held high official positions and directed the great A.E.G. electrical concern.

For Rathenau, as for Bernhardi and most other German thinkers after the war, the great puzzle was why all-powerful Germany had lost the war. Bernhardi thought that inept politicians were responsible for much. As far as immediate causes went Rathenau knew another answer since he had been responsible for co-ordinating Germany's war-time economic resources. But he went deeper and tended to read the lessons of defeat in terms of his pet bugbear, the progress of mechanization, which he had already copiously denounced before the war.

The development of mechanization had probably been the most impressive single manifestation of the new might of the Second German Empire. For Rathenau this mechanization, based on enormously increased consumption, spelt ultimate disaster in that it betokened degermanization (*Entgermanisierung*). Of Jewish extraction himself, he attributed to machines what other Germans blamed on the Jews, holding that 'anti-Semitism is the false conclusion drawn from an eminently true premise: European degermanization'. His conception of Germanity is illuminated in passing by his remark that 'the Germanic ideal, which held fast for a thousand years in the face of the assault of Christianity, is violently shaken by mechanization'. For Rathenau, as for so many other Germans, Germanity implied a harking-back to the primeval. He dwelt upon the fact that

'before the dawn of history power and courage were the highest virtues of mankind. Heroic peoples, steeled in struggle with the forces of nature, emerged from their forests; they subjected the original inhabitants who were weaker and peaceable. The clever man was the thrall of the strong.'

Socialism was one of the symptoms of this mechanistic attack against the German ideal. According to Rathenau 'socialism has never inflamed the hearts of men, and no great and auspicious deed has ever been performed in its name.' Parliamentary democracy was no better than socialism. In 1919 he wrote: 'parliamentarianism was always a makeshift, except in countries of such political maturity that the form of government is no longer a matter of concern. With us its day is past before it has begun.' The ideal state for Rathenau was an autocratic democracy based on a system of estates. He proclaimed to the German youth that

'rule everywhere should be autocratic; every government other than the autocratic is powerless and incompetent. Autocracy and democracy are not antitheses which exclude each other; on the contrary they can only become operative through union. It is only upon a democratic basis that autocratic rule can and should rest; democracy is only justified where it has an autocratic superstructure. At all times it is persons who have ruled, not corporate bodies and masses.'

Rathenau thought that this autocratic rule was peculiarly adapted to the structure of the German people. As he put it:

'Whoever saw a Prussian regiment march past and compared the mien of the troops with that of the leaders recognized the contrast between two races provided that his eyes were sharpened for the contemplation of organic existence; but at the same time he has beheld a visible symbol and image of the articulation of our people.'

And the two races were not merely metaphorical. He went on to explain that 'the whole of Germany east of the Elbe shows us that by means of conquest and colonization in times known to history it originated as a folk-structure in two layers. The conquerors were the Teutons, the conquered the Slavs; the event took place from the twelfth down to the fourteenth century.' This double structure of the German people particularly adapted them to the realization of Rathenau's ideal of rule by a popular *élite*. Indeed he sometimes thought that they went too far in this direction, lamenting that Germany lacked what the western nations possessed, the sound common sense of a stable middle-class. He revealed something of what lay behind his admiration of autocracy when he spoke with regret of 'subordination! This hard word of late Latin origin is hardly ever used in languages other than the German; we have need of it every day. . . . The inclination which subordination awakes in us is the boundless subjection of a man to the command of another man'.

Rathenau emphasized the rôle of mystery in heightening

the prestige of the ruler who enforced absolute subordination and of the state identified with him. In this connexion it is instructive to observe how nearly he approached to many of the great romantics of a century before in his opinion of Frederick the Great. Rathenau thought that

'the most convulsively subversive remark which ever proceeded from the mouth of a king was made by Frederick the Great in describing the ruler as the servant of the state. The decisive implication of this remark did not lie in the revelation of Prussian reality and sense of duty but much more in the fact that royalty was sundered from mystery and the state from mystical royalty, and that thenceforth according to the conception of the royal freethinker the state existed as the most exalted contrivance indeed, but still only as a contrivance with a view to expediency and welfare, as a human product.

'This does not prevent our own age itself from delighting to observe the mystical side of the state and of state-authority, and that indeed not merely on solemn and festive occasions.'

From the mysticism of the state Rathenau passed on to the phenomenon of nationalism and gave it as his opinion that 'decidedly the defence of nationality in the present state of civilization is a necessary, indeed an absolute 'task'. And he realized that nationalism meant total war. Before the outbreak of the Great War he wrote that 'every new industry and every new commercial connection is the equivalent to battalions. All politics are economic politics, war-preparedness. This signifies the nationalism of our time'. Rathenau thought that 'in the life of peoples modern wars are comparable to what examinations are in civil life—demonstrations of capacity'.

But Rathenau eschewed the extreme of nationalism, warning his countrymen that they were no chosen people. After the Great War he advocated international co-operation based not upon a league of nations subservient to the pluto-democratic west, still masking selfishness with *laissez-faire*, but on that social justice and general disarmament which would be the natural outcome of corporative economic co-operation based upon the hierarchic German model.

The treaty of Versailles and the decomposition of republican Germany filled Rathenau with foreboding. He foresaw to some extent the possible outcome of prevalent trends, and indeed of his own theories if the stress were somewhat shifted. (His writings had a considerable influence upon Drexler, the forerunner of the Nazis.) Beside Rathenau's notice of the late Latin origin of the word 'subordination' one may set his observation that 'the Roman Imperium vainly sought for an anchorage in the absolute, the inviolable; finally it had to satisfy itself with the oriental despotism of a bodyguard, and it went to ruin'.

Rathenau serves as an introduction to much in post-war German thought. The sense of oppression which prevalent mechanization inspired in him was shared by many thoughtful Germans. And they, like their forefathers a century earlier, tended to equate mechanization with arid intellectualism. This was an underlying reality for Rathenau and inspired his lament that the age 'cannot in the first place . . . distinguish the genuine from the false because it does not feel, but reasons'. This mechanistic rationalism was in its turn equated with western Europe. The mechanization and ultimate collapse of the second empire were held to be the symptom and effect of the degree to which this alien virus had sapped the prowess of pure Germanity. Thus the theory of the penetration of mechanization from the west was adduced in support of the wishful belief that Germany was not defeated in the Great War but betrayed, a delusion which was fostered more immediately by the legend of the 'stab in the back'. In order to effect a national regeneration it was necessary to cast back to the irrational springs of the true German spirit. Thus did the post-war years witness the rise of the new romanticism in Germany.

Neoromanticism found a most powerful focus in Count Hermann Keyserling.

This forceful aristocrat was at pains to emphasize that his significance lay at least as much in his being as in his writings. And indeed in himself he comprised much that was both traditional and actual in the Germany of his time. Born in 1880 and married in 1919 to a granddaughter of the Iron Chancellor, he came from those eastern territories which affected post-war Germany so closely, being descended from a distinguished line of Baltic barons. Keyserling sometimes called himself a condottiero, and in spirit he was of the

Baltic free-corps: in spirit only since he was incapacitated for military service by a severe wound which he received in a duel as a youth. Soon after recovering from this wound Keyserling had gone, like Chamberlain before him, to study geology at Geneva; and it was as a student that he 'read Houston Stewart Chamberlain's *Foundations of the Nineteenth Century*. The impression produced on me was tremendous. It suddenly became clear to me that if I could meet the man who had written this book, I should soon find out what my purpose in life was'. Keyserling accordingly went to Vienna, and there got to know Chamberlain, living under his influence from 1901 to 1903. He

> 'looked up with enthusiastic veneration to this man. . . . The effect of Chamberlain's continuous influence was extraordinarily fruitful. In his nature, closely related to mine in many respects, I believed that I saw myself, such as I really was, as in a mirror. I found there that centre of polarization which I needed to readjust my nature, so that, on the one hand, it could begin to unfold, and, on the other, emerge from its state of chaos to become a cosmos.'

Keyserling considered that he owed 'Chamberlain . . . an eternal debt of gratitude', although he maintained later that he 'never shared Chamberlain's racist ideas. . . . I never took those ideas seriously': which is curious in view of the tremendous impression which *The Foundations of the Nineteenth Century* made upon him, and of the fact that he expressed racist opinions not wholly dissimilar to those of Chamberlain, holding that 'the Germanic people, who destroyed the old world, were rough and cruel, but they were also courageous, loyal and ready to sacrifice; this enabled them, given their talents, to become continuously better in the course of centuries, whereas Greeks and Romans, who were refined but cowardly and false, perished through degeneration'. And again, 'quite certainly, a Germanic race exists on the plane of facts, and that race is hardly less widely spread in France and Belgium than in Germany. "Latinity", on the other hand, which only exists as an idea, is an entity of a purely cultural order'. Keyserling further thought that 'no matter how foolish anti-Semitism may be as an outlook on the world, it must for all that have its justification, because Jews are, and always have been, equally despised the world over, in the East even more than in the West'.

The logic of the last observation is not, perhaps, of the highest order. And indeed Keyserling openly scorned logic and definitions. Reasoned thought was alien to him from youth upwards, and he has described how as a boy 'in my animal nature I felt myself inferior to the intellectualized Keyserlings. In order to repress this feeling of inferiority I gave myself as little as possible to reflection'. He admitted that 'it is, in truth, a paradox that I should call myself and should indeed be a philosopher, for my whole mentality is opposed to ratiocination. . . . I have never gained anything by mere *thinking*. What I know is all brought forth from out of the Unconscious and emerges in my conscious as a revelation'. In accordance with these inner workings Keyserling 'never considered philosophy a science but an art'.

Thus did Keyserling hark back through Nietzsche to the great romantics; he championed intuition against intellect, and the unconscious against the conscious while subsuming philosophy under the head of aesthetics. And like the earlier romantics he admired the Middle Ages, remarking that 'medieval Christianity really understood human nature much more profoundly than does the modern age'.

As regards the modern age Keyserling was at one with Rathenau in denouncing 'that soullessness and mechanization which every one of any account has emphatically observed in the new Germany'. And with mechanization went intellectualism: 'We Westerners have run ahead of life with our intelligence'. In other words, 'the repression of the sphere of impulse and instinct . . . sundered conscious life from its true living roots. . . . Herein we find the true cause of that which makes us feel civilization as something in growing contrast to life'. But Keyserling distinguished himself from

'a Johannes Müller, who damns all intellectualized life as "life-in-death" . . . not to mention the innumerable swarms of minor prophets who see the proof of a higher mission in the mere possession of moods and emotions—all these are being hailed as saviours. An outlook of this type characterizes most of the latter-day regenerative movements, from the ethical and religious movements to that German youth movement which saw its ideal in the mere condition of youth as such.'

Keyserling's object, on the other hand, was to follow up Freud's psycho-analytic revelation of the unconscious and to integrate the unconscious with the conscious, eastern intuition with western intellect, whence alone true understanding could proceed. He was, in fact, making a new approach to the old problem which Leibniz had set himself.

In order to achieve practical realization of his purpose Keyserling opened the School of Wisdom at Darmstadt on the 23rd November, 1920. Disciples came flocking in. Among them two types were prominent, the earnest youth of Germany, and women. After starting the school Keyserling 'discovered what I consider to be my most original gift—that of an orchestral conductor of the spirit. From that time on, year by year, Darmstadt is taking up the fundamental themes of the universal polyphony'. According to himself 'my polyphonic style of thinking bears the same relation to that of my philosophic predecessors as polyphonic music does to homophonic (single-stranded melody)'. Keyserling evaluated his polyphonic thought in terms of 'the mystery of polarization' which he regarded as the basis of his philosophic outlook and as '*the* door of access to true knowledge'. It was a mystery which Schelling and Görres had brooded over a hundred years before, homophonic though their thought might be.

The School of Wisdom was an aristocratic institution. Count Keyserling was provided with a house by his friend and admirer the grand-duke Ernst Ludwig of Hesse and was helped in the running of his school by the grand-duke's administrator, Count Kuno von Hardenberg. This distinguished *milieu* suited Keyserling well, for he despised anything plebeian and thought that democracy had an 'ugly face'. In Europe, as he saw it, 'the proletarians aspire to nothing less than the ruin of all prosperous people'. (It may be remarked that all Keyserling's property in Esthonia was expropriated during the post-war revolution, a sad blow in view of his conviction that 'the man of spirit *must not* be forced to think of a livelihood'.) Furthermore 'the "will of the people" expresses itself on the whole as the rule of incompetence', while 'the republican form of government brings about, not liberation, but enslavement. . . . All republicans start from the false assumption that men were originally equal'. These opinions lay behind his admiration of Buddhism and contempt for Christianity. For him

'the whole teaching of Buddha bears unmistakably the stamp of . . . a princely mind. . . . Buddhism proves itself decidedly superior to Christianity. Christianity was originally a religion of the proletariat; it was in opposition to the favoured classes from the beginning. Prejudices in favour of lives which have failed and resentment against those who are happy belong to the soul, if not to the spirit, of this religion, and it therefore carries, wherever it turns, the seed of disruption.'

Keyserling, however, saw in democracy only a passing phase, since

'the democratic ideal brings about a spiritual rise of the lower strata of the people; according to the system of cross-breeding, they will very soon have been ennobled on a large scale. And once this has been attained, then the belief in equality will pass away of its own accord, and the basis will have been found for the aristocratic order of the future.'

It followed that 'it is exactly because the democratic idea triumphed in the war that a new aristocratic order is everywhere emerging'. This new *élite* would rule wisely, since 'their own self-consciousness as well as all external experience teaches them that the development onward and upward can now be achieved only by drawing once more into developed, conscious life the non-intellectual forces, the impulsional as well as the irrational and the super-intellectual'.

By a most fortunate coincidence Germany was the country peculiarly adapted to the rule of such an *élite*. 'No rule of the masses, or even of the majority, can ever be worth anything to Germany if she wishes to "keep fit". In her case a majority cannot give expression to the *volonté générale*, which Rousseau had already learned to distinguish from the *volonté de tous*'. This was evident from the fact that 'in all her great periods the German structure has, in one way or another, been aristocratic'. 'I certainly do not believe', wrote Keyserling, 'in a restoration of the princes in Germany. . . . Nevertheless its *equivalent* will have to emerge once more if Germany is again to become fit'. Only thus would Germany obtain a régime corresponding to the basic fact that 'the Germans are physiologically a caste people, in the same way as the Hindoos. And for the same reasons. As a nation, the Hindoos, too, are introverts; with them, too it is reflection that dominates. Under these conditions the only way to allow for actual differences is by an arrangement which takes into account a pre-existing framework of life.'

This outlook was reflected in 'the specific socialism of Germany, which seeks to remove competition and which would like more than anything else to turn the working class into a branch of the Civil Service, with promotion solely by seniority and the rank of *Geheimrat* as the climax of ambition'. In support of this view Keyserling related how one day at the beginning of the German revolution of 1918 he 'inquired in a certain house for the janitress. I was informed that *Frau Rat* [the councillor's wife] was not at home. *Frau Rat?* Yes, her husband had become a member of the Workers' and Soldiers' Council. All the deep significance of the revolution was contained, for this worthy family, in that fact'.

Keyserling like Rathenau looked forward to a hierarchized social state. In external affairs 'Germany must naturally continue to assert herself as a people and as a nation. . . . And particularly in the age of self-determination of peoples would it be a crime for Germany to relinquish without a struggle one jot or tittle of her rights'. But Germany was not to be nationalistic, Keyserling holding that 'all nations are of course thoroughly unpleasant affairs'. Rather was Germany to transcend nationalism by harnessing her technical efficiency to her transcendent spirit which had ensured that 'ever since Germany attained the necessary stage of development, the overwhelming majority of all great Europeans have come from Germany'. Reverting to the dream of the great romantics Keyserling proclaimed that Germany was destined to head a new international order which would adjust national tensions without eliminating them or destroying national peculiarity. He was contemptuous of 'what France and England have made out of the League of Nations. If this last is ever to become a blessing to the nations, it must be animated by the German spirit'.

Keyserling was vague as to the practical measures which should bring about and maintain this new national and international order. There is some evidence, however, that autocracy, not less than aristocracy, had his approval. He remarked that 'the Russian Czars represented, until quite recently, a higher type of mankind than the constitutional monarchs of western Europe', and went on to exclaim 'how admirably the overestimation of a superior justifies itself! No matter whether the superior originally deserves the veneration which is paid him or not'. And here again Germany was to the fore, since 'instinctively the German dreams of the leader who, by virtue of his very standing, is lifted above all comparison'.

Keyserling denied that he was influenced by Nietzsche's concept of the superman. However that may be, Keyserling's own idea of the master-nature was that of the sovereign who

> 'longs neither for peace nor mercy, neither for comfort nor compassion, for he decides; if he succumbs, he recognizes himself alone as guilty and bears the consequences with calm pride. This is the manly way. Women expect, suffer, hope and receive. Accordingly they long for compassion, mercy, peace. For this reason they are right in believing in the superior power of Fate. But a man need not trouble about God or Devil, because his initiative removes him beyond their power.'

As for gentleness, 'no one but the man who possesses the passion of a Peter the Great may profess himself to the ideal of gentleness; those who are weak . . . are made even weaker by it'. If Keyserling was severe towards gentleness he was lenient towards cold-blooded cruelty. He thought that 'where the theory that punishment is to act above all as a deterrent is accepted at all—and where is it not accepted?—torture seems justified in principle, and it depends rather on considerations of expediency than on those of humaneness, if and when torture is abolished'.

Although Keyserling minimized the influence of Nietzsche upon him, it may be noticed that his first lecture was delivered, at the age of twenty-five, in the Nietzsche-Archiv at Weimar, the house of Nietzsche's sister. Keyserling once said that 'Nietzsche's doctrine of the superman is not an expression of greatness, but an expression of the desire for greatness': a fairly shrewd remark; and a boomerang.

Less equivocal in his admiration of Nietzsche was the third

German thinker who may fitly be considered along with Rathenau and Keyserling. For Thomas Mann Nietzsche was 'a friend of life, a seer of higher humanity, a leader [leading us] into the future'; he was also, significantly, 'like Wagner . . . a later son of the romantic age'. Mann thought that 'war is romanticism', and during the Great War he drew a Nietzschean parallel between art and war in that artist and soldier both had the mission of overthrowing the false order established by the western *bourgeoisie*. He himself described his *Betrachtungen eines Unpolitischen* as an 'antidemocratic polemic' and was indignant at being subsequently accused of going back on its doctrine. He thought of himself as fighting 'a rearguard-action in the grand manner—the last and latest of a romantic German middle-class outlook (*einer deutsch-romantischen Bürgerlichkeit*)'.

Mann's championship of this romantic German middle-class outlook against the *bourgeois*-democratic west rested ultimately upon the distinction which he established between culture and civilization, a distinction from which he drew political and social deductions. He proclaimed

> 'the oneness of politics and democracy, and the naturally un-German character of this complex,that is the natural estrangement between the German spirit and the world of politics and democracy, against which it [the German spirit] sets the unpolitical and aristocratic concept of culture as its real being. It [the point of departure of the *Betrachtungen*] was an obscure feeling, and not a deceptive one, that ultimately this estrangement and insubordination was the cause of the war—that that was the reason why Germany had sunk into solitude and why the world raised armies and went into harness against us. . . . German culture [*Kultur*]! About 1914 there was nothing in the world more hated, more reviled than that; and the fact that it was written with a K provoked especial bitterness among the journalists of the Entente. But this unbridled polemic of the hostile world against the big K should not have astonished us—though understandably enough it hurt us and goaded us to the defence of our own; but we could not and should not have laughed it away and rejected it as absurd; for indeed the concept of culture really occupied the central position in our own war-ideology, just as the politico-democratic concept of "civilization" was at the heart of that of the enemy.'

For Mann this politico-democratic civilization connoted the arid intellectualism of the west. True German culture, on the other hand, was the embodiment of his ideal of the conjunction of contraries—the old formula dear to romantics from Hamann onwards. The culture of Germany, the middle land, represented the conjunction of the over-intellectualization of the west and the vital barbarism of Russia, both being welded into the higher being of the German spirit. It was, in fact, a refined version of Keyserling's attempted integration of unconscious and conscious, of intuition and intellect. And as with Keyserling, so with Mann, the tendency was to stress the anti-intellectual factor—on the political side Mann in 1917 had advocated a closer Russo-German understanding, if only as a check to the Anglo-Saxon influence.

German culture as Mann saw it was not merely hostile to western civilization in that it lay behind the Great War. That culture, he thought, was in its very being the enemy of that civilization. And that culture was in the whole tradition of Germany.

> 'The sculptors and educators of German humanity, Luther, Goethe, Schopenhauer, Nietzsche, George and the like were no democrats—oh, no. If people abroad honour them, let them reflect upon what they are doing. It was they who created the idea of culture [*Kultur*] with a big K, who formed the centre of power of the German war-ideology. People in Paris applaud the "Meistersinger". That betokens misapprehension of associations. Nietzsche wrote of this work: "—Against civilization. The German against the French."'

In connexion with German culture Mann revived the old German idea of lay piety. He noticed that 'the word "culture" [*Kultur*] is of one descent along with that other which is only distinguished from it by one letter of the termination, the word "cult" [*Kultus*]. Both signify "care"'; he went on to remark how

> 'there enters into the concept of culture an element of the wonderful and the mystical which once again renders evident its near-religious character. For in relation to what really appertains to cult "culture" is certainly a profane concept; but when compared with that of "civilization", that is, of social morality, it displays its religious character, that is, its essentially unsocial, egoistic and individualistic character.'

Pursuing this line, Mann observed that 'the religious ego becomes corporative in the congregation [*Gemeinde*]. The cultural ego celebrates its highest festival in the form and under the name of the community [*Gemeinschaft*]—a name in which the accent is heavily on aristocracy and cult, whereby it distinguishes the holiness of its idea of sociality from the profane concept of society proper to the democratic morality': he proceeded to contrast the 'cultural discipline' of the aristocratic community with the 'social sluggishness' of democratic society.

Mann devised the equation: culture is to folk as civilization is to nation—nation 'in connexion with which nobody catches the romantic ring of aristocratic simplicity whereby the word "folk",the expression "the German folk", are distinguished from the name of "nation" with its democratico-revolutionary memories and intonations'. Whereas 'the concept of the nation is historically united with that of democracy, . . . the word "folk" corresponds to genuinely German thought, that is, to cultural, conservative, unpolitical, anti-social thought'. It is fitting that this neophyte, who taught the holiness of the disciplined community and the nobility of the cultural folk, should have venerated Novalis and Adam Müller. The extreme romantics of a hundred years ago were now coming into their own.

Mann considered, and with some justice, that 'the difficulties which oppose a real, internal—and not merely legal and constitutional–"democratization" of Germany have herewith been, if not exhibited, at any rate indicated'. Superficial democratization had resulted from the defeat of 1918, a defeat which was very bitter to the German people not so much, according to Mann, because it involved 'ruin, the monstrous crash from the height of external power into political misery', as because it represented 'the shaming of its belief, being vanquished in ideals, the collapse of its ideology, the catastrophe of the centre of power of this ideology, of its idea of culture'. But despite this overthrow the Germans still clung to their cultural ideology. Therefore

'at the same time as it introduced the republican form of state, Germany was not "democratized". That German conservatism, that will towards leaving untouched the German idea of culture as handed down by tradition must, in the political sphere, reject and make war upon the democratico-republican form of state as being something alien to land and folk, as something untrue and contrary to psychic reality [*seelisch wirklichkeitswidrig.*] That rests in the nature and innermost consequence of the matter, as likewise does the fact that only he can stand by the democratic form of state, and believe in its possibility and future in Germany, who holds that the transformation of the German idea of culture in a democratic and world-conciliatory direction is possible and desirable.'

It is understandable that Mann was hostile to the spirit of socialism, which with its 'social idea of class' of 'purely economic origin' sought to undermine the holy community of the German folk. Nevertheless Mann thought that cultural conservatism stood nearer to socialism than to liberalism. He held that party-life in Germany conformed to the concept of culture and that accordingly 'talk about "liberalism" is in high degree meant only in the sense of a spiritual two-party system and not in that of a parliamentary centre and *bourgeois* outlook: a circumstance which may be clarified by an addition to the effect that it is really a question of socialism'.

Mann found the solution of the political problem in a conjunction of contraries. In practical terms it was very much the same solution as Rathenau and Keyserling had envisaged—a fusion of democracy and aristocracy, of popularity and authority into a genuinely German synthesis which would find expression in a renewed middle-class. According to Mann 'the thing which would be necessary, which could be finally German, would be a union and pact between the conservative idea of culture and the revolutionary idea of society'. It is thus apparent that, wherever the stress might lie, Mann sought to effect a real integration and equated aristocratic authority and middle-class stability not with reaction but with progress. In this Mann regarded himself as the heir of the early romantics, being at pains to point out that though their immediate political stance may have been reactionary, the trend and temper of their thought was in fact radical.

It was with this in mind that Mann gradually came to view with some concern the cross-currents of the neoromantic movement. These cross-currents derived from two main sources: first, the reaction in post-war politics, already indicated; secondly the work of Freud and the growth of psycho-analysis. Mann became perturbed at the confluence of these two currents and saw very clearly that

'today there is really . . . no brutal trend backwards . . . which did not feel itself strengthened by the irrational sympathies of the new research into life [i.e. psycho-analysis], which did not seek to establish contact with it, did not call upon it, did not deliberately enter into exchange with it and above all concern itself with politicizing it, translating it into something socially anti-revolutionary and thus making crude reaction appear in a revolutionary light.'

Thus the principle of antidemocratic authority became distorted and there 'stands in the revolutionary freshness of youth the dynamic principle, nature freed from the mind, the soul of the folk, hate, war. That is reaction in the guise of revolution, the great Backwards decked out and made up as a stormy Forwards'. Mann went on to ask:

'And the youth? Will it really fall a victim to the clumsy misuse of the profundity of the new perception of life by means of raw hostility to the spirit? Yes, it seems so—or rather it seems so sometimes, here and there. We are no longer unused to the depressing spectacle of young bodies carrying senile ideas, moving about in an alert quick-march, songs of youth on their lips, their arms raised in the Roman greeting: . . . The evil of antiquity does not become good and beautiful because it is borne by youth; it would not become righteous and lovely even if it should tragically happen that youth spilt its blood for it.'

Thus was Mann filled with foreboding as to the ultimate effect of ideas which were largely of one parentage with his own, deformed but still of the stock. Mann tried to defend his mediate position by seeking to prove that the Freudian outlook, like that of the early romantics who were its spiritual forebears, was identified with progress rather than with reaction: in itself a very tenable thesis. But none the less psycho-analysis was essentially identified with the revolt against reason: a circumstance of heavy import. Mann recognized that

'Freud, as an investigator of the depths and psychologist of the instinct, falls entirely into line with the writers of the nineteenth and twentieth centuries who, be it as historians, philosophers, cultural critics or archaeologists, stressed, cultivated and scientifically brought out the night-side of nature and the soul as the real determinant and creative factor in life in opposition to rationalism, intellectualism, classicism, in a word to the belief in the mind proper to the eighteenth and to some extent also to the nineteenth century: writers who were revolutionary in standing for the primacy of everything hallowed of earth and primal in spirit [*alles Erdgöttlich-Vorgeistigen*], of the "will", of passion, of the unknown or, as Nietzsche says, of "feeling" in precedence over "reason". The word "revolutionary" stands here in a paradoxical and inverted sense according to logical usage; for whereas we are otherwise used to associate the concept of the revolutionary outlook with the powers of light and of the emancipation of reason, that is, with the idea of the future, in this instance the message and appeal is entirely opposite: in the sense, namely, of the great impulse backward into the realm of night, of primitive holiness, of the preconscious and the pregnancy of life, into the maternal womb of myth, history and romance.[1] That is the speech of reaction. But the stress is revolutionary.'

Mann then moved off into a sentence of twenty-five lines, tracing this German growth of irrational revolutionary reaction from Arndt, Görres, and Grimm, down through Carus, embracing history, psychology, archaeology and jurisprudence, and ending up with the 'historical pessimism of Spengler'.

Oswald Spengler compressed enormous erudition within a domed skull. Born in the Harz country in the same year as Keyserling, he consumed his youth in voracious study, embracing mathematics, natural history, history, and art. The year 1914 saw him, like Keyserling, completing the first version of his major work. But the *Untergang des Abendlandes* (*Decline of the West*), like the *Reisetagebuch eines Philosophen* (*Travel Diary of a Philosopher*), came into its own in the post-war era: very much so.

Spengler, like those thinkers we have just left, had small use for rationalism. For him 'rationalism is at bottom nothing other than criticism, and the critic is the opposite of the creator; he takes things to pieces and puts them together; conception and birth are foreign to him. For this reason his work is artificial and lifeless and it kills when it meets with real life.' Spengler was also of the main line in his reverence for Nietzsche. He declared in 1924 that 'Nietzsche's work is

[1]The original German runs as follows: '. . . des grossen Zurück ins Nächtige, Heilig-Ursprüngliche, Lebensträchtig-Vorbewusste, in den mythisch-historisch-romantischen Mutterschoss.'

no piece of the past to be enjoyed, but a task which renders one liable to service'. His view of man was corresponding. He taught that

'man is a *beast of prey*. I shall say it again and again. All the paragons of virtue and thinkers in social ethics who wish to be or rise above that are merely beasts of prey with their teeth drawn. . . . When I call man a beast of prey whom do I insult, the man or the beast? For the great beasts of prey are *noble* creations in the fullest degree and are without the mendacious habits of human morals which are due to weakness.'

It followed for Spengler that 'as far as the "goal of humanity" is concerned I am a thorough and decided pessimist. For me humanity is a zoological quantity. I see no progress, no goal, no way of humanity—except in the heads of western philistines who believe in progress.'

Upon this basis Spengler reared his historical construction. The premise was, in conformity with the above, that 'in historical reality there are no ideals; there are only facts. There are no truths; there are only facts. There are no reasons, no righteousness, no equity, no final goal; there are only facts—whoever does not grasp that may write books about politics, but he does not *make* politics'. The corollary was that 'the born statesman stands beyond truth and falsehood'. And the statesman played a dominant part in Spengler's scheme of history, since for him, as for Hegel, '*the history of the world is the history of states* and always will be. The internal constitution [*Verfassung*] of a nation has, always and everywhere, the object of maintaining itself "in form" [*Verfassung*] for the external struggle, be it of a military, diplomatic, or economic kind'. This circumstance was a reflection of the fact that 'war is the eternal form of higher human existence, and states exist for the sake of war; they are the expression of preparedness for war'. Indeed war not only connoted the higher existence but life itself, since 'war is the original policy of *everything* living, and indeed to such a degree that struggle and life are one in the depths, and with the extinction of the will to struggle being is extinguished also. The ancient Germanic words for it [war] like *orrusta* and *orlog* mean earnestness and destiny in contrast with jest and play'.

This perpetual struggle found its most august expression in

the conflict between cultures which were for Spengler the highest historical entities, embracing numbers of states and social groups. In the course of the struggle cultures waxed and waned and—a special Spenglerian conceit—suffered pseudomorphosis, that is, underwent a process wherein the life of one culture was overlaid and vitiated by that of another.

For Spengler known history was primarily based on three great cultures: the Euclidean culture of Greece and Rome, the Māgic culture of the Arabs, and the Faustian culture of western Europe. This last culture was that of modern Europe and, as its name indicates, it drew its main vigour from peoples of Germanic stock. Of these peoples the two prime champions were the British and the Germans. But 'England has grown tired'. Spengler remarked in illustration that

> 'the [English] delight in enterprise is dying out, and the young generation displays spiritually, morally and in its outlook on the world, a steep decline from the height to which in previous centuries the quality of English society were bred up: an alarming spectacle and without precedent in the whole world. The old call. *England expects everyman* [*sic*] *to do his duty*, which before the war every young Englishman of good family who was at Eton and Oxford felt to be personally directed to him, now falls on deaf ears. They dally with bolshevik problems, pursue eroticism as a sport and sport as a profession and the content of life.'

That left Germany at the head. The Germans had a double warrant of pre-eminence. In the first place they were a young people:

> 'Germany is the *decisive* country in the world, not only because of its position on the borders of Asia, today the most important continent in world-politics, but also because the Germans are still young enough to experience, form, *decide* world-historical problems within themselves, whereas other peoples have become too old and stiff to hazard more than a defence. But as regards great *problems*, too, attack contains the promise of victory.'

In the second place the Germans were a Prussian people: 'Germany alone has Prussianism as a *fact* within her. With this treasure of prefigurative being it can become the educator of the "white" world, perhaps its saviour.'

The importance of Prussianism was greatly enhanced for Spengler in that he considered that the 'old Prussian spirit and socialist disposition, which today hate each other with the hate of brothers, are one and the same'. He based this identification upon the idea, already present with Thomas Mann, of a conservative-socialist front against liberalism. Spengler remarked that

'it is significant, and reveals the strength of the national instinct, that both of the parties which one may describe as specifically Prussian, the conservative and the socialist, have never lost an illiberal and antiparliamentary tendency. They are *both* socialist in a higher sense. . . . They do not recognize a private direction of government as a party affair, but assign to the *whole* the unconditional authority to regulate the conduct of the life of the individual in the general interest. That in this connection one speaks of the monarchical state and the other of the working people is a difference of words in the face of the fact that here everybody works and that the will of the individual is subjected to the common will *every time*.'

Spengler went on to talk of 'a socialist monarchy . . . a unity', and to refer specifically to Lassalle with whom, incidentally, he shared the interest in Heraclitus.

In accordance with the above Spengler expatiated upon 'the idea of socialism in its deepest meaning: will to power, struggle for the happiness not of the individual, but of the whole. *In this sense the first conscious socialist was Frederick William I and not Marx*'. In extolling the Prussian ideal of the authoritative corporative state Spengler equated socialism with bureaucracy in a manner reminiscent of Keyserling and, more remotely, of Fichte. For Spengler

'the Prusso-socialist state . . . is the *whole* folk, and over against its unconditional sovereignty both [the *bourgeoisie* and the proletariat] are merely parties—parties, minorities; both serve the commonalty. Socialism is, in a purely technical sense, the principle of officialism. Every worker ultimately receives the character of an official instead of a dealer, and the same with every *entrepreneur*. There are industrial officials and commercial officials just as much as military and transport officials. That is in the highest style of Egyptian culture. . . . It is the inner form of the political civilization of the west. . . . Marx never understood that.'

As far as Spengler was concerned Marx was quite out of things even on the economic side since according to him economics were much what Adam Müller had conceived them to be, a 'physiognomy' possessed of a 'soul' such that '*every economic life is the expression of a life of the soul*'. The economic expression of 'Prussian thought is the nonparty fixing by the state of wages for every kind of work according to the measure of the whole economic layout, graded according to plan in the interest of the whole folk. . . . It includes the *prohibition of strikes* as an antistate and chaffering expedient of a private character'. The reference to grade is significant, and it lay behind Spengler's castigation of Marx's 'total psychological lack of understanding' in that

'Marx did not know how to begin to set about distinguishing estate from class. An estate is an ethical concept, the expression of an *idea*. . . . His [Marx's] two-class system is drawn from the position of a commercial people which in fact sacrificed its agriculture to trade, and which had never possessed a state bureaucracy stamped with Prussian consciousness of station. Here [with Marx] there are only "bourgeois" and "proletarians", subjects and objects of business, robbers and robbed. . . . Applied to the sphere of Prussian state-thought these concepts are nonsense. Marx does not appear to have been capable of distinguishing the facts of English industrial slavery from the idea, issuing from the principle of "all for all", that every individual without distinction of position is the servant of the whole, of the state.'

And Marx minimized the rôle not only of the state but of nationalism, a cardinal error for Spengler who thought that 'we need a strong, daily, deep education of national consciousness' and maintained that 'we are not "men as such". That belongs to a past ideology. Cosmopolitanism is a wretched phrase. We are men of a century, of a nation, of a circle, of a type'.

Spengler bracketed Marx with England, the argument being that 'Marx . . . became an Englishman in that in his thought the state does not appear. He thinks in terms of *society*, stateless'. This was peculiarly English since 'in England *the island replaces the organized state*. A country without a state were only possible under this condition'. In England the concept of society replaced that of the state, whence the fact that

'*the English people is built up upon the distinction between rich and poor, the Prussian on that between command and obedience*. In the two countries the significance of class-distinction is accordingly quite different. In the [English] society of independent private people the lower class is determined by the common feeling of those who *have* nothing; in the [Prussian] state [it is determined] as the stratum of those who *have nothing to say. Democracy in England means the opportunity for everybody to become rich, in Prussia the opportunity for everybody to attain every existing rank.*'

Spengler went on to equate capitalism with wealth and socialism with authority. And the two were enemies. Therefore 'both the socialist parties of Germany must join against the enemy of the common idea, against England's inner self, capitalist-parliamentary liberalism'. This offensive against the decadent plutodemocracy was the natural consequence of the fact that 'Prussianism and socialism stand *together against England's inner self*, against the world-outlook which permeates, cripples and destroys the soul of our whole life as a folk. The danger is frightful'. Frightful danger demanded frightful remedy. Spengler proclaimed:

> 'We do not need any more ideologists, or any talk about the culture and cosmopolitanism and spiritual mission of the Germans. We need hardness, we need brave scepticism, we need a class of socialist master-natures. Once more: socialism means might, might, might again and again. Plans and ideas are nothing without might.'

In Spengler's world of brute fact there was no place for the moral or ideal, and the only sway was might.

Spengler maintained that in this great contest between the two ways of life the spirit of the age would range with Germany. But on the wider plane this was itself a symptom of the decline of the west. For Spengler the evolution of a culture into a civilization, which invariably occurred, was symptomatic of decay—the underlying distinction between culture and civilization being akin to that drawn by Thomas Mann. Spengler described the process thus:

> 'Finally after a measured succession of centuries each culture transforms itself into a civilization. That which was alive becomes stiff and cold. Inner expanses, soul-spaces are replaced by extension in corporeal reality; life in the sense of master Eckart becomes life in the sense of national economy; *power of ideas becomes imperialism.*'

The Faustian culture of the west was now subject to this decadent process. In such a pass the hope of Europe lay in support of Germany, not only as the foe of Britain but also as the desperate champion of the west against the coloured peoples—the yellow peril which had haunted the imagination of many Germans since the time of William II—and also against Russia, which Spengler regarded not as a state but as an embryonic culture in itself and the future seat of a new religion fundamentally hostile to all western canons of thought and belief. Germany was not singled out for leadership only by her disciplined and youthful vigour. Spengler maintained that 'history knows no folk whose way has been formed more tragically [than that of the German]'. This, then, was the folk for the age, for as Spengler saw it 'the decades in which we live are mighty, mighty—that means terrible and without happiness. Greatness and happiness are two different things, and the choice does not stand open to us. Happy will nobody be who lives today anywhere in the world'.

The very nature of the German character lent itself to the work afoot. Spengler spoke of

> 'the decisive fact: our [German] unbounded necessity to serve, to follow, to venerate no matter who or no matter what, faithful as a dog, blind in our belief despite all objections. That also is a trait laid up from primitive times which, as regards present-day matters, can be great or desperately comic; but it governs the history of our princes, churches and parties. In another country no "cause", no leader, no caricature of one even, is so sure of unconditional following [as it is in Germany]: a secret treasure of enormous might for him who knows how to use it. Historically we have lived too little to be sceptics in this matter. Every Balkan peasant, every porter in an American harbour is quicker at penetrating the secrets of politics. [The Germans are] children perhaps. More than once has history been driven out of its course by great children of this stamp.'

The fact that this leadership-complex dominated German party-life was telling for the future, since 'armies and not parties, armies of selfless devotion, are the future form of might'. Correspondingly 'the relation of the party-chiefs to the party, of the party to the masses will be cruder, more transparent, less glossed over. *That is the beginning of caesarism*'. And it was at hand. Spengler sent out his call: 'The legions of Caesar are awaking once again'.

Spengler prefaced his exposition of caesarism by observing 'the transition from napoleonism to caesarism, a general stage of development comprising at least two centuries, which can be indicated in all cultures. The Chinese call it *tschau kuo*, the time of the warring states....

I call caesarism the way of government which despite all constitutional formulation is once more wholly formless in its inner being. It is a matter of indifference whether Augustus in Rome, Hoangti in China, Amosis in Egypt, Alp Arslan in Bagdad invest their position with ancient designations. The spirit of these old forms is dead. And consequently all institutions, howsoever painstakingly they may still be maintained, are from now on without sense and importance. Significance is confined to the entirely personal power which is exercised through the capacities of the caesar or anybody else who may be in his place. It is the return out of a form-fulfilled world into the primitive, into the historical and the cosmic....

The eternal cosmic pulse has finally overcome the tension in spirit of a few centuries. Money had triumphed in the likeness of democracy. There was a time in which politics depended upon it alone, or almost alone. But as soon as it had destroyed the old orders of culture there rose up and emerged from out of the chaos a new, paramount power, reaching right down into the very elements of all becoming: the men of caesarean stamp. With them the supremacy of money is ruined. *The imperial age betokens the end of politics which depend on mind and money—and that in every culture.* The powers of the blood, the primeval, growing, germinating force of life, unbroken corporeal strength enter once into their ancient mastery. Race breaks forth pure and irresistible: the success of the strongest and the rest as prey. It seizes the governance of the world, and the realm of books and problems becomes torpid or sinks into oblivion. From now on heroic destinies in the style of antiquity become possible again.'

Spengler drew the political consequences from this great reversion to the elemental. He heralded the age of

'demagogy which is intrinsically just the same as the diplomacy of the *ancien régime*, the only difference being that instead of being applied to princes and ambassadors it is applied to masses, instead of to selected spirits, to uncultivated opinions, moods and outbreaks of the will: an orchestra of brass instruments instead of the old chamber music.'

Demagogy implied propaganda. Spengler asked: 'What is truth? For the multitude it is that which they constantly read and hear.... What it [the press] wants, is true. Its commanding officers engender, transform, and exchange truths. Three weeks' work by the press, and all the world has perceived the truth'. And since the context of operation was military, so was the character of the press: 'The press is today an army with various kinds of arms carefully organized, with journalists as officers and readers as soldiers. But it is the same here as in every army: the soldier obeys blindly and the changes in military objective and plan of operation are accomplished without his knowledge'.

This work of propaganda was rendered the easier by the fact that

'the second religiosity is the necessary counterpart to caesarism, the final *political* constitution of late civilizations. They are accordingly visible in antiquity from about Augustus onwards, and in China at about the time of Tsi Hoang Ti. Both phenomena lack the original creative strength of the early culture. Their greatness lies in the one case [of the second religiosity] in the deep piety which fills the whole waking-consciousness—Herodotus called the Egyptians the most pious people in the world . . .—and in the other [caesarism] in the unbridled might of monstrous facts; but the creations of this piety are just as little original as was the form of the Roman imperium. Nothing is built up, no idea unfolds itself, but it is as if a mist lifted from the countryside and the old forms emerged again, indistinctly at first and then ever more clearly. The second religiosity comprises the constituents of the first, genuine, early [religiosity], only differently experienced and expressed. First rationalism is lost, then the forms of the early age appear, and finally the whole world of the primitive religion . . . once more presses mightily forward.'

Such was the world to which Spengler stood as harbinger. Nietzsche had asked where were the barbarians of the twentieth century. Spengler gave him the answer. He announced that 'the time is coming—no, it is already there!—in which there is no more room for tender souls and feeble ideals. Waking once again is the age-old barbarism which lay for centuries hidden and fettered beneath the formal rigour of a high culture'. He explained that 'this barbarism is what I call strong race, the eternal warlike element in the type of man as a beast of prey. Often it seems to be no longer there, but it lies in the soul, ready to spring. A strong challenge, and it pins down its foe'. Spengler stated specifically that by race he meant 'race which one *has*, not a race to which one *belongs*. The one is ethos, the other—zoology'. According to him 'it is not a question of the pure race, but of the *strong* race which has a folk in itself.' And he went on to talk of the German folk as the least spent and most hopeful people of the white world.

The continuity of the strong race found expression in the fact that 'the woman of race does not wish to be "consort" or "beloved", but *mother*, and not the mother of one child as plaything and pastime, but of many'. Alongside the woman's duty of maintaining the strong race went the leader's task of perpetuating the caesarean *élite*. For Spengler

> 'the first task [of the great statesman] is to do something himself; the second, less evident, but harder and greater in its effect, is *to create a tradition* . . ., to release a current of unitary activity which no longer needs the first leader in order to remain in form. Thereby the statesman grows to be something which antiquity might well have described as divinity. He becomes the creator of a new life, the *spiritual* forefather of a young race. He himself as a being disappears from this current after a few years. But a minority called into existence by him, another being of the strangest kind, takes his place, and does so, indeed, for an immeasurable time. A single person can rear this cosmic something, this soul of a ruling class. . . . Such a minority gradually becomes a real race, even if it was once a party; and it decides with the certainty born of blood, not of understanding. But for this very reason everything in it happens "of itself"; it no longer needs genius. That means, if one may so express it, replacement of the great politician by great politics.'

It was in the light of this transformation of the whole ordering of society that Spengler viewed contemporary politics. He foretold 'the final struggle between democracy and caesarism, between the leading powers of a dictatorial cash-economy and the *purely political* will to order of the caesars'. In that struggle Spengler stood with the caesars. Their enemies he hated. He hated England, as we have seen; and he hated what she stood for. He hated 'the League of Nations, this swarm of summer-holidaymakers who lead a sponging existence by the lake of Geneva'. He 'hated the dirty revolution of 1918 from the first day'. But he nevertheless perceived possibilities in the Weimar constitution. He maintained that 'the German constitution of 1919, which already originated indeed upon the threshold of *declining* democracy, comprises in a wholly naïve manner a dictatorship of the party-machines; the constitutional forms really 'embody the caesarism of organizations. In this sense it must be allowed that it [the

Weimar constitution] is the most advanced constitution of the age; it already affords a perception of the end; a few small alterations, and it bestows uncircumscribed power upon individuals'. In 1921 he was already sure that 'we Germans shall not again attain to a Goethe, but to a Caesar'.

Spengler lived to see his prophecy fulfilled. And he hailed its fulfilment. Early in 1933 he wrote:

'Today this may already be said: the national revolution of 1933 was something mighty and will remain so in the eyes of the future; it was so by reason of the elementary, superpersonal weight of the pressure with which it accomplished itself, and of the psychic discipline with which it was accomplished. That was Prussian through and through, like the uprising of 1914 which transformed souls in a moment. The German dreamers rose up, quietly, impressively, as a matter of course, and opened up a way into the future. But for this very reason the participants must be clear about this fact: that was no victory, for there were no opponents. In the face of the power of the rising there vanished at once everything which was still active or had been accomplished. It was a promise of *future* victories which must be won by fighting in hard struggles for which the place was [thus] created here in the first instance. Those who lead have assumed full responsibility for this, and they must know or learn what that means. It is a task full of colossal dangers and it does not lie in the interior of Germany but outside, in the world of wars and catastrophes where great policy alone is spokesman.'

This circumstance was dictated by the fact that 'Prussian above all is the unconditional precedence of foreign policy—the successful leading of a state in a world of states—over internal policy whose sole function it is to keep the nation in form for this task'. And for Spengler the basis of foreign policy was this:

'A *genuine* international is only possible through the victory of the idea of *one* race over all others, and not through the dissolution of all opinions into a colourless mass. Let us be sceptics at last and throw out the old ideologies. There are no reconciliations in real history. . . . There is only one end to the eternal struggle, death: death of individuals, death of peoples, death of a culture. . . . We Germans . . . have rich, unspent possibilities within us and huge tasks before us. To the international which is in irrevocable preparation we have the idea of the world-organization of the world-state to give; the English that of the worldwide trust and worldwide gain; the French nothing. . . . *The real international is imperialism*, domination of the Faustian civilization and, consequently, of the whole earth by means of a single formative principle, not through settlement and concession, but through victory and annihilation.'

Spengler, in a number of ways curiously like an up-to-date edition of Rodbertus, bridged the Weimar republic and the Nazi dictatorship. The influence of this wordy prophet upon post-war Germany was enormous. And yet the intellectual link between the thought of Spengler and the Nazi creed itself was the work of one who did not live like Spengler to witness the creation of the new order, and whose influence was at first much less, as was his scope. Moeller van den Bruck was a less pretentious thinker than Spengler. With him emotion filled the place of erudition, expression of exactitude. But these very limitations made him bear towards the future. The relation between the schematic historian Spengler and the post-war neoromantics was something similar to that between the schematic historical philosopher Hegel and the romantics of a century before. But Moeller van den Bruck has been compared with Rousseau as the outrider of political revolt.

Artur Moeller van den Bruck was born at Solingen in central Saxony in 1876. His grandfather was a landed gentleman and his father an architect in official Prussian employ. As a youth Moeller was bored by the university of Leipzig and turned rather to Berlin, where he led a life of extravagance. Later he visited Paris and there came under the influence of the Russian mysticism of Merezhkovsky, and made translations from Dostoevsky. Italy next attracted him, and his first considerable book, published in 1908, was entitled *Italian Beauty*. Under the stress of the Great War and its outcome this gifted dilettante increasingly turned his attention towards political affairs. In 1923 he published *Das Dritte Reich* (*The Third Empire*). The book was a ripe product of the new romanticism and outstanding in political literature as an index to the aesthetic cult of expressionism which then prevailed in Germany.

For Moeller as for Spengler gloom was the background. But unlike Spengler Moeller was not complete and steady in his pessimism; rather was it a somewhat querulous expression of his sense of indefinite frustration. Moeller lamented thus: 'Something has gone wrong with everything; and when we put our hand to anything to set it straight, it breaks into pieces in our fingers. . . . So it was before the War, and during the War; so it was during the Revolution; so it has been since the Revolution. The whole nation lies under an evil spell'. In short, 'Germany was taken in over and over again'. This was reflected in the fact that 'our history has lost its way. Nothing of ours of late has been succeeding. Nothing to-day: nothing yesterday: nothing—if we think back—for the last generation. The last success we had was the foundation of the second German Empire'. And that was only the beginning of decay since under the second empire, according to Moeller, 'we became materialists in a materialistic age'. He went on to apostrophize: 'What an age it was, of William II: mechanized, bureaucrat-ridden and yet boastful, poor for all its wealth, ugly for all its display: an age doomed to shipwreck, doomed to see the day that swept away all its successes.'

It is thus evident that Moeller joined the other romantics in blaming the second empire, above all, for its mechanized materialism. The same critique underlay his hostility to Marxism. For Moeller 'Marx was a penetrating materialist. But he did not rise above materialism'. This condemned him, since 'the materialist conception of history, which gives economics greater weight than man, is a denial of history; it denies all spiritual values and takes as its political ideal a socialist order of society after the establishment of which the only task left to man will be to regulate his digestion'. This was an alien ideal, alien largely because 'Marx . . . was a Jew, a stranger in Europe who nevertheless dared to meddle in the affairs of European peoples. . . . Marx is only comprehensible through his Jewish origins. It is no accident that he displays Mosaic, Maccabean traits, traits of the Talmud—and the Ghetto'. Moeller observed that 'it did not occur to him [Marx] that perhaps national socialism might be a condition precedent to universal socialism'. This condemnation of Marx for such unpractical idealism came a trifle oddly from Moeller, who held that 'the whole error of socialism is latent in one sentence of Karl Marx: "Hence men set themselves only such tasks as they can fulfil." This is untrue. Men set themselves only such tasks as they cannot fulfil. It is their genius who inspires them'.

Moeller was thus at one with the other romantics in rejecting rationalism along with materialism; and like them he identified rationalism with the west, holding that 'the Age of Reason was an affair of the West'. He castigated 'our rationalists and pacifists. They all draw their conclusions from the premises of their party-political or utopian wishes, but not from the premises of the reality which surrounds us. They will not realise that we are a fettered and maltreated nation, perhaps on the verge of dissolution'. In other words those rationalists and pacifists looked to the dominant west instead of feeling with Moeller that

'we have been encaged, and the allies strut up and down outside our bars. We sought ignominious refuge in a peace which left us only an empire's rump, which dismembered our fathers' inheritance, laid hand on our rivers and even forbade us the air. We were presented with a Republic, whose basis is not the constitution of Weimar but the Treaty of Versailles. We were made serfs.'

Again and again Moeller returned to the attack of the treaty of Versailles and of its sponsor

'Wilson, who would hear nothing of a war-indemnity, but acquiesced in reparations, which the victors interpreted into meaning payment for the entire War; Wilson, who repudiated the annexation of colonies, but distributed "mandates"; Wilson, who sacrificed the "freedom of the seas", and "trade equality" and "disarmament" in order to carry home safe in his pocket his "League of Nations"'.

Of supreme concern to Moeller was the fact that 'the immediate result of the War is that the declining populations have won and the growing populations have lost'. As a matter of fact the birth-rate in Germany declined from 21·3 per 1000 in 1923 to 14·7 in 1933. In the same period the fecundity rate, that is the number of births per 1000 women aged 15 to 45, fell from 82·3 to 58·9. But then hard facts were scarcely Moeller's forte. He preferred to draw pictures like the following:

'The French . . . are helpless in face of their depopulation problems. They have been striving in vain for the last forty years to maintain their forty millions. Yet they also possess half the world which the British awarded them as the price of the World War. The self-centred Frenchman, however . . . is unaware how much behind the times his empty country is, with its sparse population and its little houses in which the rentier can thrive but not the pioneer. . . . The Frenchman is no colonizer, no imperialist; he is merely a slave-driver wherever he happens to have power. . . . On the Rhine he maintains African troops for a thrust against Germany, so that the least-populated country in Europe may politically dominate the most densely populated. Surely the day will come—must come—when this living paradox which Versailles created shall have an end.'

The probability of this development was heightened by the fact that 'the German nation is astir. Its path is blocked. It has lost its bearings. It seeks space. It seeks work: and fails to find it. We are becoming a nation of proletarians'. This problem of unemployment and proletarianization was essentially that of the folk without space—the problem which had so concerned Ratzel and German geopoliticians since. In fact for Moeller 'the population problem is *the* problem of Germany. . . . Since access to the outer world is forbidden us we must look for its solution within our borders; and since it cannot there be solved, a day must come when we shall burst our frontiers and seek and find it outside'. He told his countrymen: 'We are a country with a surplus population of twenty millions. . . . There is nothing for us but forcibly to break forth.' Moeller recognized but rejected a possible alternative, remarking that 'Neo-Malthusianism offers us counsel: to restrict our birth-rate. This is no heroic solution. Overpopulation is part of Nature's design. Nature must solve the problem'. Thus nature was equated with the expansion of Germany. But Germany was not alone in her present distress since

'even Italy is a victim; for she is driven to divert her emigration to South America, though Tunis and Algiers lie at her doors obviously destined to absorb her surplus population, did they not belong to underpopulated France. The population problem unites all conquered peoples in a common cause; and wherever it remains unsolved the nation is in effect a conquered people.'

The conquered peoples had the better hope of prevailing against their former victors in view of 'the complete absence of ideas which our enemies display: their victory brought them complacency, satiety—in spite of the economic and political peril which threatens their countries'. The threat was already real.

'Our enemies have their present success. The moment is in their favour, but everything else is against them. The secret, however, must not be revealed before its time. What we can, however, already detect is a regrouping of men and nations. All antiliberal forces are combining against everything that is liberal. We are living in the time of this transition. The change is taking place most logically from below and attacking the enemy where his power began. There is a revolt against the age of reason.'

Moeller continued thus:

'Reason turned thinking into calculating man. It corrupted Europe. The World War was the shipwreck of the age of reason. . . . The fight against the age of reason which we are entering on, is a fight against liberalism all along the line. In the course of this fight we shall realize how brief an epoch the Age of Reason has been; how circumscribed, unimportant and feeble its creation; how ephemeral its legacy. In England it has produced some practical things, in France some witty ones. But all great achievements on our side of the border were produced in the teeth of the age of reason. All eminent men with us, whether we think of Goethe or Bismarck, were un-liberal men. Every decisive event, the rise of Napoleon's power, the foundation of the German Empire, were un-liberal events.'

It will be noticed that with Moeller decisive events are acts of imperialism.

Moeller identified liberals with freemasons, his particular aversion, asserting that both 'alike appear to be men who either possess no principles, or are ever ready to set them aside; men who are always prepared—for a price—to abandon any principle, and indeed feel most at home in such barterings'. Such behaviour on the part of liberals meant that 'liberalism has undermined civilization, has destroyed religions, has ruined nations. Primitive peoples know no liberalism'. This last remark was pointed by Moeller's significant observation that 'liberalism has no magic to offer'. This had effectively prevented its growth among the German youth, since 'youth rightly craves for the romantic, and youth resented the banalities of democracy even more than its corruption. Youth's judgments were passionate and stern'. So much so, in fact, that

'there are no young liberals in Germany today; there are young revolutionaries; there are young conservatives. But who would be a liberal? There are scarcely any young democrats in the proper sense of the term, and such as there were—who a few years ago were still obsessed by yearnings towards the League of Nations and World Peace—are being swiftly nationalized. The formal democracy that posed as our state is now so discredited that nothing can save it. . . .

If we seek to discover the reasons why the young conservative and the young revolutionary have so unanimously come to the same conclusion about the principles, points of view and lines of policy that have led to the present conditions, we shall find that they share a common contempt and distrust for the liberal ingredient in political thought. . . . Liberalism is a philosophy of life from which German youth now turns with nausea, with wrath, with a quite peculiar scorn, for there is none more foreign, more repugnant, more opposed to its own philosophy. German youth today recognizes the liberal as *the enemy*.'

Something of what the nationalization of the German youth implied is suggested by Moeller's dictum that 'the German nationalist to-day as a German remains for ever a mystic, as a politician he has turned sceptic'. Germany was soon to experience the formidable effects of mystical scepticism in politics.

Meantime this mystical scepticism assailed the foundations of the enemy position. Moeller said of the western powers that

'their outward success is so brilliant that it tends to mask their moral failure. Disillusionment exists only on our side. We are the only people to enquire: what has become of the ideas of 1789; liberty, equality, fraternity? Fraternity? Versailles dealt a blow to the brotherhood of nations from which it will not readily recover. . . . Equality? Before the War, Germany was ahead of other countries in social reform. . . . Liberty? Before the War we were the freest people on the earth; we have since become the most enslaved.'

Apart from which, Moeller thought that 'it has become evident enough how ill men thrive on a political diet of Liberty, Equality, and Fraternity'; especially liberty. Moeller identified the cult of freedom, as of utility, with the 'slovenliness' which pervades liberal thought, and sneered at the way in which 'the English always talked of freedom. They always sought their own freedom at the expense of everyone else's'.

Parliamentary government was struck down along with the ideal of freedom. Moeller thought that 'this parliamentary business fettered a nation's policy. The people did not theorize about it: but they were perfectly aware that it was humbug. The Reichstag has always been despised in Germany'. That was where the German socialists had gone so astray. 'Though this Revolution [of 1918] thought it was a socialist revolution, Socialism is one of the things that it bungled. Our remarkable socialists made even more remarkable politicians. They decided in favour of western parliamentism, shrinking back before eastern terror-dictatorship'. The alternative is interesting, but Moeller did not dwell upon it. He was more concerned with explaining how natural it was 'that the attack on parliamentism should be led from two sides: by the revolutionaries with their ideal of councils, by the conservatives with their ideal of estates of the realm. The idea of "estates" is the idea of an organic structure completely incompatible with the idea of "party"'. It was therefore particularly significant that

> 'there is no party now in Germany that has not its conservative wing; all are inspired by conservative thought; liberals, opportunists, democrats, religious parties, even the revolutionaries. So far it only amounts to an impulse; we might call it a "lurch towards the Right" (*Rück nach Rechts*). It points, however, to a dawning realization that life consists in cohesion and not in disintegration and that revolutionary torrents debouch in conservative streams.'

This was necessarily the case, since '*conservatism has Eternity on its side*'; furthermore 'all great men have been conservative'.

Like Mann Moeller distinguished conservatism from reaction and like him he held that the stress was irrational. For Moeller 'the Left has reason. The Right has understanding'. This remark, reminiscent of the dicta of Schelling, Görres, and Müller, was driven home by the assertion that 'understanding and reason are mutually exclusive; whereas understanding does not exclude emotion'. It is not surprising to find Moeller associating himself with the prevalent cult of Nietzsche, asserting that when after the war 'Marxism was swamped in democratic chaos, Nietzsche with his conception

[1]The translator of the English edition of *Das Dritte Reich* admits to inventing this word in order to save three syllables over *parliamentarianism*. The frequency with which the author belabours the word may perhaps justify the expedient.

of aristocracy came again to the fore'. The movement implied recognition of the fact that 'the ninth of November [1918] was the shipwreck of leadership'. It was also implicitly the shipwreck of its origin, German democracy. For Moeller maintained that the Germans 'were originally a democratic people. . . . There was no social contract, but there was the bond of blood'; he went on to talk of 'the right of the [primitive German] tribes to assert their power inside or outside the tribe, as might seem necessary to them for their own self-preservation. This was the origin of leadership: the free choice of free men who choose them a "duke"[1] to conduct their forces to victory'.

Here at last, back in the Dark Ages, Moeller found the basis of a constructive political order for modern Germany, an indication of the way in which Germans might retrieve the failure of 1918 and still 'win the revolution'. The nation should look to a 'leader of the folk'. In accordance with this solution 'the folk will choose the leader whom it elects for itself as a nation'. Correspondingly true German democracy would find itself again, anchored in a national solidarity which would render class-war a thing of the past. For Moeller 'the only question is whether the national elements in the German working-classes will have the power and the will to wheel the proletarian battle front in a "national-socialist" direction; or rather to wheel it right round, so that the forces which were directed to class war against our own nation shall face the foreign foe. Our political fate hangs on the answer'. Moeller perceived that this great concentration of national effort might, probably would, involve wild work. He reminded his readers that 'the German people have often in the past been wellnigh imprisoned in despair. They have never found a way out except through their proverbial *furor*: perhaps it has sometimes been a barbaric way—perhaps it will be to-morrow a proletarian way'; but proletarian in a national-conservative sense: that was the novelty, the great synthesis to achieve which the Germans 'must have the strength to live in antitheses'.

National socialism would be the expression of this popular autocracy. And 'this New Socialism must be the foundation

[1]The *Herzog* to lead the *Heereszug*. Cf. the derivation of *duke* from *dux*.

of Germany's Third Empire'. The Third German Empire was the sum of Moeller's credo. It would be the corporate realm, complete in itself. It would achieve economic synthesis, co-ordinating employer and employed, submerging class. It would achieve political synthesis, co-ordinating conservative and radical, obedience and liberty, submerging party. ('Instead of government by party we offer the ideal of the *Third Empire*. It is an old German conception and a great one'.) It would achieve ideal synthesis, co-ordinating feeling and understanding, submerging reason. It would achieve national synthesis, co-ordinating Prussia and Germany, state and realm, the organic realization of the being of the folk (*Volkstum*). It would be the natural, total, final ordering of German life and spirit, the organization of organizations, the organism of estates. 'The Third Empire will be an empire of organization in the midst of European chaos': not only of organization, but of unity. The third empire would at last satisfy the age-old German craving for unity. It would at last give concrete expression to the fact that

in no country have . . . values tended so definitely towards a unity—a unity which we have never enjoyed since our first Empire, a unity which in our second Empire we failed to achieve —a unity which it must be the task of our third Empire to establish. The antithesis of our history will remain, but it is reserved for our Third Empire to bring our values to their fulfilment.'

Moeller warned his countrymen to

'be careful to remember that the thought of the Third Empire is a philosophical idea; that the conceptions which the words "Third Empire" arouse . . . are misty, indeterminate, charged with feeling; not of this world but of the next. Germans are only too prone to abandon themselves to self-deception. The thought of the *Third Empire* might well be the most fatal of all the illusions to which they have ever yielded. . . . Germany might perish of her Third Empire dream.'

But he persisted:

'The thought of the Third Empire—to which we cling as our last and highest philosophy—can only bear fruit if it is translated into concrete reality. . . . It must be as realist as the problems of our constitutional and national life; it must be as sceptical and pessimistic as beseems the times.'

This third empire, which was philosophy and politics in one, was to be the embodiment of the new spirit of German nationalism. Where that led is evident from the fact that 'German nationalism is in its way an expression of German universalism, and turns its thoughts to Europe as a whole'. This was necessarily the case since for Moeller German socialism was implicit in German nationalism, while 'the problems of socialism remain with us. They include the problem of a new world-order which shall supersede the institutions of the nineteenth and twentieth centuries: democracy, liberalism, and parlimentism, in an age of technical efficiency, of over-population; an age in which all participants lost the War'. And this problem was most urgent to the nation which

'counts twenty millions too many, twenty millions who cannot live. It may be that German socialism has a new national mission . . . to place itself at the head of the oppressed nations and show them what are the conditions under which they alone can live. When we talk now of German socialism, we do not of course mean the socialism of the social democrat . . .; neither do we mean the logical Marxist socialism which refuses to abandon the class war and the Internationals. We mean rather a corporative conception of state and economics, which must perhaps have a revolutionary foundation, but will then seek conservative stability. We call Friedrich List a German socialist.'

It may be remembered that List had, among other things, entertained somewhat expansive ideas as to Germany's place in the world. Moeller was less explicit; perhaps that was the main difference. Moeller, like so many Germans before him, gave the nation precedence over the individual in that 'there can be no justice for individuals until there is justice for nations'. And, as has been observed, he held that the German nation lacked justice most. Accordingly Moeller, again like so many Germans before him, held out peace as the ultimate ideal and war as the present reality. He said that 'the thought of enduring peace is in very truth the thought of the Third Empire. But it must be fought for, and the Empire must be maintained'. The practical implications were only partially indicated. Moeller looked back, indeed, to the first German empire not only as regards unity, but also scope. He held that 'our First Empire lost . . . lands which belonged to us by race and speech, Switzerland, and the Netherlands and the Baltic colonies'. The policy of the third empire should be to seal the west, relegating France to the European periphery, a second Portugal; Germany would further carry out 'eastern policy' (*Ostpolitik*) not in the sense of imperialism, but of a new corporative supernational order corresponding to German universalism. It was Naumann's central Europe with trimmings on.

In the international, as in the national, sphere the Third German Empire would be at once conservative and revolutionary. Conservative in that it, the middle land, would establish European equilibrium under the sign of the Germanic world-outlook, the middle term between the will of the west (more particularly of America) and the soul of Russia. Revolutionary in what this dynamic Germanic enterprise would mean to the complacent west and its outmoded way of life. For Moeller Germany is there 'in order never to leave the others in peace'. He realized what that meant, and he gave warning that 'hitherto Russia has been the danger to Europe; now Germany is the danger'.

Such was the thought of Moeller van den Bruck. It was not only the culmination of advanced political thought in post-war Germany. In a very real sense it was the climax of 150 years of persistent theory. In exploring the ideas of Moeller van den Bruck one threads a maze of romance and realism, prejudice and pessimism, bitterness and bravado, shrewdness and sentimentality, of an idealism which scales the heights of mysticism and plumbs the recesses of narcissism. And that maze leads one back past the new romantics, through the nineteenth century, by way of the historical school, back to the romantic origins. German thought had come round full circle, unbroken in its continuity, unchanged in its appeal. Moeller van den Bruck was the admiring devotee of Herder. The first and latest prophets were of one inspiration.

And now the time was at hand when that inspired belief would at last triumph into realization. But there were still a few years to go. *Das Dritte Reich* was published in 1923, but it had to wait some six years for recognition and acclaim. That time was the measure of the deceptive interlude. It deceived Moeller van den Bruck. In 1925 despair drove him to suicide.

At the end of 1923 Germany began to emerge from the sinister shadows into a brief stretch of sunlight. This development was primarily due to Stresemann in politics and to stabilization in economics.

From 1924 to 1929 Gustav Streseman conducted the foreign policy of Germany. The avowed object of this policy was, in brief, the restoration of Germany as a great power, equal in status and in rights with the other great powers of Europe. This object was pursued by means of peaceful collaboration with the nations of the west. Stresemann conducted his policy with great skill, balancing France and England, Aristide Briand and Austen Chamberlain. It was also conducted with marked success, of which the main expressions were the Locarno Pact of Western Security, signed on the 1st December, 1925, by Germany, France, Great Britain, Belgium, and Italy, and the sequel of September 1926 when Germany entered the League of Nations.

It is not surprising that this policy of fulfilment was highly distasteful to large sections of the German people, who thought it a national humiliation that this affable Berlin *petit-bourgeois*, the son of a retailer of bottled beer, should be at such pains to establish friendly relations with the statesmen of the hated *entente*. But Stresemann was much more than a liberal optimist in search of pacific appeasement. He had, after all, been a member of Naumann's National Socialist Union of democratic imperialists; thence he passed on to the national-liberal party; during the Great War he had supported unrestricted submarine warfare and had earned the reputation of being 'Ludendorff's young man'. After the war he was a firm admirer of the former crown prince, and it was in a letter to him, dated the 7th September, 1925, that he disclosed the underlying principles which inspired his foreign policy. Stresemann wrote:

'On the question of Germany's entry into the League I would make the following observations:

In my opinion there are three great tasks that confront German foreign policy in the more immediate future—

In the first place the solution of the Reparations question in a sense tolerable for Germany, and the assurance of peace, which is an essential promise for the recovery of our strength.

Secondly, the protection of Germans abroad, those 10 to 12 millions of our kindred who now live under a foreign yoke in foreign lands.

The third great task is the readjustment of our Eastern frontiers; the recovery of Danzig, the Polish corridor, and a correction of the frontier in Upper Silesia.

In the background stands the union with German Austria, although I am quite clear that this not merely brings no advantages to Germany, but seriously complicates the problem of the German Reich.

If we want to secure these aims, we must concentrate on these tasks. Hence the Security Pact [of Locarno]. . . . The pact also rules out the possibility of any military conflict with France for the recovery of Alsace-Lorraine; this is a renunciation on the part of Germany, but, in so far, it possesses only a theoretic character, as there is no possibility of a war against France. . . .

Our anxiety on behalf of Germans abroad is an argument in favour of our joining the League. . . . In Geneva we shall speak on behalf of German civilization as a whole, because the whole of the Germanic world sees in us its refuge and protector. . . .

The question of a choice between East and West does not arise as the result of our joining the League. Such a choice can only be made when backed by military force. That, alas, we do not possess. . . .

The most important thing for the first task of German policy mentioned above is the liberation of German soil from any occupying force. We must get the stranglehold off our neck. On that account, German policy . . . will be one of finesse and the avoidance of great decisions.'

In his first speech after the German entry into the League of Nations, on the 10th September, 1926, Stresemann gave assurance 'that the German Government will devote themselves whole-heartedly to the tasks of the League'. There is no sufficient reason for doubting the sincerity of that assurance, but the stress is certainly a little different from what it was in Stresemann's picture of a Germany bestowing 'protection' upon millions of Germans living 'under a foreign yoke', of a Germany bent on retaking Danzig and despoiling Poland of the corridor and part of Silesia, of a Germany united with Austria, of a Germany whose renunciation of Alsace-Lorraine was 'theoretic' in that war with France was anyway not then a practical proposition, of a Germany who lamented her lack of 'military force', and was bent on 'peace' as a means to recovering her 'strength', of a Germany driven by circumstance to resort to a policy 'of finesse and the avoidance of major decisions'.

Stresemann's letter to the former crown prince was not merely written with a view to placating the recipient. It was a genuine statement of Stresemann's policy as is evident, for instance, from an article written by him which was published anonymously a week later in the *Hamburger Fremdenblatt*; it is a more guarded, but at the same time in some respects a more radical, declaration. After anathematizing 'the diabolical quality of the Versailles *Diktat*' Stresemann went on to assert that

> 'Germany must be the champion of the German minorities in Europe; she must be the great motherland of the German cultural community. . . . The aim of German foreign policy must, further, be an effort towards the revision of the Eastern frontier, which is today recognized in all quarters as impossible. It must also consist in backing Germany's claim to colonial activity and to acquire colonial possessions. She must, finally, stand out for the national right of self-determination, which, in the question of the union of German Austria with Germany, has been treated with unexampled cynicism by the Allies, and stultified. Progress within the sphere of these foreign-political aims is not dependent on warlike resources, which Germany lacks.'

The last three words have a plangent ring. Lack there certainly was, but at the same time stocks of warlike resources were already being built up. For years past the Reichswehr had been arming secretly beyond treaty limits, chiefly by means of collaboration with Soviet Russia. The outward expression of this Russo-German entente was the treaty of Rapallo, signed in 1922. In 1926 this entente was reaffirmed by the treaty of Berlin. At the same time as Stresemann, who had few illusions as to the true nature of Russian policy, was cultivating German relations with the Soviet he made no secret of his refusal to forgo his claims against Poland. There is no doubt that Stresemann was averse from satisfying those claims by war. It is nevertheless interesting to notice that in the apologia for Locarno which Stresemann delivered in Berlin on the 14th December, 1925, he remarked that

> 'Herr Beneš and Herr Skrzynski, the Czech and Polish Foreign Ministers . . . wanted what is called in the English phrase a "non-aggression pact", that is to say a pact by which we bound ourselves to abstain from any attack. This obligation we undertook

in the West, but we refused it in the East. Membership of the League does not exclude the possibility of war.'

Such observations, guarded as they are, are not often to be met with in Stresemann's letters and speeches; for he was a very discreet and very able diplomat. His letter to the crown prince, already quoted, concluded thus: 'I would also ask you kindly to view this letter in the light of the fact that I am compelled to use the greatest reserve in everything I say.' This did not, of course, mean that Stresemann gave the impression of scheming reserve: quite the contrary. On his return from Locarno Stresemann was welcomed at the Anhalt station in Berlin by the British ambassador, who was 'specially charged by Mr. Chamberlain to congratulate you on the success of the conference at Locarno, and to say that Mr. Chamberlain will always look back with pleasure on . . . the spirit of candour and openness which the German delegates have impressed on the discussions'. A few weeks later, back in Berlin, Stresemann remarked in reference to Locarno: 'No worse nonsense has been talked lately than that about the abolition of secret diplomacy. Every man has his own secret diplomacy.'

Stresemann was a dominant figure at home, not less than abroad. In collaboration with Hugo Stinnes, the magnate who made a fortune out of the inflation and built up enormous industrial power, he had formed the German People's Party as the political organ of big business. And now economic recovery went hand in hand with Stresemann's foreign policy. The mark was stabilized and the Dawes Plan sought to substitute some kind of order, makeshift though it might be, for the confusion into which reparations had sunk. Foreign, especially American, capital poured into Germany. On this artificial foundation German industry boomed and ambitious enterprises, municipal building schemes and the like, were undertaken with a lack of moderation which the more thoughtful regarded with misgiving. But in 1929 the substitution of the Young Plan for the Dawes Plan meant further financial easement for Germany. At the same time the allied troops of occupation were evacuating the Rhineland. The first of Stresemann's three self-imposed tasks was well on the way to completion.

On the 3rd October, 1929, Stresemann died. Just three weeks later came the break on Wall Street. The great slump had begun. Germany's economic position was more precarious than that of other countries; she suffered even more than they. First it had been military defeat; then inflation, and now the slump. In the time of their distress the German people turned in ever larger numbers to those who had been held in check during the Stresemann era, but now swept forward again, pointing to present misery as the inevitable outcome of seeking to stablish German regeneration upon gold and politics that were borrowed from the plutodemocratic west.

Even under Stresemann's régime these and kindred forces had been gathering momentum. In 1925 Ebert was succeeded as president by the antidemocratic Field-Marshal von Hindenburg. Three years later Gessler, the minister for the Reichswehr, was at last forced to resign owing to scandals connected with speculation in Reichswehr funds (with a view not to personal enrichment, but to increasing the war-potential) and ventures such as the floating of the Phoebus film company with 'black' Reichswehr money. Hindenburg replaced Gessler by General Groener, his former chief-of-staff. It was ten years since the republic had been founded. Ebert and Scheidemann were gone. Hindenburg and Groener, the military pair of 1918, were together in power.

Hindenburg and the Reichswehr did not, however, command the support of all those who worked against the republican régime. The Hitler *putsch* of November 1923 had meant a break between the Reichswehr and the Nazi party. The party itself sheltered for a time behind Graefe's Popular Movement of Liberty. From 1924 to 1929 the fortunes of the national-socialists were low; but they never ceased their activities, of which the main significance was threefold.

In the first place the Nazis, however much their numbers might dwindle, never compromised with the existing régime. Unlike other parties they remained in bitter opposition and clung to their ideal of the better order of the future.

In the second place Hitler began to reorganize the party in the spring of 1925, shortly after his release from the fortress of Landsberg. On the 27th February, 1925, the leadership principle was proclaimed. In January 1926 the *Schutzstaffel* (S.S. detachment) was organized throughout the Nazi party. The stroop-troop formations were remodelled by Captain Pfeffer von Salomon. In September 1927 the first party congress at Nüremberg was held. By 1928 things were looking up. The Hitler Youth was supplemented by the Union of Nazi Pupils. The Nazi Teachers' Association, the Union of German Nazi Lawyers, and the Union of Nazi Physicians were formed. The German Womens' Order was incorporated with the Nazi party as the Red Swastika Order. Nazi administration by regions (*Gaue*) was instituted.

Among the important developments in Nazi policy and practice during these years those in the territorial sphere are outstanding. Hitler followed up his break with the Reichswehr by coming to terms with the catholics and the Bavarian authorities in order to assure himself of a base. He parted from Graefe and the other northern nationalists and sent the brothers Gregor and Otto Strasser to organize national-socialism in Prussia. This they did with considerable success, but in the course of time it became increasingly apparent that there existed a cleavage between Hitler, for whom it was the national side of the policy that mattered, and the Strassers, who held sincere socialist convictions. This was particularly the case with Otto Strasser, who had been a friend and admirer of Moeller van den Bruck and had joined with him in founding the June Club with the object of promoting the rebirth of Germany along the corporative lines advocated by Moeller. There followed protracted feud and intrigue among the party bosses, a large part being played by Doctor Paul Joseph Goebbels, who began as a follower of Graefe, was taken up by the Strassers, and went over to Hitler. Finally on the 4th July, 1930, Otto Strasser left the Nazi party. He proceeded to organize the Black Front against the national-socialists. He established contact with various formations such as the Wehrwolf and Jung Deutsche Orden, with dissident peasant bodies in Silesia and Schleswig and with the *Die Tat* (*Action*) group.

Die Tat was a group of intellectuals who were influential in military circles. They recognized the breakdown of democracy in Germany which was already apparent in 1930 with three million unemployed on the one hand, militarist parades on the other, and in the centre Brüning's government dependent upon the big business and high finance. The various members of the *Die Tat* group, intellectually contemptuous of the Nazis for the most part, fumbled for a solution along more or less authoritarian and national-socialist lines. Hans Zehrer looked to the end of parliamentarianism, revolution from above, and the formation of a new *élite*. Ferdinand Fried, the economist, proclaimed 'The End of Capitalism' in his major work, and envisaged an autocratic autarky which would reaffirm the true values of race and blood in the face of plutocratic mechanization, Carl Schmitt envisaged juridical evolution in the same sense. Giselher Wirsing brought forward the old idea of central European hegemony under the new title of the Green International, descriptive of the agricultural basis which the lesser countries would provide for Germany's supernational enterprise.

The complement to these now familiar theories was the secret organization of the Black Front, the emblem of the hammer and sword rivalling the swastika, 'Heil Deutschland' as the answer to 'Heil Hitler', the spread of street-fighting and assault, conflicts between the two in Bremen, in Stuttgart, in Rostock, Frankfurt, and Hamburg.

In this struggle the Nazi party enjoyed the great preponderance of power. This was largely due to the third main orientation of its activity at this period. At the turn of the twenties Hitler began to enter into relations with the great magnates of Germany, with Thyssen the industrialist, Schacht of the Reichsbank, and Hugenberg, the man who had helped to start the Pan-German League back in the eighteen-nineties, the capitalist leader of the nationalists, and a determined opponent of Stresemann. The support of Hugenberg was of especial value, since not only was he associated with the Stahlhelm, the nationalist paramilitary formation under Seldte, but he controlled great propagandist resources, notably the Telegraphic Union, the Ufa film company, and the Konzern Scherl which produced most of the right-wing newspapers. Such was the powerful backing which the Nazis now enjoyed. The backers looked upon the Nazis as most useful tools. The Nazis viewed their backers in the same light.

As far as the Weimar republic is concerned the rest is epilogue. Under Brüning things went from bad to worse. The socialists and communists were ineffective, as they had been for years past. Many went over to the Nazi party. The middle-classes followed where the nationalists led. In the curious presidential election of 1932 Brüning ran Hindenburg as a popular candidate against the nationalists and national-socialists. Once elected, Hindenburg dropped Brüning and substituted as chancellor the shady catholic von Papen. It is not necessary to pursue the course of the obscure and sordid intrigues which multiplied between Hitler, Hugenberg, old Hindenburg, young Hindenburg, von Papen, and von Schleicher of the Reichswehr. But one of von Papen's first actions as chancellor demands special notice. By resorting to a presidential decree von Papen dismissed the government of Prussia.

Since the foundation of the republic the government of Germany had experienced many vicissitudes. But throughout this period the government of Prussia, led by the socialists Otto Braun and Severing, had maintained a steady and democratic tradition. Two main failures vitiated this achievement. The Junkers remained unshaken in their power; and the Prussian police were never tamed. Disposed to shoot upon slight provocation, formidable with armoured cars, the *Schutzpolizei* made people fearful rather than secure. And now in 1932 these omissions on the part of the Prussian government contributed largely to its downfall. Threatened by the Reichswehr, Braun protested against the illegal procedure to President Hindenburg. Hindenburg replied that when Braun's socialist friend Ebert had been president he had sanctioned the very similar deposition of the democratic governments of Saxony and Thuringia in 1923. That deed, too, had found its lodgement. Papen himself took over the government of Prussia in addition to his direction of the central executive. This arbitrary proceeding evoked no popular resistance.

The fate of the Prussian government is indicative of an important trend in post-war Germany. It is a trend which belies the facile assumption that national-socialism is merely Prussianism anew. Militarist reaction certainly had its stronghold among the Prussian Junkers, but throughout this period popular support of nationalist and racialist policy tended to come less from Prussia, under democratic government, than from the romantic south, and in particular Bavaria. It was with reason that Moeller van den Bruck rejoiced in the fact that 'the Bavarians, from whose particularism our enemies before the War ingenuously hoped so much, are the race which have seized on the idea of national regeneration with the greatest enthusiasm'. This circumstance affords a clue to one of the, if not the, main achievement of national-socialist rule in Germany. It would seem that, for the first time in German history, particularist sympathies were largely replaced by a real feeling for German unity within the Nazi Reich. Particularist tendencies certainly remained, but lessened and overlaid by respect for the new ideal. That fact is reflected in the nature of the national-socialist system. Brutal subordination and ruthless co-ordination are not everything with national-socialism. It has progressed some way towards achieving a synthesis of the very varied elements which constitute German life and politics. National-socialism is not merely Prussian militarism, only more so. It is more formidable than that. It is organized romanticism. It is a blend of north and south, of technique and idealism, of purpose and vision. It is a truly German compound. The core is Prussian, but the *élan* is German as a whole.

This unitary *élan* now bore the movement towards its goal in dynamic tempo. In the elections of September 1930 the Nazis polled 6½ million votes, 107 seats in the Reichstag. In July 1932 they polled 14 million votes, 230 seats in the Reichstag. Those millions of Germans who voted thus for national-socialism were left in no doubt as to what they were about. At the time the fighting organ of the Nazi party, *Der Angriff*, proclaimed as follows:

> 'We enter Parliament in order to supply ourselves, in the arsenal of democracy, with its own weapons, to paralyse the Weimar sentiment with its own assistance. If democracy is so stupid as to give us free tickets and salaries for this purpose, that is its affair. . . . We come as enemies. As the wolf bursts into the flock, so we come.'

So they came. On the 30th January, 1933, Adolf Hitler became chancellor of the German Reich. Germany was set marching.

Such was the foundation of the Third German Empire.

Chapter VII

FOREGROUND

Now the historical perspective closes in, forbidding any sure survey of the structure of the Third German Empire or any competent account of how it pressed forward to meet its destiny in the fourth decade of the twentieth century.

If the perspective is insufficient to allow of any adequate record of Nazi policy, it is at the same time too full to warrant detailed examination of Nazi theory. For when the theory of national-socialism is viewed in relation to German political thought of the last century and a half it is seen to be stale stuff, stale and adulterated. It would be penance without profit to dissect the turgid unoriginality of Adolf Hitler and Alfred Rosenberg, and of their lesser company, Günther in racial theory, Darré in agriculture, and Feder in economics. The stress and presentation are novel, perhaps, but the matter is hardly more than repetition. The exaltation of the heroic leader goes back through Moeller van den Bruck, Spengler, Lamprecht, Chamberlain, Nietzsche, Lassalle, Rodbertus, and Hegel, back to Fichte's *Zwingherr zur Deutschheit.* The racial myth is only the latest edition of Spengler, Chamberlain, Lagarde, Dühring, Schemann, Wagner, Gobineau, and the adumbrations of Görres, Arndt, and Jahn. In their anti-Semitism the Nazis have merely followed Dühring in theorizing a very widespread German prejudice which goes back to the Junker following of Marwitz and beyond. The concept of the all-significant totalitarian state was cherished in one form or another as early as Schelling and Adam Müller. The idea of the ruling *élite* occurs again and again in German thought from the time when the romantics proclaimed their faith in aristocracy. The community of the folk runs from Hitler right back to Herder. The full programme of economic autarky was outlined by Fichte in 1800. National-socialism itself derives in theory from Moeller van den Bruck, Spengler, Rathenau, Naumann, Dühring, Lassalle, Rodbertus, Fichte. There is hardly a thinker in the line who was not more or less a nationalist. Spengler foretold intensive nationalist propaganda; more than a century before Herder and Novalis were urging it. The tradition of militarism—Banse, Bernhardi, Treitschke, Moltke, Ranke, Clausewitz—is only the reflection of Prusso-German history since Frederick II and before. The dynamic originality of German culture in contrast to the artificial civilization of the west was a theme dear to Moeller van den Bruck, Spengler, Mann, Chamberlain, Lagarde, Ranke, Fichte, and the romantic school at large. The polemic against reason and the intellect is Nazi, neo-romantic, romantic. The supernational mission of German culture was as evident to Novalis and Fichte as it is to Hitler and his followers. Living-space for Germans was the demand of Moeller van den Bruck, Bernhardi, Naumann, Ratzel, and List. Pan-Germanism was already a cult with Arndt and Görres and Grimm. Law that is folk-law was a concept familiar to Savigny. The abasement of the individual before the state finds precedent with Hegel. The Nazis say that might is right; Spengler said it; Bernhardi said it; Nietzsche said it; Treitschke had said as much; so had Haller before him; so had Novalis.

It is a long line, long yet compact. And in it only the major figures have been noticed; and hardly all of them. For it is better to dwell a little upon the more important figures rather than to give a breathless and insipid record of the very many second-raters and disciples: especially so in German thought, the home of dreary scholiasts and intellectual hangers-on. There is scarcely one of the thinkers previously mentioned who was not famous in his own time or after it, often both; who was not eagerly studied by thousands and taken for granted by more.

It would, however, be patently inaccurate to regard this line of German thought as an entirely compact and original national whole, sufficient to and in itself—quite apart from the obvious fact that many of the theorists differed considerably among themselves, and that in any case the Nazi leaders can hardly be said to owe their power primarily to especial capacity and research in the field of intellectual theory. The rise and triumph of national-socialism is certainly not fully explicable unless it is realized how very much its outlook was an extension of the traditional outlook of Germany; but at the same time appreciation of this factor should not prevent recognition of the cardinal importance of other more immediate factors in that ascendancy, of the personalities of Adolf Hitler, his followers and opponents, of prevailing economic conditions, of the politico-social complex of events which afforded the Nazis such scope. And other factors, more fundamental, forbid any hasty generalization as to the peculiarity and true significance of that line of German thought which is national at root, historical in growth, and romantic in impulse.

In the first place that line has clearly not prevailed unchallenged in Germany. German liberals, socialists, internationalists, and pacifists have rejected the historico-nationalist tradition. From Rotteck to Richter, from Heine to Liebknecht there stood Germans to whom that tradition was repulsive. But they have been relatively few and ineffective. We have seen how German liberalism failed in 1848, in the eighteen-sixties, and again after 1918; how it gradually became alien to the ordinary German outlook in so far as it was not the pseudo-liberalism of the national liberals. We have seen how German socialism, prejudiced at the start by Lassalle, gradually came to be state-socialism, Prussian socialism, national-socialism. Genuine liberalism and socialism were nearly always more or less in opposition to the dominant faction in thought and politics. And in Germany such opposition receives short shrift.

A more important limitation to the scope and immediate influence of the historical school was probably the fact that in Germany as in other countries, and even more than in many other countries, the majority of men and women concerned themselves with politics hardly if at all. For very many years after the rise of the historical school its theories can have meant little or nothing to the bulk of the population. Most of the German contemporaries of the romantics and their successors were doubtless quite indifferent whether the aristocracy might rightly be adjudged the female element in the state, or whether the state is in fact the manifestation of world-historical will. What did matter to them was whether the local aristocrat employed an honest bailiff, whether the petty state officials were competent. Harvests, wages, stock, church-going, and the fortunes of long-acquainted families were, most likely, the prime objects of their concern. There was, in Prussia at least, little scope even for local politics. Stein's projects for local self-government were not the start of a vigorous movement in that direction. The Junkers maintained their hold, and it was only in 1872 and the following years that local self-government came to mean something in Prussia. Such communal co-operation as there was was largely centred in the *Landschaften*, an important feature of German life since about 1770. The local Junkers and larger farmers formed economic mutual aid societies which undertook mortgage credit operations, the many leading to the one who might be pinched for a time. These societies increased local solidarity, while at the same time affording a most powerful instrument whereby the large landowners were able to keep the peasants dependent and in control.

In Germany as in other countries it was everyday life and its urgent problems, not political theory, that engaged the attention of the many. In so far as they had a distinctive political outlook it was very likely formed largely by decades of nationalistic state-education, though modified in a number of cases by an immediate sense of social injustice which might turn to socialism for coherent expression. But, after all, it is probably impossible to determine what the bulk of the population really thought of major political problems, if they thought at all. They are the silent setting of history, affording it its scope, but inarticulate. But this political abstention of the masses recoiled upon them in the end. For it meant that the theorists themselves were unhampered from below, and that they could push forward with their work and so propagate it among the educated classes that when at last the populace swarmed into the political arena they only served to swell the following. Their former indifference and inexperience provided the historical school with its most signal triumph.

If the growth and influence of historico-nationalist thought in Germany was conditioned by variations in the social strata it was hardly less affected by the factors of ethnic and political geography. German emphasis upon racial purity and cohesion does not alter, perhaps results from, the fact that the Germans are a people of very varied stock: Balts, Saxons, Frisians, and Slavs; men of Nordic, Dinaric, and Alemannic strain. These ethnographical variations are powerfully reinforced by geographical divisions, and particularly that of the river Elbe, south-west of which lie the lands familiar for centuries with the common culture of western Europe, whereas for those to the north and east it is at best a recent acquisition. Catholic Bavaria is remote in much from cryptopagan Mecklenburg, reactionary East Prussia from Baden, liberal even during the second empire. It is nevertheless a fact that the influential exponents of the prevailing political thought in Germany have been fairly evenly distributed throughout the country. Herder and Kant were East Prussians, Fichte, Wagner, and Treitschke were Saxons, Arndt and Niebuhr came from the Baltic fringe, Görres and Savigny were Rhinelanders, Lassalle a Silesian, the Schlegels Hanoverian; Schelling, Hegel and List all hailed from Württemberg. Like trends of thought all over Germany have merged into a German whole. And it has been noticed that this synthesis is far from being purely Prussian in stamp. It is none the less evident, however, that the vigour of Prussian society and the success of Prussian policy won the increasing admiration and attention of men throughout Germany, a process which was further stimulated by the economic decay of the commercial cities of western Germany during the seventeenth and eighteenth centuries and by growing industrialism during the nineteenth. This swing to the east accorded in a number of respects with the prevailing trend of German political thought. The foundations of Prussia had been laid by vigorous colonization, by clearing marches for a higher civilization; the same should be done for Greater Germany. The facility of communications over the north-eastern plains had readily promoted centralization. Situated as she had been, a state small, vulnerable and poor, and with ambitions, Prussia had almost instinctively developed administrative cohesion and military might at the expense of free trade, individual initiative, and political liberty. This decline of the western element in German life and politics is sharply emphasized if the survey eastwards is extended out beyond Prussia.

German practice and theory appear in a much less peculiar light when approached from the east instead of from the west. The interaction between German and Russian thought and politics has been marked and protracted despite the very different characters of the two peoples; perhaps just because of it. In the eighteenth century German influence in Russian affairs was exemplified by the dynastic policy of Peter the Great, the position of the Baltic Barons, the rule of the empress Anne, that of the empress Catherine II, formerly princess Sophia Maria of Anhalt-Zerbst, and her especial patronage of the encyclopaedist Grimm. Herder first went to Königsberg at the instance of the surgeon to a Russian regiment quartered in his home district during the Seven Years War; and from Königsberg Herder went on to Russia. Outside Germany the most enthusiastic disciples of Schelling and Hegel were Russians. Stein and Clausewitz entered the Russian service. After the Treaty of Vienna it was to Russia that Germany mainly looked in politics. Russia was always one of Bismarck's primary concerns. Rilke thought that Russia bordered on God. Karl Marx stood behind the Russian revolution and that in turn overshadowed the German revolution in the following year. After the Great War Russo-German treaties were concluded in 1922 and 1926. The Reichswehr viewed Russia as their arsenal, while at the same time Russian *émigrés* congregated in reactionary Munich and consorted with the national-socialists. Russian mysticism exerted a formative influence upon Moeller van den Bruck.

The examples are casual, but the tradition which they indicate is not to be overlooked. Underneath such intercourse lay conditions and experience which were largely common to both. During the nineteenth century politics in Russia as in Germany turned upon autocracy, bureaucracy, police-rule, and a Church identified with the state. Anti-Semitism flourished in both countries. Germany had her Pan-German movement; Russia cherished Pan-Slav aspirations.

The history of both countries was sombre in the main and the thought of both peoples was apt to take a moody turn which found its vent either in mysticism or in nihilism. It is accordingly scarcely surprising that there should be an obvious similarity between the communism of Soviet Russia and the national-socialism of Nazi Germany.

But Germany yet remains the middle land and many of the elements in her political outlook during the nineteenth century were only variations of general ideas which were influencing Europe as a whole and western Europe in particular. The forerunners of the historical view of politics were Montesquieu and Burke. The rise of romanticism was an international event. The nineteenth century was the century of nationalism, and it is noteworthy, and slightly ironic, that Herder gave an impetus to national thought not only in Germany but in Balkan countries also. The cult of the Nordic and the Teutonic was known to Victorian England as well as to Bismarckian Germany. Great Britain led the way in imperialism and talked of the white man's burden, while the Germans were descanting upon Nordic superiority and Germany's supernational mission. In France the Dreyfus affair and the publications of Edouard Drumont bore ample witness to the fact that anti-Semitism did not stop short at the Rhine. The syndicalist Georges Sorel, the Action Française and the Camelots du Roi showed that in France before the Great War liberal democracy did not pass unchallenged. Even more significant, perhaps, was the fact that French thinkers from De Maistre to Bergson challenged the rule of reason.

This relation between German thought and that of the west at large holds for the twentieth century also, over and above the obvious parallel of Italian futurism and fascism. Perhaps the most immediately striking feature of national-socialism is its stress upon concentration, concerted totalitarian drive, the permanent mobilization of the nation. The Nazi concentration-camps are well named. They are but the morbid symptoms of a growth that is more than purely German. Concentration is the keynote of the early twentieth century just as expansion was that of the early nineteenth. The nineteenth century was an era of expanding output, expanding markets, expanding population, free trade, free opportunity, colonial enterprise, liberalism, *laissez-faire.* It was an era congenial to Great Britain. The twentieth century is an age of concentration in its various forms, cartelization, acceleration, mechanization, specialization, mobilization, regimentation. The age has offered an opportunity which Germany has been swift to seize and skilful in exploiting. The Nazi co-ordination of Prussianism and romanticism is in some sort the co-ordination of the extreme forces of concentration and the extreme forces of irrationalism which are, perhaps, more or less complementary, the escape from reason being the necessary counterpoise to high-pitched concentration.

This achievement of national-socialism is a great and original *tour-de-force*, but it does not alter the fact that national-socialist theory is almost entirely derived from the common elements of traditional German thought during the past hundred and fifty years. For that line of thought which leads from Herder to Hitler is traditionally and typically German despite the internal limitations and external affiliations which have been noticed. The external affiliations merely show that the subject-matter of German thought was far from being invariably original and distinctive; such originality is not, indeed, a noticeably German quality; what can be and is highly original is the German approach, treatment, and development. The internal limitations, such as they are, illustrate for the most part the immaturity of the context of German thought. It was this which the Nazis seized upon, pandering to such immaturity on the one hand by popularizing and sensationalizing the corpus of German thought, and exploiting it on the other in order to establish that corpus in its most uncompromising and relentless form.

National-Socialism now stands forth in true perspective. It is novel in application, surrealist in affinity, ultra-modern in technique, but ancient in inspiration, unoriginal in its ideals. National-socialism is not artificial or exotic; it is naturally German. This, indeed, is necessarily the case, for the national-socialist leaders are not for the most part men of a profound or highly original turn of mind; they are men of small education who seized hold of the ideas and prejudices which came most naturally to them and to the bulk of the German people. The Nazis could never have won the devotion of the German folk by imposing upon it a regimen wholly alien to the German outlook; they won it, on the contrary, by calling up the German spirit from the depths. It is in this sense that the Nazis confidently claim to have brought liberation to the German folk, liberation through self-realization. These men of limited intelligence but dynamic drive achieved a splendid consummation of a century and a half of German thought. That this should be so only proves how faithful was that line of thought to the genius of the German people: a fact earlier apparent, indeed, from the way in which German thought and German politics goose-stepped together down the ages. Authority, community and totality, aristocracy, army and folk, pessimism, cynicism and idealism, they advanced as one, incorporated and transfigured within the mystic whole that was the new faith of Germanity.

A century ago a thoughtful German was already quite clear as to what the rise of this new faith would spell for the civilization of the west. In 1834 Heinrich Heine wrote:

'The German philosophy is an important matter which affects the whole human race; and our remote descendants will be the first to be able to decide whether we are to praise or to blame for having first worked out our philosophy and after that our revolution. It seems to me that a methodical people like ours must necessarily have begun with the reformation, wherever it was in a position to busy itself with philosophy and finally, after bringing it to completion, to pass on to political revolution. I find this order quite rational.... The German revolution will not prove any milder or gentler because it was preceded by the Kantian Critique, by the transcendental idealism of Fichte, or even by the philosophy of nature. These doctrines served to develop revolutionary forces that only await their time to break forth and to fill the world with terror and with awe. There will appear Kantians who will reject piety in the world of phenomena also [i.e. as well as in that of ideas]; they will mercilessly upturn with sword and axe the soil of our European life in order to extirpate the last roots of the past. There will come upon the scene armed Fichteans who, in their fanaticism of will, are to be tamed neither by fear nor by self-interest; for they live in the spirit; they defy matter like the early Christians who could likewise be subdued neither by bodily torments nor by bodily delights; yes, in a time of social revolution such transcendental idealists would be even more inflexible than the early Christians; for the latter endured earthly martyrdom in order to attain thereby to celestial bliss, whereas the transcendental idealist looks on martyrdom itself as a vain show, and is inaccessible within the entrenchment of his own thought. But more terrible than all these would be the philosophers of nature were they actively to participate in a German revolution and to identify themselves with the work of destruction. For if the hand of the Kantian smites strong and sure because his heart is moved by no traditional reverence, if the Fichtean courageously defies every danger because for him it simply does not exist in reality, so will the philosopher of nature be frightful in that he allies himself with the primitive powers of nature, being able to conjure up the daemonic forces of old Germanic pantheism; and then there will awake in him that of joy of battle which we find among the ancient Germans, [the spirit] which does not fight in order to destroy or conquer, but simply for the sake of fighting.

Christianity—and this is its fairest merit—has in some degree subdued that brutal Germanic joy of battle, but it could not destroy it; and when the cross, that restraining talisman, falls to pieces, then will break forth again the ferocity of the old combatants, the insane Berserker rage whereof northern poets have said and sung. The talisman is rotten, and the day will come when it will pitifully crumble to dust. The old stone gods will then arise from the forgotten ruins and wipe from their eyes the dust of a thousand years, and at last Thor with his giant hammer will leap aloft and he will shatter the gothic cathedrals.

When you hear the trampling of feet and the clashing of arms, ye neighbours' children, ye French, be on your guard. . . . Smile not at my counsel, at the counsel of a dreamer, who warns you against Kantians, Fichteans, and philosophers of Nature. Smile not at the phantasy of one who anticipates in the realm of reality the same revolution that has taken place in the region of intellect. The thought precedes the deed as the lightning the thunder. German thunder is of true German character; it is not very nimble, and it rumbles along slowly. But come it will, and when you hear a crashing such as never before has been heard in the world's history, then know that at last the German thunderbolt has fallen. At this commotion the eagles will drop dead from the skies and the lions in the farthest wastes of Africa will bite their tails and creep into their royal lairs. There will be played in Germany a drama compared with which the French revolution will seem but an innocent idyll. At present it is true everything is tolerably quiet; and though here and there someone creates a little stir, do not imagine that these are the real actors in the piece. They are only the little curs running about in the empty arena and barking and biting at each other until the hour comes in which the troop of gladiators arrives to fight for life and death.

And the hour will come. . . . I counsel you, ye French, keep very quiet, and, as you value your lives, do not applaud. We might readily misunderstand such applause, and, in our impolite way, somewhat roughly put you to silence; for, if formerly in our servile listless condition we could oftentimes overpower you, how much easier were it for us to do so in the arrogant intoxication of our new-born freedom. You yourselves know what, in such a case, men can do—and you are no longer in such a case. Take heed, then! I mean it well with you, and therefore it is I tell you the bitter truth. You have more to fear from a freed Germany than from the entire Holy Alliance with all its Croats and Cossacks. For, in the first place, they do not love you in Germany. . . . Once in a beer-cellar at Goettingen I heard a young Old-German assert that it was necessary to be revenged on France for Conradin of Hohenstaufen, whom you beheaded at Naples. Doubtless you have long since forgotten that. We, however, forget nothing. You see, then, that whenever we have a mind to quarrel with you there will be no lack of valid grounds. In any case I advise you to be on your guard. Happen what may in Germany, . . . be you ever armed, remain quietly at your post, your weapons in your hands. I mean it well with you, and I was seized with dismay when I heard it said lately that your ministry proposed to disarm France.

As you are, despite your present romantic tendency, a born classical people, you know Olympus. Amongst the naked gods and goddesses making merry over nectar and ambrosia, you may behold one goddess, who, although surrounded by such gaiety and pastime, yet wears ever a coat of mail, the helm on her head and the spear in the hand.

'She is the goddess of Wisdom.'[1]

That was fair warning. But its full implications have not always been very present to the nations of the west. They soon learnt, indeed, not to underestimate the military vigour and material might of Germany. But for many years they failed to heed the import of German outlook on society, either assuming that it must necessarily reflect their own or else dismissing its peculiarities with a sneer. Such an attitude is understandable. For much of German thought is pedantic and pretentious, given to inelegant excess, and apparently less concerned with sound sense than with verbal formulae. And indeed German political thought often seems hardly political at all, but more akin to poetry, prophecy, polemic;

[1]*Deutschland* in *Sämmtliche Werke* (Hamburg, 1885), vol. vii, pp. 138–42. (The translation is largely based upon the distinguished version given in *The New Statesman and Nation*, vol. xix, no. 487, p. 770.)

it tends to become so involved within itself that foreigners not unnaturally wonder whether it may not be best to leave it to its own contortions, resigning any hope of deriving objective truth from the surge of its subjectivity. But such an attitude is more facile than felicitous. Thinkers of the west who find German thought contemptible might perhaps do well to review the tenets of their own belief and to ponder a little upon those ideals which stand so close to German speculation: rule of the many by the abler few, recognition of the fact that blood will tell, a community conjoined by ties more lovable than cash and interest, a society in which all work for all, in which efficiency and enterprise find just reward, a social order that is not static but moving with the sweep of life itself, a supernational order inspired by the splendid scope of the undertaking rather than an international order dependent upon the shifts of politicians, politics that are philosophy made real, the discovery of the new faith that is to carry on where christianity left off, elevating mankind to nobler achievements and to a higher destiny.

To neglect these elements in German thought is totally to misconstrue it. It is, however, not less false to imagine that those elements, as they stand, form the kernel of that thought, and that therefore it is only needful for the western peoples to discuss with Germans their purport and application, to overlook past disagreements, and thus to clear an easy way for fruitful co-operation. For the whole tendency of German thought, its most splendid achievement, has been, even when at its most general and abstract, to impregnate itself with the subtle essence of Germanity. The inspiration that is *Deutschheit*, the mystic omnicomprehensive whole of *Deutschtum*—it is they that loom in the background when Germans themselves dwell, as they so often do, upon the mystery that makes their nation what it is and renders it obscure to others. It is remarkable that Germans who have intercourse with foreigners tend so often either to hug themselves in delight or else to falter in mistrust, for they are apt to realize, what the others generally do not, that there is no direct communication, but only through the medium of Germanity.

The fact that the German folk has developed its national ethos in such exceptional measure requires, probably, a more adequate explanation than can ever be provided. It has, however, been shown how German geography and history contributed towards that development and largely moulded it. It is now time to follow where many Germans have already led, and to take soundings within that whole which is Germanity.

The German code is stiff-girt, seemingly rigid and ritual and difficult of access. But the crust once pierced, a void is opened up within. That void is a chaos of dark thoughts. It is there because the German spirit must express itself in the German individual while at the same time the spirit lacks confidence in the individual. Here at once we come upon the fundamental cleavage between Germany and the west. A cardinal tenet of all western thought is the sanctity of the individual. The individual, imperfect as he is, is the hub of meaning and index to life's operation. But the German spirit tends to view the individual otherwise, according him no sanctity as such, dwelling upon his imperfections, and judging him insufficient. Hence the German addiction to drill, rank and organization, to the superpersonal hierarchies and formations which alone can bestow upon such an individual that poise and significance which he is incapable of deriving from, or ascribing to, himself; hence the feeling of that bookseller in Dresden who during the Weimar republic regretted the monarchy of old, remarking, 'I need a close-fitting coat to feel safe in my skin'; hence the belief that man exists for the state, not the state for man; hence the totalitarian state.

The reverse aspect of this negation of the sanctity of the individual is an exorbitant egoism. Recognition of the high claims of the individual as such imposes restraint upon a community of individuals and unites them by the common ties of humanity. Such is the basis of accepted standards of decent conduct, liberty of conscience, free expression of opinion, freedom from arbitrary arrest, equality before the law, impartial justice, representative government, and those other great instruments whereby the freedom of the indivi-

[1]To Count Keyserling. The remark is quoted by him in the chapter on Germany in *Europe* (Ed. cit., p. 115). That chapter is among Keyserling's rather more satisfactory efforts and contains a number of pertinent observations relative to the German outlook.

dual is reconciled with social order. If these claims of the individual are rejected or treated as subordinate, then the individual is thrown back upon himself and invited to exploit his ego ruthlessly against the others. Thus the individual is not at one with his fellows, but isolated among them. His loneliness in the face of others is complementary to the void within himself. The external and internal effects of the same belief, or lack of it, combine to make the German huddle for comfort into rigid hierarchies where each has his place according to arbitrary order. Loneliness craves a formal unity with others. The disturbing and unbounded relationship of man to man is thus overlaid by the fixed delimitation of tribe or class or grade. The individual can anchor himself within such a delimitation and its formal code of conduct, recouping himself for such strict observance by his freedom outside of it to give full reign to his egoism and passion, unchecked by any of those scruples which depend upon a realization of deeper community and general worth of men. Hence the German sympathy for the middle ages; hence partly the German belief in militarism; hence partly foreign denunciation of German ruthlessness and brutality. From time to time, however, great spirits dare the loneliness and scorn the stays and by a triumph of self-sufficiency win through in the face of all. Hence the fact that the greatness of great Germans is so often patiently cultivated and unrelenting egoism; hence the German admiration of that quality; hence the very common contempt of great Germans for other Germans; hence the fact that great Germans strike one so often as being self-made men, not very gentlemanly; hence the success in Germany of the leadership-principle, of rule by the master-egoist whose sovereign contempt can, indeed, embrace not only his followers, but also the forms and principles wherewith he outwardly secures and justifies his supremacy.

The negation of the sanctity of the individual obstructs direct conduct not only between man and man, but also beween man and his ideals. For if the worth of the individual and its increase by his life's process be not itself a cardinal ideal, any ideal to the realization of which the individual devotes his life and energy must be more or less external to him: not, of course, entirely external since the ideal must find expression in the individual, but external to the individual's broad humanity. Most western Europeans view social and political ideals relatively, as means, as means whereby the lives of individuals may come to achieve, however imperfectly and partially, the end; whereby they may strive to realize the absolute values of good and right and truth and beauty. Germans on the other hand tend to view such ideals absolutely, as ends, as complete embodiments of absolute values independent of, and superior to, individuals, their fortunes, and their partial standards. It is quite understandable that this German separation of the individual from the ideal should vitiate the perspective in which ideals are viewed and lead to confusion of means with ends. This confusion was, indeed, implicit in the thesis, already noted, that man exists for the sake of the state. It may then be asked for what purpose the state itself exists. The German answer is: the state for the sake of the state, order for the sake of order, power for the sake of power, the ideal for the sake of the ideal. Hence the extraordinary vehemence of Germans in their idealism, their ruthless determination to impose the superreality of the ideal upon the mere actuality of the world, to subordinate reality to their vision of it.

German talk of German objectivity generally proceeds from this divorce of the individual from the ideal. German talk of German synthesis generally proceeds from this identification of means with ends. German talk of German idealism generally proceeds from this total idealization of mere means and their transformation into a superreality.

This divorce of the ideal from the individual explains much that is very German. It explains, for instance, the fanatical quality of German idealism and the interplay of nihilism and mysticism. It explains why with Germans so much seems to depend upon the interaction of inferiority and superiority complexes. It explains the deficient German grip upon reality, the fact that, as Treitschke long ago remarked, the Germans find it difficult in times of stress to distinguish the heroic from the trumpery. The externalization of the ideal sheds light also upon the German cult of the expert, the man who immerses himself absolutely in his specialty, deriving his being from his subject, instead of his subject from his being; for a German need see nothing contradictory in an ideal being specialized and at the same time absolute. Thus the very German and usually contrasted qualities of technique and idealism, pedantry and romanticism may be intimately related as coefficient forces or, as the Germans prefer to put it, as polar coordinates. Again, if the ideal is divorced from the individual it is evident that its achievement must require of the individual a most deliberate exertion and subject him to exceptional stress: it is unnecessary to emphasize the fact that German thought and achievement again and again gives the impression of oppressive earnestness, of peculiar strain and over-exertion, lacking in spontaneity. That is largely but a reflection of the fact that if the means are total, being ends also, then the immediate effort must be correspondingly total. (Some might, perhaps, prefer to reverse the proposition, holding that the German expenditure of effort upon mere means is naturally so prodigious that they seek to justify it by proclaiming means to be ends.) This tendency of Germans to overtax themselves follows, indeed, almost necessarily, from the negation of the sanctity of the individual which implies that such worth as he may possess depends not upon what he is, but upon what he achieves. The German can rarely take himself for granted. This leads further in two directions. In the first place the necessity of overcoming this lack of spontaneity, of standing up to the strain of proving oneself to oneself by achievement, may perhaps have been responsible, partially at least, for the development of German will-power in its formidable intensity and concentration; and for its sporadic snapping in suicide or mania. Secondly, if the value of the individual as such is not high his life is naturally held cheap. Hence the German practice of wanton sacrifice of life to a cause, and willingness to be so sacrificed, both quite natural and admirable for those imbued with a sense of the insignificance of the individual in the face of the magnificence of the impersonal ideal.

The divorce of the ideal from the individual is accompanied, as indicated, by confusion of means with ends. This involves the negation of the second cardinal principle upon which all western thought has built. The German ideology denies not only the sanctity of the individual, but also the sanctity of absolute values. The main line of western thought holds that there are certain absolute and universal values, good, right, truth, beauty and the like: it is impossible for man perfectly to comprehend, let alone attain, those values: but without faith in those absolute values human life would lose its meaning. This principle German thought rejects; its faith is centred not in those absolute values, but in immediate and partial concepts which are yet held to embody those values absolutely. The divorce of the individual from the ideal now assumes a further significance. Being divorced from the ideal in his own life the individual can alter his ideals much more readily than would otherwise be the case, and since any partial political social or other ideal can be absolute, one is really as good as another. Hence the shifting and contradictory nature of German standards and enthusiasms which make all bearings difficult. This is largely a reflection of the fact that if limited ideals are treated as absolutes, means as ends, then particular expressions of a universal ideal are held to inform that ideal instead of *vice versa*. Thus for Germans the particular subsumes the universal, the relative the absolute. And since it is Germans who view matters thus, it is natural that they should foster their own particularity above all others, trying to generalize particularity itself and claiming that Germanity is the attribute which informs all absolute values and comprehends them. Thus good and right and truth simply disappear. Good is German good, right is folk-right, truth is Aryan truth. The two poles of western thought, the individual and the universal, are swept clean away. All is flux.

Men of good faith hold it to be their highest duty to hate and combat the opposites of their ideals, to subdue evil and wrong and falsehood. Just so do Germans hold it to be their highest duty to hate and combat the opposites of the attributes informing their ideals, to subdue those who are not Germans, who are not of the folk, who are not of Aryan stock. Thus Germans set out of high purpose to dominate all life and prove their total devotion to ideal Germanity by total war on its behalf. For Germans there are no wars, but only war, the total war of existence. Total war as Germans understand it implies only incidentally the bombing of civilians, the murder of women and children; much rather does it imply war in peace, war in trade, war in diplomacy, war in culture, war in education, total war everywhere and at all times until the total, German, victory.

This concept of the total war follows naturally from the German negation of the worth and brotherhood of all humanity which is the complement to the sanctity of the individual and the starting-point for the west. Germany thus rejects the very basis of western civilization. She rejects its purpose also. For her the good life of the individual does not ultimately signify. In the place of civilization German culture is set up.

German culture is a great culture. It has produced great and beautiful works. The Germans are very proud of it. It accords with the outlook sketched in above in that here as elsewhere the stress is on the dynamic element. For one thing, if the means are also the end action tends to coalesce with achievement, motion with the goal. Successive generations of Germans have reiterated their conviction that the being is the becoming. Thus from this angle also German reality is seen to be a flux. Such a concept of life naturally tends to promote synthesis rather than analysis and to emphasize the German preoccupation with synthesizing the antitheses that condition German life with a peculiar rigour; with reconciling romanticism and classicism, east and west, feeling and thought, mobile content and set form, infinity and immediacy, merging them into a whole that is superreality. It is not extraordinary that the most splendid flowering of German culture should be in the field of music.

This German culture is, as Mann noted, none the less an integral part of the German war-ideology. Such a culture sees in the good life of civilization only an artificial extract of life, insipid. It demands that life should be total like war, like the ideal itself. The longing is for life itself, life whole and in the raw, good and evil together, a life of untamed vigour, of exuberant violence and uncertainty. One is reminded here of the close connexion between Schopenhauer's will to life and Nietzsche's will to power, to domination. The German, lacking belief in the individual as the natural embodiment of life, feels that in order to enjoy life he must dominate it. His will and effort must correspond to this enormous undertaking.

It may be recalled that in Germany the twentieth century was ushered in by the literary movement significantly termed the *Lebensbejahung* (affirmation of life). That in turn recalls the constant penchant in Germany for expressionism, and the fact that along with affirmation of the whole life goes the attack upon reason and the championship of primitive emotion. And this vitalism tends further towards the contemplation of life's other side, of death.

It is this struggle for the whole life that is good and bad in one, the achievement of which is perfect power and domination, that constitutes the central theme of Goethe's *Faust* and gives it a flavour which, so Germans claim, only Germans can relish quite. And the main dealings of Faust were with Mephistopheles. This prominence of evil is likewise of general import. And now German thought comes round full circle. For if the individual be stripped of sanctity and subordinated wholly to some particular ideal, a mere means, but held by Germans to be absolute in itself, then it is not a very far step to regard man as positively evil and to hold that in the total life-struggle for power and domination all means are justified in subduing him in the name of the ideal, and in particular of the ideal of Germanity. Thus law is jungle-law, might is right, fanaticism is virtue, ruthlessness is common sense, fear is master over all, ruling in the name of the ideal.

Such is the spirit and achievement of Germanity.

That stated, the objections, scarcely restrained till now, come pressing in. It is certainly true that numbers of Germans would be horrified at the propositions thus attributed to the German spirit and outlook, and that of the German thinkers whose theories have been examined a fair proportion would be shocked at the extremer instances. It is none the less a fact that the inspiration of Germany can be detected behind the full length of that line of thought which first looked to history and began by laying such stress upon the national, the particular and the subjective; and the principles of this German faith even penetrated to the surface much earlier and more often than might have been expected. The real achievement of the Nazi movement becomes now more apparent. The complete cynicism of the Nazi leaders, their flagrant opportunism and disregard even of their own standards and professed ideals, now appear in their true light, not as the betrayal of the Nazi creed but as the affirmation of it. Hitler and his followers have for the most part maintained and realized the formal tenets of the historical school, quite agreeable to the bulk of German people and still more or less dependent upon the traditional values of the west. But this political structure and immediate programme, which some have held to be alien to the German people, was on the contrary precisely the popular façade erected by the Nazis to mask their real design, which was nothing less than the Nietzschean transvaluation of values, the education of Germans in Germanity, the nihilistic revolution which would not stop at smashing countries, but would wreck the very hearts of men and utterly destroy the civilization of the west.

This deeper purpose of the Nazis is, as has been shown, a logical extension of the more immediate teaching of the historical school. At the same time it is certainly an extension, and the fact that Germans needed education in Germanity indicates that in many cases its latent instincts were heavily overlaid. The Nazis set themselves the task of bringing those instincts to the top. They were largely evil instincts common to mankind, but steadily subdued by the process of civilization. The deepest significance of the historical school lies in the fact that its flourishing growth of one hundred and fifty years in Germany, its clear indication of what came most naturally to Germans, has tended greatly to facilitate the stimulation of those instincts and their organization within the corpus of Germanity. And here again lack of spontaneity in German thought or practice does not indicate that such thought or practice is not typically German, but rather the reverse; for, as has been indicated, spontaneity is most notably absent from the German spirit. In order to feel themselves spontaneous Germans must dwell upon their own being, they must intoxicate themselves with self. That is why Germans are so introverted. That is why Germans lust after themselves. It is this that underlies the relation of the German to Germanity. Germanity is partly the German being conscious of his peculiarity, which is the precondition to his achieving an existence which he feels to be natural and spontaneous; at the same time Germanity is also an ideal and as such distinct from the German individual and superior to him. Thus it is literally true that for the German the individual and the ideal can achieve synthesis only in Germanity; it alone enables the German to be at one with the ideal, to be of it.

The divorce of the individual from the ideal indicates at once the quite exceptional opportunities for propaganda in German thought and life. The curious and intricate relation of the German to Germanity, based on this externalization of the ideal but transcending it, indicates the quite exceptional response which propaganda on behalf of Germanity is calculated to evoke in Germany. Germanity is of the German people and yet above it. Germany is the German's way of life; it is also his fate. Germany is the mystical reality. It is Moloch and mystery in one. The German delights in explanations of what it is to be German, and he needs such explanations since it is at the same time the demonstration of the supreme ideal. It is sweet and terrible at once. Thus it is that national-socialism has led the Germans into their own. Under Nazi rule Germany has emerged resplendent in her Germanity.

And now the story draws to its close. There has been some account of the German outlook on society, and of what it meant to German life, and of what it made of it. But one problem yet remains: whether the outlook and its making were good or evil, whether, on the balance, they were of benefit to men or injured them.

To attempt any absolute and final answer would be imprudent and indeed impossible. Imprudent because praise hangs back, whereas it most often happens that they who pontificate upon the faults of others manage only to reveal their own. (A truth not very evident to Germans.) Impossible because human justice does not attain to the absolute judgment.

But in the absence of an absolute setting western civilization has been employed as the context of reference. And it is the natural one for Germany. Within this context and according to its code a judgment is possible. It must be this: German thought and German practice have for the last century and a half been undermining the civilization of the west; they are hostile to that civilization and eager to bring about its ruin; they wish its ruin because it is built upon the mean of reason, the christian ethic, the scientific spirit, and human worth—all alien to the German outlook which casts right back to barbarism. Now it appears how German thought has solved man's painful problem of the right ordering of human life in society. It has solved it in that it has denied it. Harking back by way of the particular and the subjective, through history and thence to superstition, German thought has come to deny the very value of human life within the concord of oecumenical society, holding that right order is only to be achieved by cultivation of the brutishness of tribal man and his worship of the tribal totem. Here civilization is confronted face to face with barbarism. Now it is one against the other, and the fight is to the death.

It is unnecessary to recount how the Nazi leaders have themselves gloried in their barbarism or to recall how German thinkers had earlier heralded its advent. It is enough to notice how thoughtful Germans have themselves been fascinated or revolted by the inhumanity of the German spirit. Instead of lingering over instances we will return forthwith to Hölderlin. It may be recalled that there was mention of the life of Hyperion as being in some sort similar in bearing to the train of German thought which we have traced: similar but in the opposite direction since the spirit of Hyperion's life was very rarfieed, his values sure and his perception corresponding. This is no place to trace that life, but only to notice how, parted a second time from Alabanda, and his Diotima now dead, he went away into the north-west:

'Thus came I among the Germans. . . . Barbarians from of old, become more barbaric through diligence and science and even through religion, deeply incapable of every divine feeling, spoiled right through to the marrow for the happiness that is bestowed by the holy Graces, offensive to every well-disposed soul in every degree of exaggeration and poverty. . . . It is a hard saying and yet I say it because it is truth: I can conceive of no people more dismembered than the Germans. You see workmen, but no human beings, thinkers, but no human beings, priests, but no human beings, masters and servants, youths and staid people, but no human beings—is it not like a battlefield where hands and arms and all limbs lie about in confusion, cut into little pieces, whilst the spilt life-blood runs away into the sand?'

The grisly description is capped with the affirmation: 'But the virtues of the Germans are a splendid evil and nothing further."[1]

Hölderlin was himself a German. At the age of thirty-two his mind became deranged; four years later he went insane; he clamoured horribly for death, but death was slow to come; he was madman for thirty-seven years. Those years have been called the 'benighted time' (*Zeit der Umnachtung*). The name, like the man, has a wider significance.

Looking back over the course traversed one sees at its head the age of enlightenment, the mellow light of the reason of the eighteenth century. And one sees how men rose up in Germany and set themselves against the light and called in darkness. Nor is this idle fancy. It was Herder who described the light of the enlightenment as eating round about itself like a cancer. It was Novalis who wrote the *Hymns to Night*, spurning the light 'on account of its mathematical obedience and its impudence', holding that the illusory images of the daylight and the acts of the day are merged and transformed in august and beneficent night, maintaining that day hardens and separates elements whereas intuitive night guarantees communion with the universe. It was Görres who considered that the republican principle was that of the day, and the despotic principle that of the night. It was Görres' master Schelling who also taught the medico-mineralogist Gotthilf Heinrich Schubert, a passionate admirer of Herder and the author of two works of high significance in the romantic movement, the *Ansichten von der Nachtseite der Naturwissenschaften* (*Views of the Night-side of Natural Sciences*—1808) and *Die Symbolik des Traumes* (*Symbolism of the Dream*—1814). These explorations of animal magnetism, hypnosis and the unconscious are in direct line with the work of Freud who so popularized the unconscious that many tended to think it an entirely new discovery, neglecting the lineage which goes back to Schubert through Carus. It is hardly necessary to stress the influence of this rediscovery upon post-war neo-romantics and its affinity with the Nazi

[1]The German runs: *Die Tugenden der Deutschen aber sind ein glänzend Übel und nichts weiter.*

revolution against reason. The unconscious is the realm in which the sexual and social inhibitions of individual are released. Romanticism is the realm in which the personal and political inhibitions of Germans find similar liberation.

Significant is the manner in which in a work like *Die Symbolik des Traumes* ethics and psychology tend to merge. Good and evil, the conscious and the unconscious, man and his 'other self' form neat and suggestive pairs. Schubert thought that the second self is often like a criminal twin-soul dwelling within the individual. The works of Schubert were favourite reading with the romantic author Ernst Theodor Wilhelm Hoffmann. It is remarkable how in German literature from Hoffmann and Kleist right down to Kaiser and Werfel the theme of the *Doppelgänger* constantly recurs in one form or another.[1] The *Doppelgänger* is a man's double, but the German word carries with it sinister and spiritual connotations absent from the English. A usual treatment of the basic theme is this: the *Doppelgänger* is a person's malignant self, himself but evil, the night-side of the soul. This evil spirit breaks loose, identical in form and seeming with the person himself. The double is great with evil, hypnotic, and very powerful. It sets out to dominate the real person and to subdue his virtue; nor does it desist until it has so mastered and utterly cowed that person that he makes the final sacrifice, abjuring his very personality, confessing that the substantial being is the double while he himself is nothing but his double's double, a shadow swallowed up in evil.

Surveying the German outlook on society from 1783 to 1933, and what has issued from it since, one is inclined to wonder whether that darkness which the Germans have so ardently invoked has not indeed proved very fruitful, whether their great achievement be not the triumph of the night-side of the German soul, the declared supremacy of the double who has achieved his total domination and taught the German people to see itself only in its hypnotic leader, to embody itself wholly in its self-chosen, self-emanating prince of darkness. And one wonders whether that people will see the light again.

[1]For the work of Schubert and the theme of the *Doppelgänger* cf. R. Tymms: *The Doppelgänger in Literature*, a suggestive study to which I am greatly indebted. The publication of this book is pending.

APPENDIX

I dislike and distrust bibliographies. A specialized bibliography is an illiberal compilation. But one that is ample must still be arbitrary and incomplete. This book accordingly contains no bibliography. Since, however, it has unfortunately been necessary for technical reasons to omit nearly all footnotes giving references to passages quoted from German authors and others, it becomes almost an obligation to give at least a bare list of the most important books from which these quotations have been taken directly or indirectly. Such a list is given below. It is in no sense a comprehensive, or even representative, catalogue of those books which have contributed towards the making of this one.

1783–1815 (Chapter II)

R. Aris. *History of Political Thought in Germany, 1789–1815* (London, 1936).

E. M. Arndt. *Das Ernst Moritz Arndt Buch* (Stuttgart, 1925).

R. R. Ergang. *Herder and the Foundations of German Nationalism* (New York, 1931).

J. G. Fichte. *Addresses to the German Nation* (trans. R. F. Jones and G. H. Turnbull. Chicago, 1922).
Nachgelassene Werke (Bonn, 1834).
Sämmtliche Werke (Berlin, 1845–6).
'Der Geschlossene Handelsstaat' (Vol. III).
'Reden an die deutsche Nation' (Vol. VII).

J. J. Görres. *Aphorismen über die Kunst* (Cologne, Year X).
Aphorismen über die Organomie (Coblenz, 1803).
Gesammelte Schriften (1854–60).
Wachstum der Historie (Heidelberg, 1807. Studien von Daub und Crauzer).

C. Herder. *Erinnerungen aus dem Leben Johann Gottfried von Herders* (Tübingen, 1820).

J. G. Herder. *Sämmtliche Werke* (Berlin, 1877–1913).
J. C. F. Hölderlin. *Werke* (Ausgewählt von W. Vesper. Leipzig).
I. Kant. *Werke* (Leipzig, 1920).
G. Mehlis. *Schellings Geschichtsphilosophie in den Jahren 1799–1804* (Heidelberg, 1906).
F. Meinecke. *Weltbürgertum und Nationalstaat* (Munich and Berlin, 1922).
Novalis. *Schriften* (ed. Heilborn, 1901).
Werke (Leipzig, 1931).
F. W. J. Schelling. *Sämmtliche Werke* (Stuttgart, *1856–61*).
'Vorlesungen über die Methode des akademischen Studiums' (Vol. V).
'System der gesammten Philosophie und der Naturphilosophie insbesondere' (Vol. VI).
'Uber das Wesen deutscher Wissenschaft' (Vol. VIII).
K. W. F. Schlegel. *Seine prosaischen Jugendschriften* (ed. Minor. Vienna, 1883).
Vorlesungen aus den Jahren 1804 bis 1806 (ed. Windischmann, 1836–7).
J. J. Uhlmann, *J. Görres und die deutsche Einheits- und Verfassungsfrage bis zum Jahre 1824* (Leipzig, 1912).

1815–1848 (*Chapter III*)

C. Clausewitz. *Vom Krieg* (Hinterlassene Werke über Krieg und Kriegführung. Berlin, 1867).
A. Gray. *The Development of Economic Doctrine* (London, 1931).
J. Grimm. *Geschichte der deutschen Sprache* (Leipzig, 1853).
K. L. Haller. *Restauration der Staatswissenschaft* (Winterthur, 1820–34).
G. W. F. Hegel. *Werke* (Berlin, 1832–40).
'Grundlinien der Philosophie des Rechtes.'
'Vorlesungen über die Philosophie der Geschichte.'
D. Heusler (and others). *Lebensnachrichten über Barthold Georg Niebuhr* (Hamburg, 1838–9).
F. W. Humboldt. *Uber die Verschiedenheit des menschlichen Sprachbaues* (Berlin, 1836).
K. Kumpmann. *Friedrich List als Prophet des neuen Deutschlands* (Tübingen, 1915).

F. List. *The National System of Political Economy* (trans. S. S. Lloyd. London, 1904).

A. H. Müller. *Elemente der Staatskunst* (1809).
Uber König Friedrich II (1810).
Vermischte Schriften (1812).

B. G. Niebuhr. *Geschichte des Zeitalters der Revolution.* (Hamburg, 1835).

L. Ranke. *Sämmtliche Werke* (Leipzig, 1881–90).
'Frankreich und Deutschland' (Vols. 49–50).
'Politisches Gespräch' (Vols. 49–50).
'Uber die Trennung und die Einheit von Deutschland' (Vol. 49–50).

F. K. Savigny. *Vom Beruf unserer Zeit für Gesetzgebung und Rechtswissenschaft* (1814).

1848–1871 (*Chapter IV*)

A. Gobineau. *Essai sur l'inégalité des races humaines* (1853–5).
The Renaissance (English ed., O. Levy. London, 1913).

M Lange. *Le comte Arthur de Gobineau* (Strasburg, 1924).

F. Lassalle. *Gesammtwerke* (ed. E. Blum. Leipzig).

P. Matter. *Bismarck et son temps* (Paris, 1908–14).

T. H. Minshall. *Prussian Influence in Germany* (London).

H. Oncken. *Lassalle. Eine politische Biographie* (Stuttgart, 1923).

R. Wagner. *Werke* (Leipzig, 1883).
'Erkenne dich selbst.'
'Heldentum und Christentum.'
'Modern.'
'Was ist deutsch?'

1871–1918 (*Chapter V*)

P. R. Anderson. *Background of Anti-English Feeling in Germany 1890–1902* (Washington, 1939).

F. Bernhardi. *Deutschland und der nächste Krieg.* (Stuttgart and Berlin, 1913.)

H. S. Chamberlain. *Kriegsaufsätze* (Munich, 1915).
The Foundations of the Nineteenth Century (trans. J. Lees. London, 1911).

T. Common. *Nietzsche as Critic, Philosopher, Poet and Prophet* (London, 1901).

H. W. C. Davis. *The Political Thought of Heinrich von Treitschke* (London, 1914).
E. Dühring. *Die Judenfrage als Racen-, Sitten-, und Culturfrage* (Karlsruhe and Leipzig, 1881).
Kritische Geschichte der Nationalökonomie und des Sozialismus (Berlin, 1875).
D. Halévy. *The Life of Friedrich Nietzsche* (trans. J. M. Hone. London, 1911).
F. J. C. Hearnshaw. *Germany the Aggressor* (Edinburgh, 1940).
K. Lamprecht. *Zur jüngsten deutschen Vergangenheit* (Freiburg im Breisgau, 1904).
F. Naumann. *Mitteleuropa* (Berlin, 1915).
F. W. Nietzsche. *Complete Works* (ed. O. Levy. Edinburgh, 1909–11).
'Beyond Good and Evil.'
'Ecce Homo.'
'Peoples and Countries.'
'Selected Aphorisms.'
'The Antichrist.'
'The Genealogy of Morals.'
'The Twilight of the Idols.'
'The Will to Power.'
'Thus Spake Zarathustra.'
P. Rohrbach. *Zum Weltvolk hindurch!* (Stuttgart, 1915).
H. Treitschke. *Briefe* (ed. Max Cornicelius. Leipzig, 1912–3).
Historische und politische Aufsätze von Heinrich von Treitschke (Leipzig, 1871).
Die Politik (Leipzig, 1899–1900).
Zehn Jahre deutscher Kämpfe (Berlin, 1897).

1918–1933 (*Chapter VI*)

F. Bernhardi. *Vom Kriege der Zukunft* (Berlin, 1920).
H. Keyserling. *Europe* (trans. M. Samuel. London, 1928).
The Art of Life (trans. K. S. Shelvasikar. London, 1937).
The Travel Diary of a Philosopher (trans. J. Holroyd. London, 1925).
The World in the Making (trans. M. Samuel. London, 1927).

T. Mann. *Bemühungen* (Berlin, 1925).
'Rede über Nietzsche.'
'Von deutscher Republik.'
Die Forderung des Tages (Berlin, 1930).
'Kultur und Sozialismus.'
'Die Stellung Freuds in der modernen Geistesgeschichte.'

A. Moeller van den Bruck. *Germany's Third Empire* (trans. E. O. Lorimer. London, 1934).

M. G. Parks. *An Introduction to Keyserling* (London, 1934).

W. Rathenau. *Gesammelte Schriften* (Berlin, 1925).
'An Deutschlands Jugend' (Vol. VI).
'Der Neue Staat' (Vol. V).
'Führer und Führung' (Vol. VI).
'Von Kommenden Dingen' (Vol. III).
'Zur Kritik der Zeit' (Vol. I).

A. Rosenberg. A History of the German Republic (trans. I. F. D. Morrow and L. M. Sieveking. London, 1936).

R. W. Seton-Watson. *Britain and the Dictators* (Cambridge, 1938).

O. Spengler. *Der Untergang des Abendlandes* (Munich, 1922).
Jahre der Entscheidung (Munich, 1933).
Neubau des deutschen Reiches (Munich, 1932).
Pressentum und Sozialismus (Munich, 1934).
Reden und Aufsätze (Munich, 1938).
'Nietzsche und sein Jahrhundert.'
'Pessimismus?'
'Vom deutschen Volkscharakter.'

G. Stresemann. *Gustav Stresemann: His Diaries, Letters and Papers* (ed. and trans. Eric Sutton. London, 1935–40).

E. Vermeil. *Doctrinaires de la révolution allemande, 1918–1938* (Paris, 1938).

INDEX